DATE DUE

~~SE 29 '95~~			
~~MR 22 '96~~			
~~NO 10 97~~			
~~JV 30 98~~			
~~MR 29 00~~			
~~JE 6 00~~			

DEMCO 38-296

Unbank the Fire

JANICE E. HALE

Unbank the Fire

Visions for the Education of African American Children

THE JOHNS HOPKINS UNIVERSITY PRESS

Baltimore and London

© 1994 Janice E. Hale
All rights reserved. Published 1994
Printed in the United States of America on acid-free paper
03 02 01 00 99 98 97 96 95 94   5 4 3 2 1

The Johns Hopkins University Press
2715 North Charles Street
Baltimore, Maryland 21218-4319
The Johns Hopkins Press Ltd., London

Library of Congress Cataloging-in-Publication Data will be
found at the end of this book.
A catalog record for this book is available from the
British Library.

ISBN 0-8018-4821-0
ISBN 0-8018-4822-9 (pbk.)

TO MY PARENTS

CLEO INGRAM HALE

AND

PHALE D. HALE, SR.

*If you can show me how I can cling to that which
is real to me, while teaching me a way into the
larger society, then I will not only drop my defenses
and my hostility, but I will sing your praises
and I will help to make the desert bear fruit.*

RALPH ELLISON

Contents

Foreword

V. P. FRANKLIN

What are the cultural factors that have contributed to the academic and professional success of some African Americans in a society dominated by individuals and institutions determined to keep African Americans "in their place"? How were these African Americans able to move out of the poverty-stricken backwoods of the rural South into the mainstream of American society with their identity and self-esteem intact and to pass on to their children and grandchildren values that would sustain them in the struggle against discrimination and oppression? How can we systematically introduce the values of these African American families and communities into urban public schools to improve the academic levels of African American children? This volume provides illuminating and well-researched answers to these questions and describes a successful early childhood education project that builds upon Hale's research on African American education and cultural practices.

Two of the most important elements in the formation of the African American culture are the African background of America's enslaved laborers and their American experience of oppression and discrimination. Although the Africans who were kidnapped and brought to North America in the eighteenth and nineteenth centuries came from western, central, and southern Africa, they shared a distinctive and identifiable worldview. Anthropologists and historians have examined the communication styles, artistic practices, and religious expressions among African peoples in Africa and in the United States and have noted profound continuities from the Old World to the New. Ecstatic religious rituals, musical styles, funeral rites, folklore, and other cultural expressions of sub-Saharan Africa were transferred to the New World. Janice Hale highlights the significance of storytelling, folktales, and the oral tradition in generating a faith in God and in themselves that was necessary for African Americans to survive under the most brutal and inhumane conditions.

Unlike slavery in Africa, where most slave laborers were, after several generations, often adopted by the kinship group of the slave-holders, in the United States enslaved laborers were viewed as possessing lesser mental capacities than the descendants of the European settlers and were legally deprived of the training and education necessary for their eventual incorporation into the society as free and equal citizens. As far as slaveholders were concerned, all that the enslaved workers needed to learn were the work routines and skills necessary for the production of cotton, tobacco, sugarcane, and other such crops. Some slaveholders allowed enslaved workers religious training, but the message was always, Be a good slave, do everything your master wants, and you will receive your reward in heaven.

Not only did most enslaved African Americans reject such slavehold-ing piety, but they also developed their own version of Christianity, which taught that to hold another human being in slavery was the greatest of sins and that the God of the Old and New Testaments helped the poor and oppressed. Enslaved African Americans identified with the Children of Israel, God's Chosen People in the Old Testament, and came to think of themselves as God's Chosen People in America. Negro spirituals often convey this belief in God's concern for oppressed people.

> Come along, Moses, don't get lost,
> Don't get lost, don't get lost,
> Come along, Moses, don't get lost,
> We are the People of God.
>
> We have a just God to plead our cause,
> Plead our cause, plead our cause,
> We have a just God to plead our cause,
> We are the People of God.
>
> He sits in the heaven and answers prayer
> Answers prayer, answers prayer;
> He sits in heaven and He answers prayer,
> We are the People of God.

Testimony and autobiographies of formerly enslaved African Americans reveal that spirituality was an important element in their lives.

These documents also show their strong attachment to literacy and schooling—not merely to allow them to read the Bible but also as an important element in their transition from slavery to freedom. Even though in virtually all slave states it was illegal to teach slaves to read and write, thousands of enslaved African Americans became literate.

Freedom and education were closely interconnected, and with the end of slavery, although the major objective was survival, thousands of former slaves filled the makeshift schoolhouses operated by the Union Army, the Freedmen's Bureau, and the numerous missionary societies operating in the South during and after the Civil War. When the army and missionary schools were turned over to the states' public school systems, African Americans continued to support them. From the end of Reconstruction through the first half of the twentieth century, these states failed to provide equal or even adequate schooling for African American children. Nevertheless, thousands of African Americans achieved upward mobility during that period.

In the chapters describing the lives of her parents in Mississippi and Georgia in the early twentieth century, Janice Hale provides important insights into the factors that contributed to black social advancement. Her father, Phale D. Hale, was the sixth of twelve children born to Church and Lee Ellen Hale, a family of sharecroppers in the Mississippi delta region. Phale attended the school opened for black children on the plantation in that area. Through the assistance of his family and relatives, Phale eventually migrated to Buffalo, New York, where he worked for a time before moving to Atlanta to attend Morehouse College. Phale eventually led a Baptist church in La Grange, Georgia, while he continued his ministerial studies at Gammon Theological Seminary in Atlanta. After his ordination, he returned to La Grange, where he stayed for almost four years before he was called to Mount Olive Baptist Church in Fort Wayne, Indiana, where he remained for four years. In 1950 he was called to Union Grove Baptist Church in Columbus, Ohio, one of the largest and most important black congregations in the city, and was later elected to the Ohio state legislature, where he served for fourteen years.

Cleo Ingram, who married Phale in 1943, was born in Atlanta, Georgia. Her parents, Janist and John Ingram, had migrated to Atlanta from rural Georgia in the early 1920s. John was eventually hired as chauffeur for a wealthy white banker in the city and was able to provide a middle-class lifestyle for his wife and three children. Cleo was encouraged to pursue her education and eventually graduated from Spelman College. Her family, friends, and church congregation placed great emphasis upon education as the major path for advancement for African Americans. This value was transmitted by Phale and Cleo Hale to their four children, all of whom became college graduates. Phale and Cleo Hale's professional success and upward social mobility provide an important explanation of why some southern blacks have been able to rise above both their humble beginnings and the prejudice of the larger society.

Building upon these cultural lessons, Janice Hale analyzes black life in contemporary urban America to explain academic failure among African American youth, particularly males. Upward social mobility, through skilled and semiskilled jobs in the manufacturing sector, was once possible without high educational attainment. In postindustrial urban America, however, most of these industrial jobs have disappeared, and the expanding areas of the urban economy—professional services and advanced technology—require high levels of training and education. For those African American youths who drop out of school before graduating, the possibility of getting a job stable enough to support a family ranges from slim to none.

Deteriorating housing and social services in black neighborhoods and the flight to the suburbs or to predominantly white neighborhoods by blacks who have reaped the benefits of advanced schooling limit the positive role models to which young black males are exposed while growing up. The culture of the public schools, dominated by female teachers, alienates many black male pupils, who increasingly turn to their peers and peer culture, to the streets, ball fields, and neighborhood clubs, for positive reinforcement for their social behavior and to develop feelings of self-worth. In her analysis of personality development among African American adolescent boys, Janice Hale makes it clear that they possess high self-esteem despite low academic achievement. Success in school is not highly valued among black teenage boys not merely because the school culture is dominated by females but also because the school curriculum does not reflect the patterns of acculturation and socialization in their homes and communities.

In contemporary urban America, many black youths grow up unchurched and in single-parent families. Historically, for the vast majority of nonblack Americans, schooling and education were a means to social advancement, economic security, or political power. Up until very recently, this was rarely the case for African Americans. Rather, the African American experience in the United States has been a struggle "up from slavery," and access to schooling and higher education has been an important cultural objective for other reasons.

In her early childhood education program, Visions for Children, Janice Hale includes elements of African American culture. This is justified on the basis of the importance of African American culture to late-twentieth-century Western society: just as in the late nineteenth century one would not be considered an educated person in the West if one were unfamiliar with European art, music, literature, and history, in the late twentieth century one could not be considered educated if one had not been exposed to American cultural expressions, many of which were generated by African Americans. But over and above such significance, African American culture in the school curriculum would provide African American children a sense of who they are and what their forefathers and foremothers accomplished under conditions many times more oppressive than those that exist today.

For too long, parents, teachers, and school administrators have allowed the sparks of curiosity in African American children to be smothered by excuses, denials, and sidesteps. To reverse the pattern of academic failure among urban black youth, Janice Hale makes it clear, we must first unbank the fire.

Preface

This book is a further development of theses in my earlier book, *Black Children: Their Roots, Culture, and Learning Styles*. My argument in *Black Children*, that there is a distinctive African American culture and that that culture should be considered in designing educational practice for children who are socialized in it, is fine-tuned here. In *Black Children*, I make the point that there is an African American culture and that it is expressed in child-rearing and play behavior. I focus on the mismatch between American mainstream culture and African American culture. This mismatch explains some of the difficulties African American children are having in school.

Since writing *Black Children*, I have become convinced by the argument of William Julius Wilson—that the socioeconomic devastation of the masses of African Americans cannot be ignored by social scientists belonging to the "strengths of black families" school of thought. *Unbank the Fire* continues the process of explicating African American culture but also includes a critical look at upward mobility. A central question is, How can an understanding of African American culture and socioeconomic factors create a more balanced conceptualization of the child at risk of being unable to succeed in the mainstream?

Unbank the Fire is divided into two parts. Understanding the historical context for upward mobility is the central theme of the first part. Educating African American children in the context of their culture is the central theme of the second part. *Black Children* was a celebration of African American culture and the strengths of African American families; part 2 of this book delves deeper into the cultural milieu that provides the framework for African American values and behavior. Suggestions for educational practice expand the implications outlined in the first book. An early childhood education demonstration program is described, and the design of a culturally appropriate pedagogy is explicated.

Part 1 provides a context for part 2 through biographies of my parents, which I modeled after the scholarship of James Comer's *Maggie's American Dream: The Life and Times of a Black Family*. Comer describes upward mobility patterns that were fairly typical of that generation.

My father, a sharecropper's son, grew up in the Mississippi delta. My mother, a chauffeur's daughter, grew up in Atlanta, Georgia. Both belonged to the first generation in their families to be college-educated. Their families typify the masses of African Americans in the early twentieth century, when most African Americans were agricultural workers in rural areas or domestic workers in urban areas. I examine the details of their lives not only to capture life as it was lived by African Americans in that era but also to pinpoint main currents that might be useful to educators and members of the helping professions. I seek to answer the questions, What stimulation, inspiration, motivation, and uplift were present in their families? What hardships did they have to bear?

Comer observes that upward mobility for a poor, inner-city, African American child means that he must learn to speak differently and behave differently from everyone who has raised him, known him, and loved him. Thus another key question raised in the interviews with my parents was, How did they construct a notion that they wanted to "be somebody"?

Phale and Cleo Hale, my parents, are examples of African Americans who achieved upward mobility in spite of the American educational plan for them. The intent of the American educational system was to reproduce for them the sharecropper and domestic worker status of their parents. Their success should not draw attention away from the fact that the masses of African Americans as well as members of their own families were not as successful in escaping that fate. Their biographies should not be interpreted to mean that every now and then a worthy person comes along who should be supported. Rather, I hope that my parents' biographies will deepen the reader's understanding of the "road watered with tears" that African Americans have traveled.

An overview of the volume may clarify the approach I have taken and make more explicit the connections between parts 1 and 2.

Part 1 is entitled "Understanding African American Children in the Context of Their History." Chapter 1, "Cultural Styles of African American Children," describes the situation confronting African American children. The point is made that there is an achievement gap educationally, and a shortfall in terms of life chances and quality of life, between African American children and white children.

The role of social scientists in defining the European American child as normal and the African American child as pathological is also discussed. The argument I develop is that educational gains for African American children will be enhanced only when their socioeconomic circumstances and distinctive culture are acknowledged and are used to inform educational practice.

Chapter 2, "Social Context: Historical and Cultural Factors," traces the historical and cultural factors that are responsible for the position of the African American community in American society. A review of the scholarship of James Comer, William Julius Wilson, and John Ogbu informs the discussion of how the African American experience has differed in significant ways from that of European immigrants, who voluntarily came to this country to improve their condition. It is not my intent in this section to provide new insights or to push new historical frontiers. This chapter is essentially a recap, for educators, of important background information and is designed to provide a context for the socioeconomic difficulties of African American families today.

Napoleon said that history is the story that has been agreed upon. European Americans have been taught the agreed-upon story—that African Americans have not achieved upward mobility because of a lack of individual effort. It is true that individual effort has played a greater role in the upward mobility of European Americans than in that of African Americans; African Americans have achieved upward mobility through a combination of individual effort and collective effort (civil rights activity and government intervention). Also included in this chapter is a discussion of the mismatches between American mainstream culture and African American culture that can have implications for schooling.

Chapters 3, 4, and 5 deal with the upward mobility of Rev. Phale D. Hale, Sr. They describe the way my father rose from being a sharecropper's son in Mississippi to graduating from Morehouse College, obtaining a graduate degree, becoming a leading Baptist pastor, serving in the Ohio state legislature, and serving as chair of the Ohio Civil

Rights Commission. The factors accounting for his being the only one of the twelve children in his family to attend college are examined. My interviews with him and other informants lend credence to my theory that a combination of unusually high intelligence and a surprisingly stimulating environment has been the prerequisite to African American upward mobility.

The African American role models in Phale's life are highlighted: his father was poorly educated but amazingly charismatic, proud, and inspirational; another male relative, born three years after slavery ended, invented the helicopter. My father was inspired by the most outstanding African American men of his generation: Rev. E. J. Echols, Sr., Dr. W.E.B. DuBois, Dr. Benjamin E. Mays, Dr. Mordecai Johnson, Dr. Martin Luther King, Sr., and Dr. Howard Thurman, to name a few. Identifying the factors that shaped his development may enable members of the helping professions to assist the youth of today in achieving upward mobility.

Chapter 6 deals with the upward mobility of Cleo Ingram Hale. Her parents migrated from the rural South to Atlanta. Her father was a chauffeur for a white investment banker. Her mother was a housewife, who also did laundry in her home for whites.

My mother, her sister, and two cousins became the first generation to be college-educated. In this chapter, I explore the factors that accounted for their upward mobility. The story of Cleo is interwoven with the sociological theory of William Julius Wilson and the history of African Americans living in Atlanta during that time.

Chapter 7, "Unbank the Fire: Toward Upward Mobility," serves as an epilogue to part 1. It reiterates the meaning of the biographies and extrapolates the lessons to be learned. Issues that Jonathan Kozol has brought to our attention are reviewed, such as inequities in school financing. This discussion captures Kozol's insights and makes them readily accessible for the reader. It is not intended to be an exhaustive or new treatment of disparities in educational opportunities. Unequal school financing creates a continuity between the education of today's inner-city children and the segregated education provided for their forebears earlier in the twentieth century; thus the schools today play the same role they were intended to play for my parents in Mississippi and Georgia during their childhoods—reproducing for children the status of their parents.

Part 2, entitled "Educating African American Children in the Context of Their Culture," comprises the final four chapters. Chapter 8,

"The Transmission of Cultural Values to African American Children," suggests that there is a distinct African American culture, which has given rise to a particular worldview, and that this worldview has contributed to the survival and advancement of African American people. The chapter describes that culture and how it has been transmitted through the generations. Here I make suggestions to parents and teachers on how to use this culture to help African American children maintain their faith, resiliency, and perseverance. Chapter 9, "The African American Schoolchild in a Strange Land," describes the way in which the transfer of this culture is interrupted because of an ethnic conflict between white teachers and lower-income African American children.

Chapter 10, "Visions for Children: An Early Childhood Education Program," describes a demonstration school, Visions for Children, designed to facilitate the intellectual development of African American preschool children. The school operates in Warrensville Heights, Ohio, a suburb of Cleveland. The research associated with this program was funded by the Cleveland Foundation, and I served as president of the program from 1985 to 1992.

This demonstration program, which operates in a day-care format, is designed to articulate a pedagogy that begins in early childhood and includes a learning environment drawn from African American culture, teaching strategies that complement African American learning styles, and materials relevant to the African American experience.

Chapter 11, "Culturally Appropriate Pedagogy," proposes an approach to the education of African American children that springs from an understanding of their development: the interplay between the socioeconomic factors that have shaped their fate in America and the cultural characteristics that are their spiritual essence.

My discussion of issues related to African American male and female development in *Black Children* is extended in this chapter. It also includes a review of the work of Reginald Clark, which outlines strategies that lower-income African American families have used to produce high-achieving children. The importance of increasing the numbers of African American children who take higher-level courses in math and science and pursue scientific and technological careers is noted.

Recommendations are made about humanizing inner-city classrooms so that skill-and-drill instruction can be transformed into instruction that is developmentally appropriate, hands-on, conceptually

and contextually interrelated, culturally salient, appropriately accelerated, interesting, and motivating. Instructional strategies are described
that incorporate the arts and employ artistic teaching.

The most important unit in the educational process is the activity
between the teacher and the child. Artistic teachers identify ways to
unlock the potential of every child, provide more human contact in
the classroom, enhance the spirituality of the classroom, and incorporate the arts in all aspects of instruction.

When artistic teaching is employed, children are motivated by the
interesting manner in which subject matter is presented; children are
given opportunities to explore ideas and content in meaningful collab-
oration with their teachers and peers; and the children are given choices.
Children should be given a multidisciplinary exposure to the curriculum so that they are able to develop their interests and talents in the
process of mastering information and skills. The identification of talents and interests is the first step toward building careers that lead to
lifelong satisfaction and self-actualization.

The title of this book was drawn from the text of a sermon of my
father's. I have included an excerpt from that sermon here, so that the
explanation of the expression "unbank the fire" can unfold in his own
words:

Unbank the Fire

Let me go back to Mississippi.

I saw my daddy cut down trees; we would help him cut the trees
into hard wood. Wood was a very important commodity in our
family. It was used for cooking, heating the house, heating the water
for washing the dishes, heating the water for bathing, and in any
other capacity where heat was needed. This was the source for all the
heat that came into our house.

At bedtime, I would see my daddy take a shovel and scoop up the
ashes that had accumulated in the fireplace. He would lay them on
top of the burning flames.

I asked, "Daddy, what are you doing?"

He replied, "Son, I am banking the fire. These ashes will hold the
fire until morning comes."

O Glory!

My Daddy just kept putting ashes on the flames until you could
no longer see the fire. It looked as though the fire was completely
out.

We would go to bed.

The next morning, he took a poke iron and came back to the same fireplace and raked in the same ashes; under the ashes, the wood had continued to burn slowly. There were little chunks of wood with fire on the ends of them.

O Glory!

He pulled those little chunks of wood together, matching the hot ends, then he got down on his knees and began to blow air on those ends.

He blew until little sparks began to fly.

He blew until a little flame was started.

He blew until a fire began to burn.

Then, he laid new fresh wood on the flame.

The fire was *unbanked!* The fire began to burn. My daddy had unbanked the fire. God told me to tell you to unbank the fire! The fire is here, but it is banked.

Put together your pieces of wood with the heat on the ends.

Get down on your knees and blow on it with prayer, faith, and love.

Blow on it until the sparks start flying.

Blow on it until a little flame leaps through the ashes.

Blow on it until the fire starts burning.

Blow on it until the Holy Ghost comes.

Blow on it until the church catches on fire.

Oh Glory!

Blow on it until your soul catches on fire.

Oh Glory!

When the church catches on fire, the world will come to see it burn.

Then the world will catch on fire.

Unbank the fire of prayer.

Unbank the fire of love.

Unbank the fire of faith.

Unbank the fire of service.

Unbank the fire.

I titled this book *Unbank the Fire* because I do not believe that extraordinary measures are called for to assist African American children in reaching their potential. All that is necessary is for this society to remove the ashes that historically and currently stunt their development and to allow what is there to come forth.

Acknowledgments

This book was made possible by contributions from many people to my personal and professional life. I am grateful to Dr. Donna Evans for recruiting me to join the faculty at Wayne State University when she was dean of the College of Education. I appreciate the support I have received from the administration of Wayne State University, especially Dean Paula Woods, Assistant Dean Sharon Elliott, Associate Dean for Research Steve Illmer, and Provost Garrett Heberlein, in providing me the time and resources to complete this book and in assisting me to launch my research career.

I thank also my mother, Cleo Ingram Hale, for researching the family photographs; Ella Hale Warren for providing the photograph of Smith William Penn Hale; my research assistant, Teri Vago, for coordinating the other photographs and for assisting me in seeking permission to quote material from other sources. Thanks to Rick Bielaczyc and M. J. Murawka for the photographs of contemporary educational settings.

I thank my mother, Cleo Ingram Hale, my father, Rev. Phale D. Hale, Sr., my cousins Clemmon Hodges and Ella Hale Warren, and Dr. Charles Leonard for allowing me to interview them. I am especially indebted to my mother, Cleo Ingram Hale, my brother Phale D. Hale, Jr., my sister Marna Hale Leaks, and Dr. V. P. Franklin for reading the manuscript and for their advice and editing. Thanks to Dr. Franklin and Dr. Asa Hilliard for writing introductory material.

I would like to acknowledge here the support I received in founding Visions for Children, an early childhood education demonstration program in Warrensville Heights, Ohio, which is described in chapter 10. I am deeply grateful to Steve Minter, director of the Cleveland Foundation, for his support of my research. I thank Goldie Alvis, program officer for the project, for her invaluable support at critical moments. The project would not have been possible without the contributions of the following persons: Visions for Children trustees Steve Bullock, Betty Pinkney, and Barbara House; Visions for Children staff persons Eric Johnson, Milton Wilson, Laura Chaves, LaRhonda Garrett, and Gwendolyn Baker; Cleveland community leaders Rev. Otis Moss, Jr., Bernard Greene, Lem Roberson, Rev. Charles Reese, and Joseph Meissner.

I am especially grateful to numerous persons in the Cleveland, Ohio, community who virtually saved my career when I needed them, especially four African American men: George Forbes, Dr. John Harris, Rev. Otis Moss, Jr., and Steve Minter.

I thank my former professors in the Early Childhood Education Department at Georgia State University for their friendship, advice, and support, especially Dr. James Young, Dr. Martha Abbott-Shim, and Dr. Joanne Nurss. I have received support and encouragement from mentors and colleagues such as Dr. James Comer, Dr. Sandra Scarr, Dr. Asa Hilliard, Dr. V. P. Franklin, Evelyn Moore, Dr. Carol Phillips, Dr. Valora Washington, Dr. Deborah McGriff, Gerald Smith, Dr. J. D. Andrews, Dr. Marilyn Smith, and Dr. Kay Lovelace.

Countless friends have been supportive throughout the years, but especially while I lived in Cleveland and Detroit working on this book: Dr. Sharon Milligan, Monica Kaufman-Lott, H. Gray Underwood, Karen Overstreet, Christine Carter, Patricia Coley, Sherry Stamps, Jacqueline McCutcheon, Alveda Beal, Pamela Hoffman, Caroline Jackson, Dr. Barbara Jackson, Dr. Ellen Pinderhughes, Dr. Patricia Maryland, Edwina Moss, and Dr. Brenda Terrell; my pastor and his wife, Dr. and Mrs. Charles G. Adams, of Hartford Memorial Baptist Church; my siblings, Phale D. Hale, Jr., Marna Hale Leaks, and Hilton Ingram Hale; my brother-in-law, Emanuel Leaks; my nephew, Richard Pace, Jr.; and my aunt, uncle, and cousin, Dorothy, Raymond, and Ralph Grier.

I thank my son, Keith Anderson Benson, Jr., for inspiring me to continue to believe that all African American children deserve everything that I desire for him.

I thank Dorothy Winbush Riley, for giving me a copy of her book of quotations from African Americans, *My Soul Looks Back 'Less I Forget.* I have used many of these quotations in this volume. I am also grateful to Laura Chaves (former director of Visions for Children) for compiling the list of children's books that appears in chapter 8.

Finally, I thank Jacqueline Wehmueller, my editor at the Johns Hopkins University Press, for her patience, encouragement, and support as I prepared this manuscript.

Chapter 8, which appeared in shorter form as "The Transmission of Cultural Values to Young African American Children" in *Young Children* (1991) 46: 7–15, is reprinted by permission of the editors. Chapter 10 is reprinted by permission of the publisher from Shirley A. Kessler, *Reconceptualizing the Early Childhood Curriculum* (New York: Teachers College Press, © 1993 by Teachers College, Columbia University. All rights reserved), 205–24.

The following gave permission to quote previously published material: James P. Comer, *Maggie's American Dream: The Life and Times of a Black Family* (New York: New American Library, 1988); Jonathan Kozol, *Savage Inequalities* (New York: Crown, 1991); Nicholas Lemann, *The Promised Land* (New York: Knopf, 1991); "Walkin' Blues" by Robert Johnson © 1978 King of Spades Music, used with permission of the publisher, all rights reserved; "I Can't Be Satisfied" by Muddy Waters © 1959, 1987 Watertoons Music (BMI), administered by Bug Music, used by permission, all rights reserved; "Stardust" by Mitchell Parish and Hoagy Carmichael © 1929, renewed 1957 by permission of CPP/Belwin, Inc., Miami, all rights reserved; Langston Hughes, "Mother to Son," Alfred A. Knopf, used by permission of the publisher.

PART ONE

Understanding
African American
Children in
the Context of
Their History

Cultural Styles of African American Children

A basic premise of this book is that African American children need to be regarded, nurtured, and educated in the context of their culture. In this chapter, I hope to encourage educators to understand the African heritage, which has been ignored in traditional educational practice.

Let us begin with the Pulitzer Prize–winning playwright August Wilson, who warns African Americans about the danger of separating from the African heritage. An *Ebony* magazine interview (November 1987) quotes: "Woe to the fellow who can only sing other peoples' songs and has none of his own. He a man done forgot his song," warns Wilson's root worker in *Joe Turner's Come and Gone*. "He a man done forgot his song. Forgot how to sing it. A fellow forget that and he forget who he is. Forget how he's supposed to mark down life" (Wilson, 1988).

Wilson uses *song* as a metaphor for the cultural heritage that African Americans should retain and celebrate:

There is an Africa in each of us that we have to get in touch with to understand our relationship to this society. When white folks look at us, they see everything that they are not. If they can make everything we are bad, that makes everything they are good. If they look at us and see "dumb," that means they must be intelligent. If we accept that, then we look at them as being intelligent and conclude that we are dumb. When we do that we have no identity, no self-determination, no self-respect.

But all we have to do is to claim that part of ourselves which I think is the strongest part—our Africanism. It has nothing to do with putting on beads or dashiki's. It's simply understanding who we are in the world, understanding our relationship to this society and claiming a responsibility for ourselves and our salvation instead of letting other people claim that for us. (p. 68)

Wilson's words echo a question that is being raised by African American scholars: Can we bring about an improvement in educational outcomes for African American children without recognizing their culture? Since the 1950s, desegregation has been a focal point for educational reform that is designed to benefit African American children. But how can we create schools that educate African American children effectively wherever they are found? Early childhood is the time to begin examining learning and care-giving settings.

The education of white children proceeds relatively more smoothly than that of African American children because their learning experience complements their culture. To achieve equal educational outcomes for African American children, it will be necessary to design an educational system that complements rather than opposes African American culture.

Further, when African American children experience educational difficulties, they are diagnosed more harshly than white children with comparable difficulties. Asa Hilliard points out that categories of special education that lend themselves to objective assessment reflect no disproportionate assignment of African American and white children (quoted in National Black Child Development Institute, 1985). For example, auditory tests show whether or not a child hears a tone, and he receives a score based only on that. Vision tests show whether or not a child accurately reads a line on the eye chart, and he receives a score based only on that. In auditory and vision tests, African American and white children score consonant with their representation in the population. In contrast, in categories of special education where the subjective judgment of the teacher or the examiner enters in, African American children are disproportionately classified as educable

We must create schools that effectively educate African American children wherever they are found. (Richard Bielaczyc, Photography-Media Services, Wayne State University Libraries)

mentally retarded (EMR) and white children disproportionately as learning disabled (LD). Of the African American children classified as EMR, 80 percent are males—for a variety of reasons.

One of the realities in the African American community today is that babies are being born to girls as young as twelve years old. The fertility rate of African American middle-class women is lower than that of white middle-class women, and African American professional couples are not even reproducing themselves. But lower-income teen-aged girls bear children disproportionately to their numbers. Their bodies are not prepared for childbearing, they receive inadequate pre-natal care, and their children receive inadequate postnatal care. African American male children have a higher rate of infant mortality, which suggests infant vulnerability. They also have a high rate of prematurity, which gives rise to neurological vulnerability. African American male children are also placed with adoption agencies and end up in foster homes to a greater extent than African American female children. These sociological, physiological, and neurological factors result in a disproportionate number of these children being assigned to lower ability tracks in school.

Any category with a large proportion of African American chil-dren always is vaguely described and calls for even vaguer treatment. EMR, for example, is a global designation. LD, a category with more white children, is precisely delineated: an LD child may be dyslexic, aphasic, or a host of other designations, each clearly defined and spe-cifically treated. An LD child could eventually be moved into a main-stream designation. An EMR child is so designated for life. Also, there is a disparity between the resources that school systems invest in EMR children as opposed to LD children.

Further, on the spectrum of special education, at one end of the continuum are African American children, who are disproportionately classified EMR, a global, undelineated designation. At the other end of the continuum are white children, who are disproportionately classi-fied as gifted, another global, undelineated designation.

There is also a need for educators to be honest about the politics of programs for the gifted. In evaluating our approach to these programs, we need to consider whether any child is gifted in every realm of human expression. If not, why do gifted programs operate on this principle? Children may be gifted in athletics, art, music, mathematics, science, language, or human relations, but few are gifted in all of these categories.

In Seattle, Washington, a desegregation team was concerned that so few African Americans were in gifted programs. The team devised culturally appropriate assessment procedures and criteria, using the work of Asa Hilliard (1976) as a guide. The team found that white children in the gifted programs did not meet these criteria. In fact, the most important common denominator the team found was powerful parents, who had gotten their children into the gifted program. For most of these children, placement in the gifted programs was detrimental to them, at least as the programs were designed. Although a child might benefit from an accelerated program in mathematics, he might be pedaling hard to keep up in language arts. Such a child is under enormous pressure in a globally accelerated program. Fortunately, many such programs are being renamed "gifted and talented," and enrichment and acceleration are being differentiated into distinct subject matter areas for individual children.

In our society, when Johnny can't read, it is suggested that there is an inappropriate match between his level of development and the curriculum or instructional strategies. When Willie cannot read, it is suggested that he is culturally deprived and genetically inferior. And even though Japanese children are outperforming white American children in school, there has yet to appear a journal article by a white American suggesting that the Japanese are genetically superior to white Americans. Instead, the number of hours Japanese children give to their schoolwork and the transfer between the Japanese business and educational ethos are considered. In other words, the inference is that some distinctive educational practice is being brought to the educational enterprise that accounts for the outcome.

When we study ways of closing the achievement gap between African American and white children, we must focus on devising curriculum and instructional strategies that will produce equal educational outcomes for all children. Lines of inquiry that suggest some inherent pathology within the child, the African American family, or the single-parent family should be forsaken. One promising line of inquiry lies in the thesis that there is a distinct African American culture. Educational practice will be improved only when educators identify mismatches between the culture that African American children bring to school and the culture of the school.

White children have strengths and a pattern of abilities that teachers "take to." In other words, white children come to school ready to receive the education that the schools are prepared to deliver. Further, there is symmetry between white children and their teachers; we know that the children most likely to go to college are those most like their teachers. Consequently, their education proceeds relatively smoothly. African American children also have strengths and a pattern of abilities. However, these emerge from their African American culture, and because we do not have an adequate developmental psychology of the African American child, teachers are not prepared to recognize and extend those strengths. Joe Kretovics of the University of Toledo commented to me that the school does not *dignify* the experiences of African American children.

An area of special cultural divergence is language. White children are rewarded at school and on standardized tests for the words they know for objects and concepts. Their culture emphasizes verbal fluency and vocabulary breadth. The African American culture emphasizes a different aspect of language—it is not what you say, but how you say it, that is important. That is, the African American culture emphasizes charismatic and stylistic uses of language.

Charismatic language emanates from the southern religious tradition and is exemplified by the preaching style of Dr. Martin Luther King, Jr., and Rev. Jesse Jackson. But even though these two preachers are outstanding, there are about twenty thousand African American preachers who are equally dynamic—they just have never been on television. The preaching style of the African American preacher, utilizing distinctive inflection, rhythm, intonation, rhyme, and emotional overtones, is used by African American female orators as well—Barbara Jordan and Shirley Chisholm, for example.

Stylistic uses of language are also found in the verbal rituals of northern African American urban males. Examples are "woofin'," "soundin'," "signifyin'," "playin' the dozens," toasts and chants like the "shine" stories and the signifying monkey. These stylistic devices evolved into the rapping songs of the 1980s. The early rappers were the Last Poets of the 1970s and were followed by Gil Scott-Heron.

The lyrics of rap songs, delivered in their characteristic quick tempo, certainly requires a quick mind and good language skills. The high-school son of Jerlean and Jack Daniel, for example, rewrote Shakespeare's *Macbeth* into a rap performance, which he called *MacRapper,* and through it was able to convey the essence of that play to his classmates. We also know that fortunes have been made in earnings from this genre. The problem for African American children is that there is no place on school tests for rap skills.

Another example of language divergence is the emphasis on oral expression in the African American culture and on literary expression in the European American culture. These differences can be found in church. I am a member of a primitive, missionary (bench-jumping)

Baptist church, which uses an Afrocentric worship service. When I recently attended an Episcopalian worship service, I was surprised that every prayer was read, either from the printed church bulletin or from a prayer book. In my church, there are no prayer books; people are appreciated for a dramatic, colorful, emotional, dynamic, extemporaneous prayer. Prayer is second only to the sermon as the most dynamic and emotional part of the worship service.

Of course, there is no right way or wrong way to pray. The point is that a child who worships regularly in an Anglocentric church grows up accustomed to seeing a significant portion of his experience expressed in print. The African American child grows up observing the expressive oral styles of his community: the dramatic flair of the African American preacher, the dynamic delivery of gospel songs, and the theatrics of the choir director and the soloist (who may be a future Aretha Franklin or James Brown). The African American child grows up in an environment that encourages extemporaneous speaking, memory development, musical genius, and oratorical flair.

Furthermore, the white child probably grows up in a household where phone messages are written down; in an African American household, messages are more likely to be memorized and delivered verbally. The white child might grow up in a household where messages to family members are written on a chalkboard and where grocery shopping is done from a written list; in the African American family, the grocery list might be memorized or items selected on site.

The point is that the white middle-class child has a whole compendium of experiences that prepare him to take meaning from print. The experiences that are planned for him in school assume such a background. When they encounter African American children, educators have no prism for seeing the wealth of experiences and abilities these children bring to school. The only conclusion current educational science can come to is that African American children are language and cognitively deficient.

It is imperative that we elevate to the level of science an understanding of African American cultural styles so that we can create cultural continuity for these children at school.

Consider four remarkably successful African American males. Michael Jackson is the No. 1 selling recording artist in the history of the world. Michael Jordan has been hailed as the most exciting basketball player ever known. Bill Cosby is the No. 1 draw on television. And Eddie Murphy is the No. 1 box office draw at the movies. These four

African American males are financially successful, generating billions of dollars for the American economy. Think for a moment if these men had, as children, been together in one kindergarten classroom. It would be every kindergarten teacher's nightmare: she would have to tell Michael Jackson to sit still, Michael Jordan to sit down, and Bill Cosby and Eddie Murphy to shut up! But in fact such African American male children are exactly who we have in our classrooms. But our classrooms and styles of instruction are so monocultural that far too many of these children achieve in this society *in spite of* school, instead of *because of* school. School becomes a hurdle they must jump over in order to achieve in out-of-school arenas.

CHAPTER TWO

Social Context: Historical and Cultural Factors

The historian is the prophet looking backward.

CARTER G. WOODSON

The grandchildren of European immigrants like to tell how their grandparents came to America with little education but a strong work ethic and how, in spite of numerous hardships, they progressed. The implication is that, if African Americans would just work hard, they would also succeed. Let me use this viewpoint as a springboard for a discussion of the historical realities that create roadblocks to upward mobility for many African American families. This chapter condenses for educators the events in American history that created problems for the African American children we serve. It is essential because, in my view, the version of history most Americans receive is distorted and sanitized: it has been said that history is the story that has been agreed upon.

James Comer (1988) contrasts the experience of white immigrants with that of African Americans in seeking upward mobility in this country. Most families whose forebears entered this country with few skills and little education have college graduates in about three generations. But most African Americans who attain the baccalaureate degree stand on the shoulders of uneducated or working-class parents.

The vast majority of African American college students are the first generation in their families to attend or graduate from college.

The period 1815–1915 saw large numbers of European immigrants come to the United States; the industrial revolution was in full swing, and agents of industrial entrepreneurs literally went to Europe to convince workers to emigrate. These immigrants settled in their own communities in the United States. Even today, these pockets of immigrants still exist—Greek Town, German Village, Little Italy.

By settling in such communities in large numbers, immigrants were able to use strong family and ethnic ties to decode the culture, to learn the language, and to become upwardly mobile. They created a support system. Because the economy was booming, they immediately had jobs and were able to connect with the larger economy. Even though they had little education and few skills, these were enough to get farm or factory jobs to meet their adult responsibilities.

These immigrants could vote as soon as they were naturalized and were able to organize politically, using their numbers to create political power. Consequently, by the turn of the century they had successfully used the public schools to give their children the educational and cultural foundation to move into the twentieth century. These children entered the industrial era (1890–1950) with a level of education that allowed them to be economically viable. When U.S. factories virtually closed in the 1950s, their grandchildren were ready with a level of education required to move into the postindustrial era (1950–80). Their great-grandchildren are ready, subsequently, with a level of education that allows them to move into the so-called information age (from 1980 into the twenty-first century), a highly scientific, technological era. A higher level of education is required today for a person to meet his adult responsibilities than has ever been required in the history of the world. Never before have educators been called upon to educate *everyone* with such high academic and social skills.

Comer contrasts the experience of the European immigrants with that of African Americans. Where the immigrants had a sense of community and the support of ethnic culture, African Americans had isolation. On the slave ships, Africans who spoke the same language were separated, unable to communicate with anyone. Upon arrival, babies were sold away from their mothers, marriage was not permitted, and families were often separated. There evolved a science of breaking slaves.

While European immigrants immediately participated in the economy, African Americans marked time in slavery. This would not be as significant if we lived in a socialistic economy. However, *in a capitalistic economy, the name of the game is the accumulation of capital,* which then works to produce more wealth. The period during which African Americans were in slavery was a very bad time to have been inactive economically, and the consequences were severe. It is no accident that the most famous U.S. millionaires made their fortunes around the turn of the century; the robber barons whose names are household words—the Rockefellers, Vanderbilts, Astors, Mellons, Carnegies, Kennedys—made their fortunes because the economy was relatively unregulated.

In *The Fitzgeralds and the Kennedys,* Doris Kearns Goodwin (1987) chronicles how those families made the American system work for them. Joseph Kennedy made his fortune primarily in the stock market, using insider information that would be illegal today. These financiers and industrialists played havoc with the economic system, which ultimately led to the Great Depression.

Consider for a moment that the income tax was not instituted until the 1920s. This means that these individuals did not pay any taxes on all this money. There was also no inheritance tax. Consequently, they passed all their money on to their progeny.

SLAVERY AND SHARECROPPING

Meanwhile, African Americans were in slavery. Notice that I describe African Americans as being in slavery long after the history books say that slavery ended. We have been taught that slavery ended in 1865, with President Abraham Lincoln's Emancipation Proclamation.

The truth is that Abraham Lincoln freed the slaves legally but not economically: cotton still had to be picked. Economic slavery did not end until 1948 with the invention and refinement of the mechanical cotton picker by International Harvester. Nicholas Lemann (1991) reports that the first cotton picker was demonstrated in 1931, but it could not be built on a factory assembly line. The development of the machine then passed from its two inventors to International Harvester, and by October 2, 1944, picking a bale of cotton by machine cost $5.26, whereas picking it by hand cost $39.41. A machine thus did the work of about seven people.

Sharecropping, which was nothing but an extension of slavery, was

Cotton picking in the South, 1930s (Memphis/Shelby County Public Library)

made obsolete by the mechanical cotton picker. Thus the formal end of slavery in 1865 had little consequence for the masses of African Americans, since the planters then devised sharecropping to meet their need for a great deal of cheap labor. "The issue of the labor supply in cotton planting may not sound like one of the grand themes in American history, but it is, because it is really the issue of race. African slaves were brought to this country mainly to pick cotton. For hundreds of years, the plurality of African-Americans were connected directly or indirectly to the agriculture of cotton" (Lemann, 6).

Slavery was created to support the antebellum cotton economy, sharecropping was created to support the postbellum cotton economy, and segregation was created to support sharecropping. To support the cotton economy, African Americans were thus denied the social and legal rights of ordinary American citizens. Sharecropping was in many ways worse than slavery. When slavery ended, African Americans were at least "in the black." They did not have any assets, but they did not have any debts, either. But because of the "creative" accounting of southern planters, as sharecroppers African Americans sank into debt. Two other factors made the sharecroppers' lives difficult: during slavery, the planter took care of all his slaves, even those too young or too old to work. During sharecropping, although sharecroppers' incomes were practically nil, the young and the elderly were their responsibility. Also, lynching was a real concern because of clashes with poor whites. When African Americans were owned by planters, they were protected against life-threatening conflicts. So sharecroppers found themselves in an economic system that made them even more vulnerable than slavery had but without the protection from poor whites they had been afforded when they were a planter's property.

The slave status seemingly made whites feel comfortable with the intimacy customary between whites and African Americans. However, with Emancipation, Jim Crow laws were necessary to define social intercourse, particularly for poor whites, who did not have the money or the privilege to maintain social boundaries. "Segregation strengthened the grip of the sharecropper system by ensuring that most blacks would have no arena of opportunity in life except for the cotton fields. The advent of the cotton picker made the maintenance of segregation no longer a matter of necessity for the economic establishment of the South, and thus it helped set the stage for the great drama of segregation's end" (Lemann, 6). The mechanical cotton picker came into widespread use by 1948, which I suggest is the functional end of slavery for African Americans.

> In 1940, 77 per cent of black Americans still lived in the South—49 per cent in the rural South. The invention of the cotton picker was crucial to the great migration by blacks from the Southern countryside to the cities of the South, the West, and the North. Between 1910 and 1970, six and a half million black Americans moved from the South to the North; five million of them moved after 1940, during the time of the mechanization of cotton farming. In 1970, when the migration ended, black America was only half Southern and less than a quarter rural; "urban" had become a euphemism for "black." (ibid.)

One could challenge my suggestion that slavery ended in 1948 by stating that all African Americans were not incarcerated on southern plantations until then. However, the economic fortunes of most African Americans are tied to the condition of the African American masses. So, even though there were African Americans who became educated and entered the professions, they still were not able to enter the mainstream. As Comer points out, most well-educated African Americans achieve upward mobility through the professions, not the primary job market. "This is the reason that the black middle-class is largely from the professional rather than the business sector, and only recently from the government sector" (214).

White people, in general, do not go to African Americans for professional services they can obtain from whites. Consequently, any African American's economic fortunes are going to be limited by the economic situation of the community that is their only market—other African Americans. An African American physician will not have an economic base comparable to that of a white physician; an African American entrepreneur, lawyer, or minister will be likewise tied to the economic situation of the African American masses.

DISENFRANCHISEMENT

Until 1965, when the Voting Rights Act was passed, the states where the majority of African Americans lived did not allow them to vote. Certainly, one of the most significant contributions of Dr. Martin Luther King, Jr., was his part in the passage of this act. It is easy to see why there was such resistance to granting African Americans the franchise in the South: it represented a major transfer of political power, given the large numbers of southern African Americans.

It goes without saying that, for an ethnic group to achieve parity in the U.S. political system, it must have the vote and representation in government. White immigrants enjoyed a considerable advantage in being allowed to participate in the political system soon after their arrival in this country. This point is brought home by noting the changes that occurred in the South once African Americans were enfranchised. After George Wallace was elected governor of Alabama with the support of African American voters, he hung the portrait of Dr. Martin Luther King, Jr., in the state capitol building. I am not certain whether he developed a sudden admiration for Dr. King or whether this was in response to his African American constituency. What is important is that southern politicians blocked school doors and spewed racial epithets only as long as they had to depend upon a poor white constituency to get elected. Dr. Melvin Drimmer, a noted professor of African American history, has commented that the Civil Rights Movement liberated not only African Americans but also upper-class southern whites, because both were held hostage to the poor white electorate. V. P. Franklin has noted that this observation is not exactly correct. His analysis is that, while upper-class whites did not have a majority of votes, they did have political influence.

QUALITY EDUCATION

While white immigrants were taking advantage of free public schools for their children after the Civil War, African Americans were struggling for basic literacy. It is safe to say that the education of African Americans has been inferior to that of whites since the beginning of their sojourn in America.

> Racist social policies led to massive undereducation of blacks during the period when most Americans were preparing for life in the late and post-industrial era. In the 1930s, in the eight states that held eighty percent of the black population, four to eight times as much money per person was spent on the education of white children as black, and some twenty-five times in areas that were disproportionately black. The same disparity existed in higher education. As late as the mid-1960s, the endowment of Harvard was more than twice the endowment of the one hundred-plus black colleges combined. (Comer, 214)

Even today there is a disparity in expenditure on education between communities where a majority of African Americans reside and mostly white suburban school districts. Americans apparently believe that the quality of education a child is entitled to is determined by where his family can afford to live. A more equitable system would be to pool all of the money available for educating children and divide it equally among all children.

Comer notes that, in the 1930s and 1940s, the inferior education of African Americans in the southern states, where the majority of African Americans lived, crippled an entire generation. When the factories closed in the 1950s, African Americans were not prepared, as the grandchildren of the white immigrants were, to move into the postindustrial economy. Even though some African American families overcame their lack of readiness, most families foundered under such stress.

> These conditions locked ninety percent of them into the bottom of the job market—sharecroppers, tenant farmers, domestics, the lowest-paid industrial laborers—and to the margins of the society, without the political, economic, and social opportunities in the mainstream.

Despite this, through the social organization provided by the black church, minimal incomes, and the controls that were a part of small town rural life, most black families functioned reasonably well until the 1950s. In fact, the 1950 census shows that only twenty-two percent of all black families were single parent—now about fifty percent. And black neighborhoods across the country were reasonably safe. (ibid., 213)

Lemann suggests that, when African Americans left the plantations and moved to urban areas, what had been essentially a southern problem became the No. 1 issue on the national agenda. For the millions of rural African Americans who moved into urban areas, there was no planning for housing, employment, and social services. This social cauldron burst into flames in the 1960s in many U.S. cities. William Julius Wilson (1987) attributes the contemporary difficulties of African Americans to this overmigration to the urban North between 1920 and 1970 and to the subsequent lack of African American male employment.

After World War I, the Congress passed legislation to limit the immigration of Europeans, even though the capitalists still needed workers. This was the first time that African Americans could secure industrial jobs without having to compete with immigrant workers, and millions of African Americans migrated to industrial areas. But when the factories closed in the 1950s and the nation shifted from an industrial to a postindustrial economy, the federal government did nothing to prepare a new generation of African American men for employment. Essentially, African American men were used as an employment buffer in the economy.

The message here for educators is that African American males were disconnected from the economy after the 1950s. The inferior education that Comer describes and the shift from an industrial to a postindustrial economy that required even higher skill levels left African American males prepared for only the lowest level of industrial jobs, and these were no longer available.

Among the far-reaching consequences of this situation is the high number of single-parent households headed by African American women. Wilson documents this direct relationship. He also notes a growing number of African American women who have never married, pointing out that having a job is generally the minimum criterion for a desirable marriage partner. The average African American woman wants a BMW—black man working—but according to Wilson the species is becoming as extinct as the dinosaur.

Joblessness among African American men feeds into another problem Wilson analyzes: the crime rate in the African American community. Teenaged African American males do not have the opportunity to work and are unlikely to see older African American men work. It is estimated that the unemployment rate among African American men between the ages of fifteen and thirty-five years is 50 percent. Wilson suggests that when any ethnic group's numbers grow as a result of migration, the population will include a large number of people under age twenty-five. This automatically results in an increase in crime by that ethnic group. It does not mean that any particular ethnic group has a predisposition to commit crimes compared to another ethnic group; it just means that, statistically, more crimes are committed by that age group.

Wilson also examines the consequences of the departure of middle-class and working-class African Americans from the inner city. In the 1940s and 1950s, inner-city communities were heterogeneous in social class, and a child had a variety of adults who interacted with him and assisted him in becoming upwardly mobile. These middle-class and working-class families served as a social buffer and provided uplift for

A sharecropper family, 1928 (Rockefeller Archive Center, Tarrytown, N.Y.)

Recent migrants from the South to Chicago during World War I

poor families. But in many present-day inner-city communities, these poor families are isolated. There is a concentration of people at the same social and cultural level and little opportunity for children to be exposed to family forms, lifestyles, and values that promote moving into the mainstream.

VOLUNTARY AND INVOLUNTARY IMMIGRANTS

John Ogbu and Ann Woodard (1989) suggest a contrast between immigrants and African Americans that carries Comer's analysis a step further—that one's belief in the fairness of the American system is shaped by the circumstances of one's immigration to America.

They divide immigrants into four categories: we will examine the two that are germane to this discussion. One category is *voluntary immigrants;* these are the white European immigrants who came to

America to improve their condition. *Involuntary immigrants* are divided into three categories: ethnic people who were enslaved, such as African Americans; ethnic people who were conquered, such as Native Americans and Mexicans; and ethnic people who were colonized, such as Puerto Ricans and Hawaiians.

There is no question that white immigrants experienced discrimination upon their arrival in America. However, the way they coped with that discrimination colored their attitude toward the role of individual effort in upward mobility. For example, when an immigrant applied for a job and was not hired, he could say to himself that he was not hired because he was a foreigner. He could also reason that he could understand that the employer might prefer to hire an American. He also knew that he did not speak English very well.

His response, rather than anger, could have been that he would go to night school and improve his English. He might also vow that his children would be well educated so they would speak good English.

Improving his English was a bread-and-butter decision, a cosmetic change he could make that did not do violence to the deep structure of his culture. He could improve his English, but he could continue to observe the festivals of the old country, enjoy ethnic foods, and worship as he chose. His decision to improve his speech was the same as an American tourist who bones up on his French because he is planning a vacation in Paris. Improving his fluency in that language will not change anything fundamental about himself.

Furthermore, the European immigrant had a memory of how things were in the old country and, when times got hard in America, he had memories that reminded him that he was making progress. He also stayed in touch with Uncle Cicero back in the old country, so he could continually assure himself that he was doing better than the relatives he had left behind. Over time, through hard work, he had excellent opportunities to progress as an individual, and he began to believe that the American system was just and fair.

Contrast the different experience of an involuntary immigrant, the African American. First, African Americans can seize on no one characteristic to change, like acquiring good English, that will end discrimination. African Americans perceive discrimination in America as being enduring and institutionalized.

Second, African Americans do not have a memory of how they were doing before arriving in America to help them endure when things get tough. They do not still know Uncle Kwame back in Africa to compare themselves to. African Americans compare their progress to that of middle-class white people. Their logic is expressed by, I have a degree and my white counterpart has a degree. Then, why do I live down here and she lives up there? Or, I have a degree and my white counterpart has a degree. Then, why am I training her to be my supervisor?

White immigrants emerge from their immigration experience feeling that the American system is fair and that the individual can achieve within it. African Americans emerge from their immigration experience believing that there is a ceiling on how far a lone African American can progress. Consequently, African Americans believe in collective struggle, civil rights activity, and affirmative action.

Valerie Cook is a white professor at San Diego State University. She is highly conscious of and sensitive to issues in African American culture. She has also made important contributions in training African American school psychologists. She once commented that, even though she has an understanding of African American culture, she understands most whites at a different level of consciousness, because, as she says, "I was *raised white.*" That is a salient concept: that a person who was raised white has a very different worldview than a person who was raised African American. If interracial understanding is going to be achieved, it is very important for members of the helping professions to understand that those two perspectives on the American system of "freedom and justice for all" exist.

Ogbu and Woodard suggest that African Americans are less willing to make cosmetic changes—in their language, for example—because such aspects of their culture have a boundary-maintaining function or an identity-maintaining function that separates them from white people. There is great concern in the African American community about whether one is speaking standard English to enhance economic success or whether one is "talking white." There is great concern about whether one adopts mainstream behavior to enhance upward mobility or whether one is "acting white." And there are terms for those who become confused about where the boundaries are drawn, such as *Uncle Tom* or *Oreo* (black on the outside and white on the inside).

Ogbu and Woodard point out that this can be an important concern for African American children, particularly adolescents who decline to enroll in gifted classes because they do not want their African American peers to think they are acting white. African American male adolescents report that they often become the class clown to make fun of the fact that they scored high on a test. These adolescents must devise elaborate strategies to become achievers and at the same time not be ostracized by their peers. African American children have difficulty in school because they have the *burden of acting white.*

African American children grow up receiving a comprehensive education on how to be an African American child. They do not receive an equal education on how to be white; they receive fragments on how to be white. They must put what they know about being African American and what they know about being white into some kind of harmonized presentation so that when they encounter their first teacher she will respond to them with reasonable expections that they can achieve.

There would be no need for this book if African American children had until they were twenty-one years old to achieve this. But they must achieve this by the time they are three years old and encounter their first teacher and, as Ray McDermott (1987) says, begin to amass their institutional biography, which is passed from teacher to teacher throughout their educational career. We need to elevate to the level of science the study of the development of African American children. Further, this exploration should not be restricted to lower-income children, because middle-class African American children are not achieving up to their potential either.

As Ogbu and Woodard point out, an African American child in a family with an income of $50,000 a year scores in standardized tests like a white child in a family making only $5,000 a year. Educators in affluent school systems report that the African American children in their district are not like the inner-city African American but are just like white children. The African American child in their classrooms, whom I will call *little Willie,* has parents who are professionals. He lives in a $300,000 house in the subdivision around the corner from the school.

But according to Comer's study about upward mobility in African American families, even though little Willie's parents are both college-educated, they are probably first-generation college-educated and may be the only ones in both families of origin to be professionals. Consequently, when little Willie goes to his grandmother's house on the weekends, he plays with his cousins and the children in the neighborhood who represent the African American masses. When he goes to church on Sunday morning, he probably does not go to the Congregational church around the corner from his house. He goes to the church his mother grew up in back in the inner city with the "real" African American people—meaning a cross-section of the community. When he wants to play basketball (with those who can "really play"), he will go back into the inner city to the court around the corner from his grandmother's house.

And when he makes these forays into the African American community, little Willie had better not go there talking white and acting white. In fact, he probably should not wear his school jacket if he wants to get home in one piece.

The point is that little Willie has to become bicultural. If he talks to his friends and relatives the way he talks at school, they will think he is talking white. If he talks to his teachers the way he talks to his friends and relatives, they will think he is ignorant. Can we then wonder why he is not scoring on standardized tests in a manner that would be expected given his family income and occupational level? So it is that we will not achieve equal educational outcomes for African American children until we conceptualize them in the context of their culture.

CHAPTER THREE

The Upward Mobility of Rev. Phale D. Hale, Sr.: Mississippi

Walkin' Blues

Well I woke

Up this mornin'
feelin' 'round

'round for my shoes

You can tell by that,
man, I've got them
old them old walkin'
blues.

Woke up this morning

Feelin' 'round, feelin'
'round, for my shoes

Well you can

Tell by that child

Hey

I've got the walkin'
blues.

ROBERT JOHNSON,
*sung by Muddy Waters
(born McKinley
Morganfield)*

When I was a child, our family took long automobile trips from Columbus, Ohio, en route to our vacations in, usually, Buffalo or Atlanta. While we rode, my father told us stories about his childhood and his struggles to "be somebody."

My father, Rev. Phale D. Hale, Sr., graduated from Morehouse College in 1940 with a bachelor of arts degree in religion and philosophy. He holds a master's of divinity degree from Gammon Theological Seminary, now part of the Interdenominational Theological Center, also in Atlanta. He has been pastor of the Union Grove Baptist Church in Columbus, Ohio, since 1950. Phale Hale served as a representative in the Ohio state legislature for seven terms and retired undefeated. He has also served as the chairman of the Ohio Civil Rights Commission, president of the Columbus NAACP, and member of the national board of Operation Push. I might add that he is the smartest person I know. When he told us about his childhood as a sharecropper's son in Mississippi, it was hard for me to imagine how he became who he turned out to be.

I always felt that his story should be told.

Phale and Jesse Jackson, 1976

However, I thought of it as a biography, a novel, or a screenplay, none of which I felt qualified to write. Later, I read James Comer's *Maggie's American Dream: The Life and Times of a Black Family,* the story of his mother's struggles to obtain an education for her five children. His comments on upward mobility in the last chapter helped me conceptualize how I could tell my father's story and highlight the themes that were interesting to me as a developmental psychologist. One question I wanted to answer for myself was whether he was an accidental product of a deprived environment or the fruit of a rich and stimulating environment.

Phale was the sixth child of twelve children. Besides him, only the

Phale and Robert Kennedy, 1968

two youngest finished high school. He was the only one to attend college.

My older brother, Phale, Jr., estimates that Phale, Sr., has an IQ of about 150, and that this was an important factor in his attaining an education. But I am very interested in the fact that Phale, Sr., was the sixth child; all of his siblings were bright, so perhaps birth order was an important factor in his receiving an education.

June Dobbs Butts mentioned in a lecture that, in sharecropping families that were usually large, they spoke of "wasting" one child by letting that child obtain an education. They would have enough children remaining to work the land and be economically productive. I wonder whether Phale was in a good position in terms of birth order to be the one "wasted."

Because Phale was the sixth child, there were enough older children to work the land, and as they gradually left the plantation to seek their fortunes, there were enough younger children to allow him to be spared from farmwork. He was surrounded by boys close to his age: one a couple of years older and four slightly younger, a strong cadre of workers who could compensate for his absence.

I received validation of this birth-order hypothesis from Virginia Henderson of Madison, Wisconsin, daughter of the late Wade McKinney, who pastored Antioch Baptist Church, one of the largest churches in Cleveland, Ohio. Dr. McKinney graduated from Morehouse College in 1925. Virginia and her sister, Mary, were the famous McKinney twins who were validictorian and salutatorian at Spelman College in 1953. Dr. McKinney was a mentor to my father.

I discussed my theory with Virginia on a visit to her home and discovered that her father was also a sharecropper's son, one of twelve children, the only one to pursue higher education, and the sixth child. This strengthened my interest in birth order as a factor in my father's achievement. Psychological theory posits that the oldest child is usually the highest achiever in the family, and this was the case with my mother, as chapter 6 reveals. But my mother grew up in an urban environment. It may be that the exigencies of agricultural life better position a middle child to be the highest achiever.

So the intent of this chapter is not just to tell a story. It is also to uncover the factors that allowed my father to rise above his beginnings in a different way from his siblings but similar to that of other African American achievers of his generation. A central consideration for today's educators is how to achieve upward mobility for the masses of African American children. I hope my father's story offers some answers.

THE HALE FAMILY HISTORY

Two brothers from the Upper Volta region of Africa were captured and placed on a slave ship in the early 1800s. Family history records that they were very intelligent men. They were not placed in chains but worked as mess boys. One brother became ill, died, and was buried at sea. The surviving brother married after landing either in Virginia or in one of the Carolinas (the couple was married by jumping over a broom). At least one son was born of this union. This son had at least two sons and two daughters.

One of the sons, Silas George Hale, became the grandfather of Phale. He was born in October 1852 and died in February 1929. Silas married Eliza Lawson in 1877. There were fourteen children born to this union.[1] Phale's father was Church, the second-born child.

Eliza's parents were Church and Betsey Lawson.[2] Church Lawson and his brother, along with their families, were brought to Mississippi from Cuba as slaves in the middle or late 1850s. Church Lawson's brother went back to Cuba in 1865, when slavery ended. Church Lawson was a progressive person who bought land in the 1800s.

Silas Hale actually first dated Eliza's older sister. However, she contracted a fever and died. Eliza was then about twelve years old and too young for courtship, so Silas waited until she was old enough and returned to marry her.

Silas and Eliza bought 360 acres of land in Lowndes County, Mississippi, near a hamlet called Penn Station (near present-day Columbus). They also owned 165 adjoining acres in Oktibbeha County. The family moved to Lowndes County in 1897.

Eliza eventually inherited the Lawson family property in Oktibbeha County. She sold this land and used the proceeds to pay the remaining amount owed on the land she and Silas were purchasing. This land was farmed by Silas and Eliza and their fourteen children. They sold 125 acres of their Oktibbeha County holdings in the 1920s. The remaining 40 acres in Oktibbeha County and the 360 acres in Lowndes County remain in the Hale family to this day.

Church Hale married Lee Ellen Roberts (1885–1937). (My own middle name, Ellen, is for my grandmother Lee Ellen.) Lee Ellen was the daughter of Carl and Margaret (Peggy) Roberts. There were eight children in the Roberts family.[3] Church Hale was a deacon in Brownridge Missionary Baptist Church, which was founded in 1863.[4] According to Clemmon Hodges, the Hales were the "movers and shakers, who ran the church."[5]

Church Hale lived in Lowndes County and worked on his father's farm. Lee Ellen Roberts lived in Sessum, in Oktibbeha County, near Starkville, where her family owned a farm. Young people met through church activities in those days, and Church would ride his horse four-and-a-half miles to St. Matthew Baptist Church along with other young men to meet the young ladies of Sessum. Clemmon Hodges's

The Hale family on the Pillow plantation, 1925 *(Phale is on the far right, first row)*

family were members of that church, and he reports that the Roberts family "ran" St. Matthew.

My father, Phale Hale, was born on Silas and Eliza's farm in Lowndes County, near Columbus, as were his five older siblings.[6] When he was about three months old, Church and Lee Ellen moved their family to Sessum, to a farm called Asku, where Lee Ellen's parents lived.

My informant, Ella Hale Warren, is the family griot (historian). She is Phale's first cousin (her father was Tannie Hale) and lived on Silas Hale's farm. She graduated from high school in the 1930s. Ella is not certain about why the family moved. Her guess is that Church was dissatisfied with their house, which was small and had a dirt floor and that Church requested a larger house from Silas but was turned down. Although Ella never saw the house in Sessum, she supposes it was larger than the one the family left.

Juanita, Phale's younger sister, was the only child born in Sessum. When Phale was two years old, the family moved to Greenwood. Ella is not certain why the family left Sessum for Greenwood but observes that, by the time they moved, Church and Lee Ellen had seven children probably ranging in age from an infant to thirteen years old, a large enough family to do a substantial amount of farming.

I was always curious about why, with both of their parents owning their own land, Church and Lee Ellen sharecropped a white-owned plantation. Ella visited the family on their farm outside of Greenwood and tells me that the house they lived in, although a sharecropper's shack, was more spacious than the one they left in Columbus. So there may have been some belief in Church's mind that he had advanced.

Phale, however, finds it odd that Ella thinks the three-room shack outside of Greenwood was more spacious than the house in Columbus and wonders if she is counting the smokehouse and the shed. Clemmon saw the house in Sessum and the one in Greenwood. After the Hales left, Margaret (Aunt Mug, Lee Ellen's sister) moved into the house, and he visited her there a number of times with his father. He notes that in Sessum there was more land around the house, which was nicely landscaped with shrubbery. However, inside, the two houses were about the same.

Clem also observes that Bob Pillow was one of the wealthiest plantation owners in the Mississippi delta and the mansion he built in the 1940s was a showplace. Clem photographed it once.

Clem believes that Church and Lee Ellen left their families' farms to sharecrop in the delta because they could not support their family on these holdings. They had land but not an extensive amount. Even though Church's father had more land than the Roberts, Church could not have supported his family adequately on either farm. Land in the delta was more fertile, so the family left what they called "the hills" for the delta in order to make an independent living. Somehow, Church became connected with Bob Pillow's plantation in the Mississippi delta near Greenwood. He became what Ella describes as a "straw boss," sharecropping himself but also recruiting other sharecroppers from Lowndes County to move to the Pillow plantation.

Nicholas Lemann (1991) sheds light on the attraction of the delta for Church and other African American farmers during that period. "The Delta is the richest natural cotton-farming land in the United States. Its dark black-brown topsoil, deposited over eons of springtime floods, is more than fifty feet deep. Like an oil field or a silver mine, that holds the promise of big, big money, and so the agricultural society that grew up on top of it was dominated by farming tycoons, not yeomen" (10). The delta was not farmed before the Civil War; it was mostly uncleared and undrained. The clearing and draining of this land was a big undertaking. The flooding of the Mississippi River was what made the land rich, but that very flooding could ruin crops. For the land to be farmed, levees had to be built to protect the land from the floodwaters. Twenty years after the end of the war, a reliable system of levees was built. Lemann writes:

> The Delta is remote, even now, and in its state of nature it was wild— swampy in some places and densely forested in most others, and populated by Choctaws and panthers and bears. It was the last area of the South to be settled; the mythic grand antebellum cotton plantation did not exist there. The leading planter families of the Delta consider themselves to be members of the Southern upper class—which is to say that they are Episcopalian, of British or Scotch-Irish extraction, and had ancestors living in the upper South before 1800—but they were never so well established somewhere else as to have precluded a move to the Delta when it was frontier. (ibid.)

According to the Greenwood-Leflore Public Library Genealogy Department, William Reese Pillow was the father of Bob Pillow, the planter Church Hale worked for. William Reese Pillow, a native of Columbia, Tennessee, came to Mississippi in 1868 when he married Elizabeth Scales. In Mississippi he bought Double Oak, part of the Scales plantation, from his wife's aunt, Mary Walton. He afterward sold it and moved to Greenwood, where he had a dry goods store. His home was on the site of Mrs. W. T. Fountain's present home; the Fountain's store site was once the garden. A year after moving to Greenwood, William Pillow lost his money and moved back to the country. He built the family home, Elmwood. His father, Walter, and his mother moved to Greenwood from Columbia, Tennessee, two or three years later and remained with their son until their deaths.

Elizabeth's father, Nathaniel Scales, was originally from North Carolina and his wife was from Woodville, Mississippi. He owned a great deal of land in the Greenwood area.[7] He was killed in the Civil War somewhere near Memphis. His grave was never found because of the number of casualties.

William Reese Pillow was at one time sheriff of Leflore County. He died at the age of forty-seven. Robert Pillow married Frances Peebles and had two daughters, Helen and Elizabeth. Their descendants still live on the plantation.

According to Lemann, "The planters' houses, most of them, are quite modest, with small lawns and a few shade trees, evidence of a desire not to divert too much arable land to other uses. The big money made in the Delta is usually spent outside the Delta, on parties in Memphis and tours of Europe and Eastern prep schools" (ibid.). Lemann also sheds light on the attraction the delta had for Church Hale.

> The planters of the Delta had . . . created a significant, though unpublicized, black migration of their own, from the hills of northern and central Mississippi to the Delta. The most common family history among black families in the Delta [was of] . . . the family scratching out an existence in the mediocre soil of the hills; the Delta plantation manager painting his enticing picture of the bountiful cotton crop in the Delta and the economic promise of the sharecropper system; and then the move. (ibid., 17)

But the migration almost always ended in disappointment because it was nearly impossible to make any money sharecropping. "The sharecropper's family would move, early in the year, to a rough two- or three-room cabin on a plantation. The plumbing consisted of, at most, a washbasin, and usually not even that. The only heat came from a woodburning stove. There was no electricity and no insulation. During the winter, cold air came rushing in through the cracks in the walls and the floor. Usually the roof leaked. The families often slept two and three to a bed" (ibid.).

Before the Depression, cotton was the least mechanized crop in American agriculture and extremely labor-intensive. Acreage planted to cotton steadily increased after the Civil War, peaking in 1929. This created an enormous demand for field hands, which was met mainly through sharecropping. The number of sharecroppers grew in lockstep with the number of acres of cotton. By 1930, eight and a half million people were living in sharecropping families. "The Delta, as home to the biggest and richest plantations in the cotton belt, was the capital of the sharecropper system—at least in its most extreme form, in which all the sharecroppers were black and lived in self-contained plantation communities that were home, in many cases to hundreds of people, and where the conditions were much closer to *slavery* than to normal employment" (ibid., 11).

Although some scholars attribute present-day urban pathology to the aftereffects of slavery, William Julius Wilson (1987), citing work of Herbert Gutman (1976), shows that African Americans overcame the legacy of slavery through strong family ties. Other scholars attribute urban pathology to deficiencies among the former sharecroppers themselves. Wilson discounts that theory also, pointing out that share-croppers were hard-working people with strong moral values, strong families, and strong ties to the church, and were accustomed to the controls of rural living. They also were a hale and hearty people who came to the cities with strong bodies. Wilson's views are confirmed by my interviews with my father.

The central activity on the plantation was the planting and harvesting of cotton. Lemann describes cotton picking as follows:

> Picking was hard work. The cotton bolls were at waist height, so you had to work either stooped over or crawling on your knees. Every soft puff of cotton was attached to a thorny stem, and the thorns pierced your hands as you picked—unless your entire hand was callused, as most full-time pickers' were. You put the cotton you picked into a long sack that was on a strap around your shoulder; the sack could hold seventy-five pounds, so for much of the day you were dragging a considerable weight as you moved down the rows. The picking day was long, sunup to sundown with a half hour off for lunch. There were no bathrooms. (8)

School on the Pillow plantation did not start until all of the crops were gathered. Only after the crops were in in the fall did school open. This was usually around the middle of November, depending on how large the harvest was. School closed when the weather broke in the spring and it was time to plant.

Church plowed his fields. Then the family planted the cotton, and as the plants grew they "worked" the plants (pulled weeds). The Hales had enough land to keep them working every day; Church worked a large acreage compared to the other families on the plantation. The family was thus able to loan or give food and supplies to the other families and their comparative prosperity sometimes created jealousy among the other families. There were eighty or ninety sharecropping families on the Pillow plantation; the Scales plantation, which was nearby, also had a large number of sharecropping families.

The house the Hales lived in was a shotgun house, which meant that there was a long hallway from the front door through to the back door. There were three rooms off that hallway and a kitchen. There were two beds in two of the rooms. The children slept two to a bed, so Phale slept in a room with three other children. The parents' bedroom contained a bed for them and a bed for the very young children. One of the rooms was used as a guest room; in addition to a bed, there was furniture for the guests to sit on. Whoever slept in the guest room vacated it when there were guests and slept in one of the other rooms on a pallet made of quilts. Because of the age spread of the children, all fourteen members of the family did not live at home at the same time, so sleeping four to a room generally accommodated everyone.

In Phale's bedroom there was a kitchen table and a bench on which the family sat for meals: a bench was a space saver because there was not enough room for all of the chairs that would have been required. There was also a woodstove. For fuel, the family felled their own trees, cut them into small pieces, and allowed them to dry in a woodpile.

In the backyard, a huge metal pot sat on legs and a fire was built under it to heat water for washing. The hot water was poured into zinc tubs, in which the clothes were washed and the Saturday night baths were taken in preparation for church on Sunday. Everyone had to take baths on the same evening, so it was quite an undertaking, heating water, pouring it into the tubs, and taking turns bathing. Phale remembers lying on his bed, waiting his turn, thinking that, when he grew up, he would never again bathe on Saturday night. Now he always bathes in the morning.

Since there was no running water, the family had an outhouse behind the house; it consisted of a deep hole in the ground, a seat made of two boards placed side by side with a space in the middle, and a structure around it all.

There also was a lockup, or pen, for the mules and cows. The Hales had the use of two of Bob Pillow's mules, supplied to them along with the house, the land, and the equipment. Church eventually acquired a cow and a horse and buggy. Also behind the house were peach and apple trees and a garden with every kind of vegetable one could imagine: white potatoes, sweet potatoes, beans, peas, turnips, mustard greens, cabbage. Lee Ellen canned these vegetables for winter, storing them in the smokehouse. The children picked blackberries, which Lee Ellen made into wine and jelly. These were also stored in the smokehouse. They also raised Louisiana cane, which they cut and took to the mill to grind. They then cooked the juice down to molasses.

The house was on pillars over a hole in the ground. Wagon loads of sweet potatoes were stored in this hole, ready for use anytime.

They also had a smokehouse. In the fall, they would kill hogs and cows, put the meat into one of the zinc tubs, cover it with salt, and leave it for a couple of weeks. Then they would wash it off and hang it from the ceiling of the smokehouse. They would build a small fire on the floor, which was dirt, and the smoke would surround the meat, season it, and keep it from spoiling. In their smokehouse all winter long were bacon, ham, pork shoulders, pig's feet, pig's ears, and pork ribs.

There was a corn shed where dry corn was stored. They let the corn harden and dry in the field and then, before winter, filled the shed. They also ground the dried corn into cornmeal.

Thus the only foods that had to be purchased were flour, sugar, pepper, and salt. Occasionally they bought light bread; however, normally they baked bread, corn bread, and biscuits.

The milk from their cows they churned into butter. They drank the buttermilk, rarely drinking what they called sweet milk.

Ellen would rise first in the morning and cook bacon and eggs or ham and eggs with biscuits (served with molasses) and rice. (Phale later noticed that in Georgia they ate grits for breakfast, but in Mississippi, they ate rice.) The Hales were never hungry; they had plenty to eat and plenty to share with others who were less fortunate. Essentially, they lived in a noncash economy. They did not know there was a Depression, because they had all the resources they needed to live comfortably.

Lee Ellen made most of the clothes for the family, especially the overalls all of them wore in the fields. The girls made their own clothes. The family never used or even heard of blankets; they used quilts instead, pieced from worn-out clothes by the women when they sat around the woodstove in the evenings. Shoes and clothes for church were bought with money earned selling excess produce. Church would load the wagon with watermelons and go to Greenwood to sell them, calling, "Watermelons, watermelons, the Georgia rattlesnake, red to the rind!" He would also sell cantaloupes, peas, butterbeans, and corn.

In Phale's family, at least one parent was always at home, and often both. They rose before the sun came up: the old saying is that sharecroppers worked from "can to cain't"—from when you can see to when you can't.

After breakfast, which they always ate together, the older children and Church went to the fields. Children too young to work played in the yard. When they got older, they played in the pasture. Their mother was always home with them. When they were old enough to differentiate between the grass and the cotton or the corn, usually around six years old, they were given a hoe and taken to the fields. If Lee Ellen was working in the fields, she would return to the house around 10:30 A.M. to prepare dinner. Around noon, everyone else would return to the house, and then go back to the fields about 1 o'clock.

Lee Ellen would return to the house about 5:30 P.M. to prepare supper. When the sun went down, everyone else came in from the fields and had supper. After suppertime, the family would sit together and hold family conversations, usually about the family, the neighbors, the church, Sunday school, and events in the community.

THE CHURCH

Both Lee Ellen and Church were able to read and write, in spite of a limited education. Church was the person in his family of origin who corresponded with family members and passed along news. Lee Ellen also corresponded with members of her family of origin. There were no telephones, and the distances were difficult to cover by horse and buggy. So, letters were the primary means of communication.

The reading material in the household was an occasional newspaper printed in Memphis, an almanac, Sunday school literature, the Bible, and a calendar. Usually the Bible was read on Sunday mornings before breakfast. Church led the prayers and Phale read the Bible, probably because he was the best reader.

In his role as Sunday school superintendent, Church had the opportunity to travel throughout Mississippi to attend Sunday school conventions. Often Phale was permitted to travel with his parents to those meetings. This experience differentiated him from his siblings, who were not as interested in going along.

Church bought his first automobile, a model-T Ford, in 1925 for $444.10. When Phale asked him what the ten cents was for, his father replied, "Well, I guess that is for the keys." He bought the car to drive to conventions. Sometimes other people rode along and shared the expenses. In Mississippi, African Americans were not allowed to stay in hotels, so they stayed with other families.

The Hales were well-respected members of their community. The Hales were very dignified, Clem says. In those days, farmers were not looked down upon as they were in later generations; farming was considered hard, honest, dignified work. Church was, according to Clem, "a tall stately looking gentleman. He was tall and big—not fat, but imposing. If you saw him walking down the street, he looked important. He didn't look like a farmer, he looked like a country doctor. He had a strong imposing voice. He was very likeable, kind and distinguished looking. He conveyed being smarter than you would expect, given his educational level. As he became older, even the foremen on the plantation called him Mr. Hale."

Lee Ellen, Clem says, "had queenly qualities. People respected her presence. She always dressed well and was well groomed. You would never believe that she had given birth to twelve children if you saw her. She had great carriage." Lee Ellen's daughter Maggie describes her as an emaculate housekeeper, and my mother considered all of Lee Ellen's daughters excellent housekeepers. Maggie was more like a mother-in-law to my mother than a sister-in-law, and I was fascinated to see my mother anxiously ironing the sheets on the bed in preparation for Aunt Maggie's visits.

Lee Ellen was president of the missionary society. In addition to being superintendent of the Sunday school, Church was also chairman of the deacon board of Brooklyn Chapel Baptist Church, the church attended by sharecropper families on Bob Pillow's plantation. Later in life, the Hales joined New Zion Baptist Church in Greenwood, where they were "movers and shakers . . . as they had been everywhere else," according to Clem. The Brooklyn Chapel Baptist Church was a wood frame building used for both worship and school. Phale is not sure about the history of the church; however, he believes that Bob Pillow had it built.

The Hales were the object of some jealousy among other church families. As a teenager, Phale was selected to serve as the church janitor. His duties were to clean the church and to ring the bell calling the parishioners to worship. Even though his salary was only seventy-five cents a month, some of the church members grumbled that the Hales were taking over the church.

Phale tells a story of an admonition he received from his father in racial folkways. His father explained to him that, if any white boys pushed him or tried to make him fight, he should not fight back. He explained that, if the white boys' fathers came seeking to punish Phale, he could not stop them. Phale was devastated that his father, his greatest hero, was powerless to protect him from whites. However, the racial realities were balanced by Phale's opportunity to see his parents in leadership roles on the plantation, specifically in church. He saw his parents as leaders in their elected offices and as speakers before the congregation, giving reports from conventions they had attended.

Phale recalls walking a long distance home from a baseball game and feeling faint from hunger. He had no money, but he stopped at a store and asked the owner for an advance of food, promising to return later and pay him. Phale was proud when the owner remarked that, since Phale was Church Hale's boy, he would make him the loan.

I asked Phale to describe his father. He was a good man, he said, and a good husband and father. He never saw his father chew tobacco or smoke a cigar, cigarette, or pipe. He never saw him drink liquor. He was a good role model for his children—and a good disciplinarian, whom his children obeyed.

Church established curfew hours. Wherever you were, you were required to be home by sundown. If you needed to stay out longer, you had to go home, get permission, and return. Everyone had household chores. Phale remembers once when he saw his father approaching before he had done his assignment and how he rushed to begin it, while assuring his father he was working on it. Phale also remembers Church as being a good provider for his wife and children. Lee Ellen's responsibility was to take care of the house; she worked only short hours in the fields while she had children too young to work.

I asked Phale to reflect on his mother. He said that she was a good mother and that she was always there. He had a great deal of contact with her because, after he told her he wanted to learn how to do everything she did, she taught him to cook, wash, iron, sew, and clean house. She was a soft-spoken woman who rarely became angry or raised her voice.

A story from Phale's childhood reveals her love for him. Phale contracted typhoid fever as a young boy. His mother had tried all of the home remedies she knew but was not able to break his fever. Finally, Church hitched up the mules and they rode the four miles to town to the doctor. They carried him up the steps into the colored waiting room, where they waited until the doctor had seen all the white patients. The doctor examined Phale and told them that he had typhoid fever and was going to die. Lee Ellen burst into tears and cried uncontrollably. The doctor asked, "Auntie, don't you have ten children at home?" Lee Ellen said yes. "Well," the doctor said, "when this one dies you will have nine left!"

Sadly, Lee Ellen and Church carried Phale back down the steps and took him home; there was no hospital in Greenwood that would accept a colored boy. She placed him on the bed and wrapped his body in leaves. When she had done everything else she could, she knelt by the side of his bed and prayed to God all night long. "Lord, you said in your Word, that if a shepherd had one hundred sheep and one went astray, that he would leave his flock and find that one which was lost. Father, the doctor said that when my child dies, I will have nine children left. I know that, but dear God, *I want this one too!*" Lee Ellen prayed until her soul was satisfied and then went to bed.

As Phale tells it—often in sermons—something moved in that room that "the doctor had not figured on; something was touched that the doctor and his medicine couldn't heal." Early the next morning, Phale opened his eyes, called his mother, and told her that he was hungry—a sign that the fever had broken and he had begun to recover. Lee Ellen fell to her knees and thanked God for saving her child. Phale remembers his mother as a deeply religious woman who loved her family very much.

Phale does not remember Church administering corporal punishment to him or any of the other children, but he is sure it was probably done occasionally. It was not often necessary, because Church taught the children, and it was reinforced in Sunday school, that they were to obey their parents. This meant not only their biological parents but anyone old enough to be their parents. Any neighbor had permission to punish them if they needed it, and they would again be punished by their father if he discovered they had done something that warranted a neighbor's punishment.

The minister who pastored the church, Rev. Alvin L. Hill, had a traveling circuit and preached at their church once a month. When he came, he stayed at the Hale home in the guest room. Phale recalls Rev. Hill as one of the first persons to raise Phale's own sights beyond the farm. He remembers once, when he was five or six years old, standing beside the minister, who was sitting on the swing on the porch. Rev. Hill put his hand on Phale's head and said, "Young man, let me tell you something. If you develop your brain, there are people in Chicago who will pay you five thousand dollars a year for your brain."

Phale said that those words made a great impression on him. Rev. Hill had a son in Chicago at that time, and this also impressed him. I asked how it was that he happened to be talking to the minister; why was he drawn to hold conversations with the person who came in from the outside world with stories to tell? Where were his brothers and sisters? They were playing in the yard, he recalls, and he was not sure why he often sat and talked with the minister when he visited. He just knew that he was an interesting man.

The family was very close to the church, so much so that Phale's friends teased him by saying that his father *was* the church, his mother *was* the missionary society, and his sister *was* the BYPU (Baptist Young People's Union). They all attended Sunday school at 9:30 A.M. They arose early, as was their daily custom, and had a big breakfast. When they were small, Church hitched up the mules and rode them to Sunday school. When they were old enough, they would walk. They would go barefoot and carry their shoes, because it was hot and they were more comfortable without shoes. Just before they arrived at the church door, they would dust off their feet and put their shoes on.

Inside the church there was one aisle, down the center to the pulpit. On one side of the pulpit was the choir stand, where Lee Ellen sang. By the time he was seven or eight years old, Phale sang with her. The deacons' board sat together, the mothers' board sat together, and the deacons' wives sat together. They also had a mourners' bench, which was where you sat until you had accepted Christ as your savior and became a Christian. During revivals, sinners also sat on the mourners' bench.

The church was the center of social intercourse for plantation families. After church, the families would eat from picnic baskets they had brought. Family members would move from bench to bench, sampling each other's food. It was a time of fun and fellowship. Young women could send tickets to young men and choose them as recipients of food they had specially prepared. When Clem Hodges tried to explain his blood and marriage ties to my family, he recalled many marriages between members of our families. "Basically, you married who was there," he said.

EDUCATION

Nicholas Lemann (1991) describes the quality of education for share-croppers' children:

> Their children walked, sometimes miles, to plantation-owned schools, usually one- or two-room buildings without heating or plumbing. Education ended with the eighth grade and was extremely casual until then. All the grades were taught together, and most of the students were far behind the normal grade level for their age. The textbooks were tattered hand-me-downs from the white schools. The planter could and did shut down the schools whenever there was work to be

done in the fields, so the school year for the children of sharecroppers usually amounted to only four or five months, frequently inter-rupted. Many former sharecroppers remember going to school only when it rained. (18)

For Phale, there was no school until all of the crops had been gathered. School was held in the church, and all grades were taught in one room. When he was in the third grade, for instance, he asked the teacher whether he could return to the second grade because his friend was in that grade. The teacher gave him permission without a second thought. The teacher came from town, not from the plantation. How did the teacher teach when everyone was in a different grade? She told you to shut up and sit still until she got to you, Phale says.

The sole purpose of education in those days, Phale says, was to teach you to read and write by the time you were about fifteen years old. Then you could marry, get a mule, and go out and plow. As Lemann says, "whites kept the black school system in Mississippi infe-rior in part because they didn't want sharecroppers' children to have career options beyond sharecropping. Senator James K. Vardaman once said that educating the black man 'simply renders him unfit for the work which the white man has prescribed, and which he will be forced to perform. . . . The only effect is to spoil a good field hand and make an insolent cook'" (47).

The event that seemed to have the most impact on Phale's future life was the return to Mississippi of a Mr. Powell, the grandfather of John Harris, who later married Juanita, Phale's sister. Mr. Powell owned real estate in Chicago but lost it during the Depression and returned to the Pillow plantation with his grandson, John, who was about Phale's age.

Phale and John attended Sunday school together at Brooklyn Chapel and learned about the friendship of the biblical characters David and Jonathan. John said, "Let's you and I be friends like David and Jonathan," Phale agreed, and they shook hands. When John's grandfather allowed him to go to school in Greenwood to the eighth grade, Phale, who was only in the third grade even though they were close in age, was given permission to go to Greenwood too. Phale says he had never even heard of the eighth grade.

The school year was longer in Greenwood than on the plantation, but Phale was surrounded in his family by boys who could compensate for his absence. Thus Phale's birth order probably was a factor in his father being able to spare him from the farm. Of course, Phale still had chores to do and cotton to pick when he was not in school. He would rise as early as 3:00 A.M., while the family was still sleeping, prepare his breakfast, and complete his homework before leaving for school. He would walk four miles to school, attend school all day, even play basketball, and walk four miles back home, where he went to bed early. Phale remembers never being late for school and being amazed that his schoolmates were often late even when they lived across the street from the school.

Phale also prepared his lunch to take to school with him. However, because he was embarrassed for his schoolmates to see his bacon or ham and biscuits, which were considered "country" in comparison with the hamburgers and hot dogs his classmates could buy, he would hide his lunch on the path to school and eat it on the way home. He remembers how desperately happy he was to see that lunch when he returned to it.

I asked Phale whether he felt he was smarter than his siblings and whether that is why he succeeded in school. "I don't know," he said. "I do know that I was smart enough to know that I needed to go to school!" I also asked Ella Hale Warren and Clem Hodges why they thought Phale went to school while his siblings did not. Ella says that Phale always just seemed interested in school. Clem believes that Phale had a brilliant mind and was always questioning things and seeking stimulation. He observes that one went to school in those days at great sacrifice, since everything was structured to maintain the status quo and to keep you on the plantation. The whole system was designed to encourage large families (through Christmas gifts) and to keep African Americans productive, generation after generation, as sharecroppers. After long hours in the field, there were numerous temptations, such as girls all dressed up and looking for a man to marry. People focused a great deal of energy on their social lives because there was little else to occupy their minds. So a person who wanted to be upwardly mobile had to work incredibly hard and move past innumerable temptations.

In those days, Clem says, you almost had to obtain permission from the plantation owner for your children to go to school past the sixth grade. And it was easier to justify a girl going to school than a boy, because every able-bodied male child was needed to work the fields.

Once Bob Pillow picked Phale up as he was walking to school and gave him a ride into Greenwood. He asked Phale why his father let him, a younger child in the family, go into Greenwood to school and whether that created a problem with the other children. Why was his older brother, Buddy, not going? Phale answered that his daddy had asked Buddy whether he wanted to go to school, and Buddy didn't want to go—he preferred to plow. Willie B., whose nickname was Buddy, married as a teenager, got a house, and stayed on the plantation. His first child was born on the plantation. He and his wife and family eventually moved to Chicago.

Phale says that there was no perception among sharecroppers that education provided you any advantages. There was no encouragement to go to school and no envy on the part of one's siblings because one went. Buddy did go to school in Greenwood for a short while but was absent so much he eventually quit. Phale's older sisters went to the plantation school, married when they became old enough, and eventually left the state. Years later, after Lee Ellen's death, Anne lived with her sister and brother-in-law Juanita and John Harris and finished high school in Chicago. C.H., the youngest child, lived with Phale in Fort Wayne, Indiana, where he finished high school.

When the children were not in school, in addition to seasonal work in the fields, they worked around the house. The girls canned. The boys cut, hauled, and stocked wood. They also picked blackberries and anything else they could find for their mother to can. In the fall, they cut cane to be ground and made into molasses. They killed hogs, fed chickens, and picked apples, peaches, and pears for canning.

ECONOMIC STAGNATION

Phale had friends in Greenwood whose families owned land in the delta, and Phale remembers exhorting his father to buy his own land. The family, he notes, was at its peak labor force, with five of the sons old enough to do considerable work. He was very disappointed when his father did not respond favorably.

I asked Clem why Church made no effort to buy his own land. In those days, he says, people did not make drastic changes. They were very cautious. Church felt he was doing all right economically, given where he and his contemporaries had come from—slavery. Also, an African American could not just buy land at that time; he had to go to the white people for that. There was no economic development apparatus to assist sharecroppers in becoming landowners, and banks and mortgage companies operated in concert with plantation owners to keep African Americans working as sharecroppers.

Lemann describes the economic cycle for sharecroppers: cotton was picked in October and November and ginned (separated from the seeds) in the plantation owner's gin and weighed. It was then packed into bales and sold. A couple of weeks later, the owner did his accounting for the year. Just before Christmas, he met with the sharecropper for the "settle": the sharecropper would be handed a piece of paper, showing how much he had made from his crop, and would be paid this share.

From the crop earnings would be deducted the "furnish," the monthly stipend the planter provided the family, usually between fifteen and fifty dollars. An exorbitant interest rate was usually charged for the furnish. Phale remembers that his father received a furnish of forty dollars a month and was charged 25 percent interest. He estimates that his father cleared about a thousand dollars at the end of the year. That money was used to purchase items that could not be made.

The furnish was to cover the family's living expenses until the crop came in in the fall. "The planter provided 'seed money' for cotton seed, and tools for cultivation. He split the cost of fertilizer with the sharecropper. Thus equipped, the sharecropper would plow his land behind a mule, plant the cotton, and cultivate a 'garden spot' for vegetables. Between planting and harvest, the cotton had to be regularly 'chopped'—that is, weeded with a hoe—to ensure that it would grow to full height" (Lemann, 18). The furnish would buy only "cheap homemade clothes and shoes, beans, bread and tough fatty cuts of pork—but nonetheless the money often ran out before the end of the month, in which case the family would have to 'take up' (borrow) at the commissary," whose goods were usually marked up (ibid.). Sharecroppers were charged exorbitant interest rates for buying at the commissary on credit.

When tractors came into use in the 1930s, sharecroppers were charged for their use without being told what the charges would be. "For most sharecroppers, the settle was a moment of bitterly dashed hope, because usually the sharecropper would learn that he had cleared only a few dollars, or nothing at all, or that he owed the planter money" (ibid., 19). And there was indisputable cheating. "There was no brake on dishonest behavior by a planter toward a sharecropper. For a sharecropper to sue a planter was unthinkable. Even to ask for a more detailed accounting was known to be an action with the potential to endanger your life. The most established plantations were literally above the law where black people were concerned" (ibid.).

Lemann estimates that only about a quarter of the planters were honest in their accounting. He gives tragic accounts of sharecroppers who had managed to buy their own mules and plows, giving them some measure of independence, and of having them seized by planters after the settle. One sharecropper was told that he would be paid nothing for the entire year because the planter had to use the money to send his son to college.

I asked Phale whether his father was treated fairly in the settle. The most glaring injustice he saw had to do with the differing prices of cotton. Cotton picked in the early fall, when it was clean, garnered a prime rate. It was priced lower in the late fall, when it was dirty from rain and leaves and was not as white. His father was given the lower price regardless of the condition of the cotton or when it was picked.

Phale had occasion to observe a sharecropper challenge the settle by bringing his own figures to the accounting. He was threatened by the manager and told never to bring any figures in there again. There was talk among the sharecroppers that Mr. Pillow had threatened to put this man off the plantation. Once, Phale attempted to discuss his father's settle with the plantation manager, who told Church not to bring that boy in there again. "I'm your boss," he said, "and this is all you get." After that, his father restrained Phale from challenging the accounting.

I wondered whether Church gave any thought to his economic fortunes when his children grew up and left. I assumed that the planters did not have a retirement plan. Phale doubted whether his father, in his prime, considered the future. When his children were grown and he was no longer able to work the land, he moved to Memphis and lived with his daughter Rosalie. Phale sent a monthly allowance to his father and eventually went to Memphis and secured what was called an old age pension for his father.

GREENWOOD

One fact emerges clearly from my interviews with my father: the events that lifted his sights were associated with his experiences in Greenwood, Mississippi. Although he was close to his older brother, Buddy, and got along well with all his siblings, as he was growing up, most of his ties were in Greenwood. He felt especially close to John Harris; the two boys played together, visited each other, and walked together the eight miles to school and home each day. Phale was so inspired by John being in the eighth grade that he set as his goal making it to the eighth grade. Later, he set as his goal graduating from high school and, later, going to college.

School in Greenwood was quite an advancement over school on the plantation. Phale was amazed that there was a real school building, schedules, and different classes. He was accustomed to children of all ages sitting in one room all day, with boring, unmotivating instruction. In Greenwood, he set goals for himself. On the plantation, he went to school because his parents told him to go; here, a whole new world opened up for him.

Phale worked on the farm during the summer and whenever he was out of school, and there seemed to be no tension for Phale in deviating from family custom—no teasing or ostracism for being different. This is consistent with his adult relationships with his siblings; they respect him and have a warm, loving relationship with him. Thus upward mobility did not extract a price of distance from his family. (This is in contrast to my mother's experience, which is discussed in chapter 6.)

Phale remembers having to buy his books. He paid for them by picking cotton. "I could pick five hundred pounds of cotton in one day. Not many people could do that. When I needed extra money, I could pick cotton for other people and be paid." Once Phale borrowed an ink pen from the niece of Mr. Threadgill, his teacher and coach. But while Phale was making a fire, the pen accidentally fell into it. He remembers getting up very early in the morning, "when you could barely see. But the cotton was white, so I could see it. By noon, I had picked over three hundred pounds of cotton."

He had other opportunities for making extra money. For example, when the Yazoo River flooded, workers were needed to move the cotton stored in the flooded area. Here, as he watched the other workers work, he learned that cotton could be moved more expeditiously by hand truck than by hand. This knack of observing other workers allowed him to catch on quickly to new jobs.

Phale speaks very matter-of-factly of his prowess as a cotton picker and seems to have no bitterness about it. I asked whether it hurt his back to stoop over and pick cotton. "You could stoop over or get on your knees," he says; "when your cotton sack became full, you went over and emptied it." He later worked in the steel mills in Buffalo to earn money to go to college and felt that work in the steel mills was harder than picking cotton.

Why then did African Americans hate picking cotton so much, if it wasn't that hard? Phale believes it is related to the pay—people wanted to make more money. "I wanted to get the nuts and bolts of my life in my hand. I wanted to get an education. I never bothered about work being hard. If the work was there, the job was to be done, I just took it and I just did it."

Did he feel as smart or smarter than the children he encountered in Greenwood? Were the children grouped by ability? He says that he made very good grades in school; however, he was never concerned about how he compared to the other children. I rephrased my question several ways, but he could not remember any comparing of his abilities with those of others. My mother says that this attitude is consistent: "He really does not compare himself to other people." The only thing he felt sensitive about in Greenwood was his lunch.

One thing stands out, however: he created a peer group for himself with other strivers, forming a fellowship with five other boys, who called themselves the Daddy-Cot boys. At that time a popular saying in the community was that no one had ever graduated from Greenwood (colored) High School and amounted to anything. The Daddy-Cot boys made a pact to change that; they were going to be different. And they were: they all graduated from high school and, later, from college.

Although Phale was inspired by his fourth-grade teacher, his first teacher in Greenwood, the person he identified with most strongly was L. H. Threadgill, his mathematics teacher and basketball and baseball coach, who came to Greenwood in 1929, after graduating from Knoxville College. Phale describes Mr. Threadgill as a good friend who motivated them in the classroom and in athletics.

When I lived in Jackson, Mississippi, I had a chance meeting with Charles Leonard, a dentist who came from Greenwood, Mississippi. Dr. Leonard graduated from Stone Street High School in 1947; it was the former Greenwood High School, where fourteen years earlier Phale had graduated. Charles knew of Phale Hale, because Phale occasionally returned to Greenwood and spoke to school assemblies. Mr. Threadgill, who became principal of Stone Street in 1941, and Phale enjoyed a close relationship for the rest of Mr. Threadgill's life, and he frequently invited Phale to return to his old school. Charles recalls Phale as a local boy who had done well and who wanted to remember where he came from and to inspire the young people there. Phale was highly respected by people in Greenwood. Charles taught at the school after obtaining a B.A. degree from Florida A. & M. University.

Mr. Threadgill, according to Charles, was a kind of Benjamin E.

Mays of Greenwood. He motivated young people; he was a rugged individualist; he had a severe facial expression but inside was soft and caring. He was fair-minded and honest and a great leader.

Clem describes Mr. Threadgill as being hard on his students, strict; he pushed them to succeed. He was also a sharp dresser. He eventually married a woman named Bessie, a classmate of Phale's whom Phale had a crush on in high school. Prior to Mr. Threadgill, Mr. Wilkes was the principal, a kind, fatherly figure who resembled Church Hale.

Phale excelled in baseball and basketball. And Charles so excelled in football that Mr. Threadgill contacted A. S. Jake Gaither, the legendary coach at Florida A. & M. University, and arranged for Charles to receive a football scholarship to college.

Charles feels that the African American community of Greenwood motivated and supported the young people. The men encouraged the athletes with support, attention, and money. It was not a lot of money, but it expressed their care and concern. Charles remembers the postman, a Mr. Dickerson, who had come to Greenwood in 1922; he came to see the games and encouraged the athletes. (Mr. Dickerson had also graduated from Knoxville College.) Charles also remembers Willie J. Bishop, who owned a café bar, as a man who loved athletics and was a strong backer of young people. Mr. Bishop had five daughters. He had attended Alcorn College for two years and was the Grand Master of the International Order of Elks for the state of Mississippi. Such support and visibility made the athletes accountable for their behavior. They were very concerned about disappointing the people who encouraged and believed in them.

Clem agrees that the African American community in Greenwood was supportive of the educational aspirations of young people. "They were people who had come from plantations of one kind or another. They understood the value of acquiring an education. They were convinced by the messages of teachers and preachers that education was the way out of slavery and poverty. Everywhere you went, the older people were encouraging you to do well."

Although African American boys were barred from joining the Greenwood Boy Scouts, white people in Greenwood established the Lucky Club for these boys. Phale was a member of the Lucky Club. Also, when the school basketball and baseball teams traveled to competitions, the boys would eat dinner together and listen to inspirational speakers. Phale also continued to be active in his church's Baptist Young People's Union and assumed a leadership role. He represented the group at state conventions, where he had the opportunity to broaden his horizons.

Phale also remembers white people in the community coming to school assemblies and speaking to them. One white man talked about the educational value of travel and encouraged them to travel whenever possible. Phale was very impressed by that advice. Even though he did not have much interaction with whites in the community, he did work during the summer for a white family, cutting their lawn, working in their garden, and plowing. When school started in September, the woman of the house offered to raise his pay if he would quit school and work for them full time. He declined, because he wanted to go to school.

Charles Leonard notes that all African Americans had decent relationships with individual white people on a one-to-one basis. It was when African Americans as a group had hopes and aspirations for advancement that whites became defensive. Any challenge to the racial folkways that maintained the dominant-submissive relationship was swiftly crushed. He reminded me that Emmett Till was killed in Money, Mississippi, in the early 1950s, and that Money is only eight or nine miles from Greenwood. When he was fourteen years old, Emmett, who was visiting his grandfather for the summer from Chicago, allegedly whistled at a white woman and was brutally beaten to death. Those charged with the murder were acquitted by an all-white jury. If that heinous crime occurred as late as the 1950s, it doesn't take much imagination to guess what the Hales were up against prior to 1933, when Phale departed.

Phale was less charitable about whites during another interview, when I pressed him for his reasons for leaving Mississippi. He says that he was aware of the beatings and lynchings of African Americans and that he wanted to get as far away from Mississippi as possible. He says that whites called African American men "boys" until they were old enough to be called "uncle." They called the women "girls" until they were old enough to be called "aunt." People who left Mississippi and returned to visit told of the promised land up north. What impressed them in particular was that white people called them "Mister" and "Missus." No African Americans were given titles by white people in Mississippi.

Charles Leonard says that the quality of education at the high school in Greenwood was superior, that the teachers were extremely dedicated and inspirational, and that he felt well prepared for his studies at Knoxville College and subsequently at Meharry Medical School. So, the chances for success for graduates of Greenwood High School seemed to be limited only by the lack of opportunity in Greenwood, not by the quality of their high school education.

Phale's fervent desire was to leave Greenwood; he felt that he would be nobody if he stayed there. I asked him what occupations were open to African American high school graduates in Greenwood. "You could cut grass," he said. "You could sweep floors—serve as a custodian. You could cook. You could be a busboy. The best jobs available to black people were mailman, or you could work on a train as a Pullman porter, a busboy, a waiter, or a chef. That is just about all there was." Charles Leonard's father was a plumber. When he was growing up, other African Americans worked at the compresses, which were storage areas for cotton that had been ginned and baled, and at the Buckeye, a mill that processed cottonseeds into cottonseed oil.

Most of the property in Greenwood was held by old families, he says, and was not available for development, which prevented the economic development of the whole community. The city was also landlocked to the south. Farming was the major industry, and there were few factory jobs. There was a café; there were some juke joints; some people made bootleg liquor. In other words, there was little in Greenwood for a black person with any degree of intelligence or enterprise. By 1955 to 1960, there were one or two insurance agents and morticians.

The county agricultural agent, a respected position, usually had a college degree. The agent helped farmers with crop rotation, financing of property, and so forth. And in 1953 Mississippi Vocational College became Mississippi Valley State University, an African American college established by the state and accessible to young people in the delta. But in 1933, Phale felt that his only hope for achieving a college education was to leave Mississippi. An essential ingredient was to find a job that would pay well enough to allow him to save the money he needed to work his way through school. Such employment was unavailable in Mississippi at that time. He had to go. As Muddy Waters sang,

> If I'm feeling tomorrow like I feel today,
> I'm gonna pack my suitcase and make my getaway.
> Lord, I'm troubled, have a worried mind.
> And I've never been satisfied,
> And I just can't keep from cryin'.
>
> —Muddy Waters, "I Can't be Satisfied"

NOTES

1   The names, nicknames, and birth and death dates of Silas and Eliza Hale's fourteen children are as follows: Richmond (Bud), October 1879–March 1960; Church (Bro), July 1881–June 1955; Tannie (Dime), December 1882–April 7, 1951; Layden (Mammy), 1884–1953; Smith William Penn (Penn), 1886–1949; Edmonia (Sister), 1888–1940; Brotop (Daddy), 1890–1982; Mondelphia (Eliza), 1893–1950; Mary Etta (Pudden), 1893–1950; Manassa (Shack), 1895–April 7, 1951; Ned Franklin (Betsy), 1896–1949; William Daniel (Nib), 1889–1955; Pensacola (Minerva), 1900–1943; and Adelle (Baby or Tootsom), 1902–1961.

2   Church and Betsy Lawson had five children: a first-born daughter, who died in the 1870s; Eliza (Big Ma), 1862–September 4, 1922; Ida; Richmond; and Travis. Travis was one of the first African American schoolteachers in Oktibbeha County when schools were set up for African American children. He taught at Lyde Grove School. He and Richmond eventually moved away from Mississippi and never returned.

3   Carl and Margaret Roberts had eight children: Carl, Lee Ellen, Doc, Anna Belle, Margaret (Mug), Azalee, Mister, and Willie Lee.

4   Ella Hale Warren (1983) writes that the founder of Brownridge Missionary Baptist Church was Rev. John Lyde, who pastored until his passing in 1912. Before the Civil War, he and another young man from Jackson invited a few slaves to the Lyde home for prayer meeting on Sundays. When the news spread to slaves on surrounding plantations, the meetings grew. Eventually, the meetings were too large to be held in a home. The minister sought help from the owner of the plantation in arranging a larger place to worship. Eventually, a white woman named Miss Edwards gave the members a triangle of land near the Mobile and Ohio Railroad in what was then the hamlet of Penn Station, Mississippi.

The minister and his members built their first church out of sticks, mud, pieces of wood, and tree branches with green leaves. They called their church Brush Harbor. After the green leaves turned brown, the top of Brush Harbor resembled a brown ridge. The members voted to rename their church Brownridge. Eventually, the building became too small for the congregation. Assisted by outside contributors from the area, they built a larger church beside the old building in 1869. This building served a dual purpose, as a house of worship and as a secular school. It was the only school in the vicinity.

By the 1880s, the building again was too small for the congregation. A larger church was built, with only contributions from members, on a plot of land in the same area—facing the railroad, now called Gulf, Mobile, and Ohio Railroad (GM&O). Over the course of the next eighty years, the building was remodeled several times.

5   Clemmon Hodges of Buffalo, New York, is my father's cousin. He regards Phale as his inspiration for moving from a sharecropping family, himself, to achieve a baccalaureate degree from Morehouse College and a master's degree in social work. He was an especially valuable informant because he is related to Phale on both the Hale and Roberts sides of the family and provided valuable history and insight on both.

He grew up in Crawford, Mississippi (near Starkville), and followed in Phale's foot-steps in attending high school in Greenwood and Morehouse College in Atlanta.

6   Church and Ellen Hale had twelve children: Rosa Lee, Magnolia, Elizabeth, Rebecca, Willie B., Phale Dophis, Juanita, Jonathan, Fred, Jethro, Anne, and Church, Jr.

7   William and Elizabeth (Scales) Pillow had seven children: Mattie, Elizabeth Addie, Annie, William, Robert, Mary, and Walter. Nathaniel Scales and his wife had three children: Leslie, Elizabeth, and Addie.

CHAPTER FOUR

The Upward Mobility of Rev. Phale D. Hale, Sr.: Buffalo

When Phale was a child in the cotton fields he promised God that, if God would just take him out of Mississippi, he would preach the gospel. The year before he graduated from high school, a friend of his was killed riding a freight train. But Phale told God that, even if he died trying to get out of Mississippi so that he could get an education, then so be it. When he asked his parents to let him leave, Lee Ellen said to Church, "I don't know what Honey wants to be, but we should let him go." This was 1933. Phale received his high school diploma on Friday and caught a freight train the following Monday.

He set out on his journey with his friend Rusty, one of the Daddy-Cot boys. Rusty had also finished high school. Their destination was Chicago. John Harris had married Phale's sister Juanita (Doll) and had returned to Chicago where he had family members. John had finished high school and had gotten a job in the postal service, a top job for African Americans at that time. Doll initially worked in a slaughterhouse, one of the jobs readily available to migrants at that time. The couple invested in real estate, John moved on to higher jobs, and

Amazing grace! How sweet the sound
That saved a wretch like me
I once was lost and now am found
Was blind but now I see.

Through many dangers, toils, and snares
I have already come
'Tis grace that brought me safe thus far
And grace will lead me home.

JOHN NEWTON, *1779*

they prospered. Doll eventually was able to quit her job. They had no children.

Phale and Rusty walked and hitchhiked from Greenwood to Clarksdale, which took all day. Once they realized how slow they were progressing, they decided to ride the freight train. It was illegal to ride the freight trains, but there were a lot of people, colored and white, who did. The other hobos on the train taught Phale and Rusty how to stop the train by reaching under the car and pulling a line. It was important to get off the train before it reached the town where it was unloaded and where there was a danger of being caught. They would go on to the town on foot through the woods and swamps, and by the time the train was unloaded and ready to depart, they were able to jump on again.

In a town in Kentucky, while they waited for the train to be unloaded, Phale and Rusty went into a restaurant to eat. All the customers, colored and white, were lined up to be served. A white man stepped ahead of Phale, but the white man waiting on them said, "I'm sorry, he's ahead of you," and he served Phale next instead of the white person. Phale says that that was the first time he ever experienced being served before a white person. In Mississippi, he never ate in white restaurants. However, in any instance where blacks interfaced with whites, whites came first: blacks rode on the back of the trains; the doctor served white patients before he came to the colored waiting room.

Phale and Rusty stayed the entire summer with Doll and John in their apartment. They looked for jobs and filed applications, but they were unable to find jobs. They were told that they were too young or too inexperienced. Phale's father wrote telling him to come back home, and Rusty's parents wrote telling him to come back home. Rusty decided to go back, probably because he felt he was imposing on Phale's relatives. Also, Rusty's family had more economic resources than Phale's, and there was hope that he could attend college in Mississippi. In fact, Rusty did eventually graduate from Alcorn College.

But Phale declared that he was not going back to Mississippi except for a visit and then not until he could buy a train ticket and ride as a passenger. He and Rusty had jointly saved seven dollars and fifty cents, which they split between them. When Phale offered his half to Rusty, realizing the dangers Rusty faced hoboing back to Mississippi, Rusty refused. Phale slipped the money into Rusty's coat pocket without his knowledge. Rusty departed Chicago in time to enroll in Alcorn College in September.

Phale left Chicago in September, shortly after Rusty left, and traveled to Buffalo, where his sister Maggie (Magnolia) and her husband, Allen Spivey, lived.

THE HALE FAMILY IN BUFFALO

The first member of Phale's family to live in Buffalo was Church's brother Smith William Penn Hale, who had wanted to get as far away as possible from Mississippi and everyone from Mississippi. He had attended the Ministerial Institute and College (MIC) in West Point, Mississippi, and then lived in Louisiana, Florida, and Omaha, Nebraska, before settling in Buffalo in 1925. Smith worked for a time in the steel mills; he was also a preacher and founded a Pentecostal church, which he named Hale Chapel. The church still exists, though it is renamed.

Allen Spivey had grown up on the Pillow plantation with his mother and brother. He had traveled to Seattle to seek his fortune, but was unable to find a job, and returned to Mississippi to marry Maggie.

Three of Phale's sisters—Maggie, Rebecca, and Elizabeth—wrote to Uncle Smith asking whether they could come to Buffalo and stay with him until they could get on their feet. Reluctantly, Smith gave them permission to come. Maggie and Allen went first, in 1927. The next year the twins (Rebecca and Elizabeth) and their husbands followed: Elizabeth and Tom White Johnson and Rebecca and Tom White. Smith rented rooms to them.

Uncle Smith was very unhappy that his relatives from Mississippi had followed him. He often said that he had left Mississippi to get away from Negroes, and he felt his nieces and their husbands were not on his cultural level. Smith did not treat them as relatives. He ridiculed them, treating them as his inferiors. He had very strict rules for the household: they could not use the living room, which was reserved for Smith and his wife and their friends. His relatives were restricted to their bedrooms but were allowed to visit between their rooms. Making this even more difficult, Elizabeth and Tom had two small children to share their room with. When Cleo first visited Buffalo as Phale's wife twenty years later, she couldn't believe how small the rooms were in comparison with those in the South. She remembers the bedrooms in Smith's house as the smallest she had ever seen. Even in the nice house Maggie and Allen moved into later, the bedrooms were small.

Smith William Penn Hale, 1920

Maggie and Allen
Spivey, 1933.

Further, the Mississippi relatives were required to enter the house
by the backdoor; and Smith established a schedule for using the kitchen.

On the plus side, the men immediately found good jobs. Allen got
a job working for American Brass, which he kept until his retirement.
The other men also got jobs at American Brass. In those days, men
were hired for their physical strength and willingness to work. Allen
was the epitome of the sharecroppers William Julius Wilson (1987)
describes as emerging from the farm with strong bodies, strong moral
values, and a strong work ethic.

Wilson and Stanley Lieberson (1980) provide a sociological inter-
pretation of the relationship between the three couples and Smith

Hale. The plantation-to-ghetto migration picked up steam in the 1920s when Congress curtailed the immigration of whites from Southern, Central, and Eastern Europe. Never before were African Americans able to secure jobs and not be discriminated against in favor of white immigrants. Lieberson points out that Chinese and Japanese immigrants were also discriminated against because of skin color, but legislation also curtailed their immigration. Furthermore, those Asians who were here solidified their ethnic networks and created occupational niches in small, relatively stable communities.

It is Lieberson's position that the curtailment of European and Asian immigration worked in favor of those already here: there was no regulation or curtailment of African American migration, creating a situation in which whites muffled their negative attitude toward immigrants and instead directed their antagonism toward African Americans.

The sheer numbers of migrants, however, made it difficult for African Americans to follow the path of the Europeans and Asians in finding occupational niches. Furthermore, the continual stream of new arrivals made it difficult on the African Americans who had arrived earlier, like Uncle Smith. As Lieberson points out,

> sizable numbers of newcomers raise the level of the ethnic and/or racial consciousness on the part of others in the city; moreover, if these newcomers are less able to compete for more desirable positions than are the longer-standing residents, they will tend to undercut the position of other members of the group. This is because the older residents and those of higher socioeconomic status cannot totally avoid the newcomers, although they work at it through subgroup residential isolation. Hence, there is some deterioration in the quality of residential areas, schools and the like for those earlier residents who might otherwise enjoy more fully the rewards of their mobility. Beyond this, from the point of view of the dominant outsiders, the newcomers may reinforce stereotypes and negative dispositions that affect all members of the group. (380)

The three couples probably had enough resources among them to rent a house together. However, they were also probably very naive in negotiating their new environment. In addition, Uncle Smith spent more time ridiculing them than teaching them. He was also consumed with building his church, and had to work in the factory to earn his living. And he lived well; he owned his own home, which was beautifully decorated, so evidently he had worked hard.

Elizabeth and Tom became discouraged first and returned to Mis-

sissippi. They continued to farm until about 1948, when they moved to Chicago. Rebecca and Tom left for Mississippi in the 1920s and, in the late 1940s, went to Memphis and, eventually, to East St. Louis, Illinois, where Tom had relatives. They remained there for the rest of their lives. It is easy to see why they were discouraged. Buffalo is so different from Mississippi; just the cold and the snow were difficult enough. Allen and Maggie stayed on in Buffalo, where they bought a home as a first step toward economic stability and progress.

Even though Uncle Smith is depicted as somewhat of a Simon Legree, I appreciate him for laying the foundation for urban migration for the Hale family—he was the first one to establish any place in the North for others to follow. Ella says that he moved to Buffalo in 1925; Doll and John moved to Chicago probably in the early 1930s. So at the time the Hale sisters moved to Buffalo, there was no place else to go, since it was essential to have a relative to room with and to show you around the town. That is probably why Allen was unsuccessful in finding a job in Seattle, where he went seeking his fortune in the years before his marriage. Phale's achievement of his dream was inextricably bound to the establishment of Maggie and Allen in Buffalo. Later, Manassa, Smith's sister, moved to Buffalo, and she was followed by countless other members of the Hale family (including Clem Hodges) from Mississippi.

Cleo doesn't recall anyone else staying with Smith Hale. In fact, Smith eventually left Buffalo to distance himself again from the Hales. Only Church Hale had news of Smith. Smith is dead now; Cleo doesn't know when he died; Ella Hale Warren has recorded that he died in 1949. As far as she knows, he never went back to either Mississippi or Buffalo. He never attended family funerals or weddings.

Aunt Maggie has said that Smith was a very unusual man, very smart, and the most outstanding of Church's siblings. She also said that Smith's spark was passed on to Phale. Phale's cousin Clem Hodges may have gotten the spark from Phale. Clem's uncle Ed Hodges was married to Manassa, Church's sister; they were in the second wave of Hales to go to Buffalo. Clem eventually followed them.

The fact that Smith started a church is evidence of his creativity. Maggie and Allen did initially attend his church, but they probably were not comfortable there, given the discomfort at home. Cleo says they almost feared Smith—probably because they were so dependent on him.

According to Maggie, Smith was a good preacher, his sermons

were dynamic, and he knew the Bible. (This was one of the only books African Americans had in those days, so they learned what it said.) When Phale began to preach, Maggie said, he preached a lot like Uncle Smith, even though Phale had never heard him preach and does not count him as an influence.

Smith was the first person in Phale's family to attend college; Smith's father, Silas, had sent him, perhaps even recruited him, to be the one in the family to attend college. Given the fact that Silas was a landowner, he was able to pull together the resources. Ministerial Institute and College (MIC) at that time (Smith graduated in 1907) actually provided the equivalent of a high school education. At that time, African Americans graduated from high school at the end of tenth grade and whites at the end of twelfth grade. Ella, when she finished high school in 1933, was in the first class to complete twelve grades.

MIC was founded by African Americans to provide a secondary education for their children. It was not supported by public funds but by individuals, churches, and state religious associations. MIC still exists today, but it no longer is a degree-granting institution. It offers Bible study and religious education training. But when Smith Hale attended, he received formal training for his entry to the ministry and the highest level of education achieved in his family. Typically, his brothers finished only sixth or seventh grade. His accomplishment was so noteworthy that the family folklore evolved that he had actually finished college. The fact that the school was called an "institute and college" added to the mystique. Furthermore, the Rev. E. J. Echols, Sr., the leading pastor in Buffalo, also graduated from MIC (it was called the Howell Institute at that time), which Smith was able to capitalize on.

Interestingly enough, Smith was a middle child, a birth-order position that allows one to be "wasted." He was the fifth child, with four boys older than he and three younger, which meant that he could be spared from working the fields.

Phale is more sympathetic toward Smith than Maggie, but of course Phale did not have to live with him. He sees Smith as very generous in allowing eight extra people to live in his home. Smith's nieces and their husbands all had strong personalities and were not especially flexible and able to make adjustments. He also had to satisfy his wife in bringing his relatives into his home.

Eventually, Allen met Mr. Hackney, who worked with him at

American Brass and was chairman of the deacons' board at Trinity
Baptist Church. Allen and Mr. Hackney became good friends—the
Spiveys did not have many friends—then Mrs. Hackney and Maggie
also became friends. The Hackneys invited Maggie and Allen to join
their church, because they loved their church and it was a growing
church. Maggie and Allen went, and they liked it. The Hackneys were
very warm people, friendly and intelligent. Mrs. Hackney was a high
school graduate (a high level of education for African Americans in the
1920s). The two couples remained friends until their deaths.

Maggie and Allen had a guest bedroom in their new house, and
they had a boarder. Everyone had boarders then, as a way of supplementing their income. Maggie and Allen served as surrogate parents
to Phale (and as grandparents to us children) for the rest of their lives.

Cleo describes Maggie and Allen as living the righteous life like no
one she had ever seen and attending church like no one she had ever
seen—and she grew up in a family of faithful churchgoers. But although her parents were active in the church, they had other outlets as
well, socializing with other families, having card parties, and so forth.

The church for Maggie and Allen, however, was their total life.
They attended Sunday school on Sunday morning, stayed for worship
service, and returned for the Baptist Training Union in the evening.
On Monday during the day Maggie attended the missionary society;
in the evening Allen attended the deacons' board meeting. On Tuesday they attended the Sunday school teachers' meeting (a big night).
On Wednesday evening was prayer meeting. On Thursday evening
Allen went to the church for choir rehearsal; he did not sing in the
choir but was there in his capacity as a deacon, to oversee the activities
of the members. Friday was the only day that was free. On Saturday
they attended church socials, such as picnics or church suppers. Cleo
recalls that when she and Phale visited them, Phale was right in there,
attending everything.

PHALE ARRIVES IN BUFFALO

Phale caught a freight train in Chicago and hoboed to Buffalo. He got
off at Spring Street and walked to Maggie's house, a sight to behold,
covered with soot from head to toe. Maggie said, "I thought you were
coming on the train." Phale replied, "I did." (Of course, Maggie
meant as a passenger on a commercial train.)

The next day, Allen took Phale to Seaton's men's store and bought him a suit of clothes, shoes, socks, a shirt, and a tie so he could go to Sunday school. Phale fell in with the church program on the second day after his arrival and after that never missed a Sunday. There was some tension between Phale and Uncle Smith, who wanted Phale to join his church and help him with his congregation. However, Phale was staying with Maggie and Allen and felt that he should accompany them to church. Allen was his Sunday school teacher at Trinity.

Phale in Buffalo in the 1930s

Educationally and in terms of church management, the people at Trinity were not much more advanced than the parishioners Phale had left behind in Mississippi. He began to suggest changes to Allen, which the congregation resented when Allen passed them on to them. The feeling was that Allen felt superior to them because his brother-in-law was a college student. Eventually, Phale realized that his suggestions were not appreciated, and he did not want to create tension for Allen.

Allen was a role model for Phale. He was a good man. Cleo feels that Allen made a strong impression on Phale because of the way he provided for Maggie. Phale had the opportunity to observe Allen turning his paycheck over to Maggie on payday for her to manage. Of all the things Phale saw in his life, Cleo was most grateful that he saw that, because when he married her, he emulated that behavior. As we reflect upon the role models in Phale's life, we have to ask where young African American men of today formulate their images of what a man is and does. How many Allen Spiveys do they have the opportunity to know and emulate?

Allen was a real resource to Phale because he was a working man in a fellowship with other working men; he therefore belonged to a network that was very valuable to Phale in finding work. Phale arrived in Buffalo in September 1933 and had a job in the steel mills by December. From that time on, he had a well-paying job whenever he needed one, even during summer vacations when he returned to Buffalo after the school year at Morehouse.

Phale first enrolled in evening classes at Buffalo State Teachers' College. He later enrolled in the University of Buffalo. It was a more prestigious school, and its schedule was more compatible with Phale's working schedule. At the University of Buffalo, he met three other African American students, one of them E. J. Echols, Jr. Phale and E.J. became fast friends. E.J.'s father was Rev. Elijah J. Echols, Sr., pastor of First Shiloh Baptist Church.

Rev. Echols had also grown up near Starkville, Mississippi, and was pastoring there when he was called to pastor Shiloh. (In those days, when significant numbers of African Americans migrated from the same place, it was common practice to call their pastor to join them.) Rev. Echols was a dynamic preacher and an outstanding pastor in the community. He impressed Phale because he had a college degree and because he was a good father, a good preacher, and a good pastor. Phale looked upon him as a father, and Rev. Echols treated Phale like a son.

Phale had grown disenchanted with Trinity and attended worship services at a church pastored by Rev. Mason, who had graduated from Colgate Rochester Divinity School. The members of his church were on a higher socioeconomic level than the members of Trinity, but Phale found the worship services "cold," less expressive. E.J. invited Phale to Shiloh, which he liked better; it was more a church for the masses. Phale walked to Shiloh, a longer walk than to Trinity. He attended Sunday school, church services, the Baptist Young People's Union, and many church activities. He has a picture in his photo album of himself as a member of a literary society sponsored by the church. So, they seemed to have a variety of enrichment activities for young people.

Rev. Echols took Phale under his wing and became his mentor. He appointed Phale president of the youth group at Shiloh. He also took him and E.J. to conventions. At one of these conventions, Phale had the opportunity to meet the legendary Rev. L. K. Williams, president of the National Baptist Convention, U.S.A., Inc., when he and E.J. drove Rev. Williams to the railroad terminal after a meeting. Rev. Williams was a powerful preacher and the most influential Baptist of the time.

Phale frequented a YMCA for African Americans across the street from Maggie and Allen's house. This put him and E.J. in a position to obtain jobs as stewards on a steamship that sailed on Lake Erie. Initially, the children of the white stockholders had been hired as stewards. However, when the ship would dock, they would disappear to enjoy the sights and would not return to work. The officials decided to find some hungry, hardworking African American youths who needed the money and would be reliable. Phale and E.J. met these criteria.

Phale appreciated this opportunity to earn money, and he and E.J. were hard workers. Phale seemed very adept at creating a peer group for himself with young people who shared his vision of upward mobility. He swore off alcohol and cigarettes; he noticed the drunks on skid row in Buffalo and vowed not to have drugs influence him at all.

Often the whites who rode on the steamship would leave behind bottles of alcohol as a tip for him and E.J. But there was a cook on the ship, named Stud, who enjoyed spirits, and they would give Stud the alcohol in exchange for the best from his kitchen. The other stewards were amazed when they were served chicken wings and Phale and E.J. were served T-bone steaks.

At the end of the summer, Phale left the Great Lakes Transit

Company with more money in his pocket than he had ever had in his life. Growing up, he had never had a bicycle or a pair of roller skates. (He once had one roller skate, which he skated on.) Now he had enough cash in his pocket to buy a motorcycle, which he longed for. But after spending two and a half hours looking at a motorcycle, sitting on it, touching it, walking around it, he walked outside, looked back at it, and walked down to the corner and decided to use his money to pay his tuition to college.

E.J. married and had a son before completing his education. He got a job in the post office, which as I have noted was a good job for African Americans in those days. He ended his education, even though Rev. Echols tried to persuade him to attend Morehouse College, as his younger son Walter did. Phale was the godfather of E.J.'s first child. Rev. Echols enlisted Phale's help in trying to persuade E.J. to go to Morehouse and offered to take care of his wife and son if E.J. would go to Morehouse. E.J. declined. In the late 1940s, E.J. was called to preach at, and eventually to pastor, Shiloh. Much later, he became president of the Empire (New York) State Baptist Convention. He and Phale remained close friends until E.J.'s death.

Earlier, Rev. Echols was vice president of the Empire State Baptist Convention. Phale and E.J. became friends of George Sims, Jr., the son of Rev. George Sims, president of the Empire State Convention, and Phale and E.J. spent a great deal of time in the Sims household. Phale recalls a conversation between Rev. and Mrs. Sims as Rev. Sims was trying to decide how much money to send George, Jr., who was a student at Virginia State University. He finally decided to send him a blank check. Phale thought about how different their situations were. While he was agonizing about how he could earn enough money to send himself to college full time, George was being sent a blank check by his father. I commented that I was sure he also felt it was ironic that, while all he thought of was going to college, E.J.'s father was willing to send him and he didn't want to go. Did the comparisons between himself and his friends bother him? He says that it didn't. Did he regret that his father could not send him to college? He says that he never held it against his father that he couldn't help him; he realized his father's situation. He believed that the Lord would help him make it. His focus was on what it would take for him to pursue his dream.

Even though Phale had promised God that he would preach if He delivered him from the cotton fields of Mississippi, he fought the ministry. "Fighting the ministry" is an expression people use who have been "called" by God to preach but feel ambivalent about being a preacher. One can resist the "call" for years before accepting. Some never accept it. Phale had had second thoughts about becoming a preacher even as a teenager in Mississippi. Church people felt that preachers should not dance, for example, and he enjoyed dancing. He considered being a lawyer but worried about the ethics of defending someone he knew was guilty. He also considered becoming a mortician.

Then one day he realized that he was "fighting the ministry." He woke up one morning and talked with Allen and told him he was going to be a preacher. He felt as though a load had been lifted off of his back.

After Phale accepted the call, Rev. Echols licensed him to preach. He preached his trial sermon in the basement of Shiloh. It was Rev. Echols who suggested that he go to Atlanta and attend Morehouse College. Phale had heard of Morehouse College when he was in Greenwood; they must have sent recruiters, he thought. However, he never considered going. He didn't have the resources and couldn't even conceptualize obtaining them.

CHAPTER FIVE

The Upward Mobility of Rev. Phale D. Hale, Sr.: Morehouse

Going to Morehouse College in 1936 meant packing your suitcase and showing up. When his children went to college, my father was amazed at all the tests there were to take and forms to be completed a year in advance. In his day, you got there any way you could and registered.

When Phale was attending the University of Buffalo, he worked as a busboy in a restaurant. A white woman named Mary, who attended Shiloh and worked as a chef at the same restaurant, found out that Phale was a college boy and organized a fundraiser to help Phale with college expenses. She also gave him the opportunity to work as a waiter and let the customers know he was putting himself through college. He was thus able to earn extra money in tips. Phale was so grateful to Mary that, when he left for Morehouse, he made pans of soap (a skill his mother had imparted) and left them at the restaurant for her.

There were three men at Morehouse whom Phale knew from Buffalo—Walter Echols (E.J.'s younger brother), King Peterson, and Ike Meadows—and they shared a room. (Here he was again, sharing a room with three other

> To be unshackled, to improve the mind, to mold the character, to dream dreams, to develop the body, to aspire for greatness, or to strive for excellence is the birthright of every child born into the world. . . . And no society has the right to smother ambition, to curb motivation, or to circumscribe the mind.
>
> BENJAMIN E. MAYS
> *President Emeritus, Morehouse College*

people.) Because Phale had worked in Buffalo in the steel mills and as a waiter, he was able to buy a very natty wardrobe for his campus debut. He knew it would be a long time before he could afford to buy more clothes, so he bought everything he thought he would need before leaving Buffalo. Phale was so sharply dressed that no one would believe that he was as poor as Joe's church mouse. Even Cleo had the erroneous impression that he had money, by the way he dressed and carried himself.

His friends from Buffalo eased his transition to Morehouse, introducing him to their friends; he thus met upperclassmen, unusual for a freshman. Also, Phale no doubt had a certain savoire-faire gained from his three years of city working experience. Of course, at that time it was unusual for any Morehouse man to go to college straight out of high school, so many of them were older students.

Phale was deeply inspired by the atmosphere at Morehouse. Many of his professors were African American, and they called him "Mr. Hale." At white schools, you were limited by what whites would allow you to become, but at Morehouse, you could achieve or accomplish anything you could envision. Sara Lawrence Lightfoot (1988) describes her father's impression of Morehouse during his years there between 1932 and 1936 (Phale arrived in 1936). The environment freely mixed education, social life, and religion. Students were required to attend chapel Monday through Friday and on Sunday morning and Tuesday evening. Chapel was a highly ritualized, religious occasion. The students grumbled about having to attend chapel, but it was a student gathering place and so built an esprit de corps among the students.

Charles Lawrence, Sarah's father, reported that John Hope, the first colored president of Morehouse, would speak at morning chapel. And at the Tuesday evening chapel, Samuel Archer, a popular professor and Hope's eventual successor, would address the students.

> Hope and Archer were opposites. Dr. Hope, graduate of Brown University, classics scholar, a handsome, elegant, light-skinned man with silver-gray hair, gave insightful restrained homilies to the Morehouse men. Dr. Archer, a large imposing man, a former football star at Colgate, shook the rafters with his big booming voice, his straight talk, and his hyperbole. "Both Hope and Archer were admired by the student body—John Hope for his depth of mind and Archer because he liked to, as they say today, 'tell it like it is.'" Despite the contrasts in their oratory, both men used the pulpit to preach about "character building," advice that combined intellectual, moral and religious

training. Their renditions were offered as "a very practical kind of advice." (Lightfoot, 144–45)

In 1946 Clem Hodges followed Phale to Morehouse. Phale had told him so much about Morehouse that he felt he was entering the promised land. He was, of course, immediately disappointed in the physical plant—heaven was supposed to look better than this. He kept his bags packed for two weeks, unsure about whether to stay.

There was no room for Clem to live on campus, so he roomed with a Mrs. Johnson, who boarded students. One of his fellow roomers was Robert (Bob) Johnson, who is now an editor and associate publisher of *Jet* magazine. It was Bob who persuaded Clem to stay a little longer.

Clem went to orientation, where they told him the meaning of being a Morehouse man. He heard Benjamin Mays speak in chapel on Tuesdays, which boosted his ego; after that, Tuesdays couldn't come around fast enough. Clem matriculated with Martin Luther King, Jr. They both majored in sociology and minored in religion. (Clem almost followed Phale into the ministry. Fortunately, he says, he caught himself in time.) Clem and M.L. jointly authored a paper for Walter Chivers, a legendary professor of sociology. The assignment was to write a paper on rural sociology, but Clem and M.L. got permission to write their paper on urban sociology.

Daily chapel was an inspiration for Phale, as it was for Charles Lawrence and Clem Hodges. The speakers for chapel were some of the most prominent African American men of that generation: Howard Thurman, philosopher and mystic; C. D. Hubert, professor and interim president of Morehouse; William Holmes Borders, professor at Morehouse and pastor of Wheat Street Baptist Church; James Nabrit, executive secretary of the Georgia Baptist State Convention (his son, James Nabrit, Jr., later became the president of Howard University); Mordecai Johnson, president of Howard University; W.E.B. DuBois, professor of sociology at Atlanta University; Alonzo Herndon, founder of Atlanta Life Insurance Company; and C. A. Scott, publisher of the *Atlanta Daily World*.

Samuel Archer was president of Morehouse during Phale's freshman year. He passed on soon thereafter, and C. D. Hubert was named interim president. Benjamin Mays became president in 1940, the fall after Phale's graduation.

C. D. Hubert, who taught Phale religion and philosophy, became his friend and mentor. Morehouse students were required to take one year of Bible studies (Lightfoot, 1988), a course taught by Dr. Hubert. Charles Lawrence reported that the students called Dr. Hubert "Big Boy Hubert" because of his girth. Cleo says he weighed about three hundred pounds. Dr. Hubert, a graduate of Morehouse, had received his graduate degree from Colgate Rochester Divinity School, where he had been influenced by Walter Raushenbusch. According to Lawrence, "Raushenbusch, a central figure in the development of 'the social gospel,' influenced Hubert's views about the connections between theology and ideology. The social gospel has to do with the here and now . . . with considering the relationships between labor and management . . . with the Christian socialist movement. . . . It was the tradition from which Martin Luther King, Jr., came" (ibid., 145).

Hubert enthusiastically transmitted these ideas to his students through his teaching and in his sermons as the pastor of Providence Baptist Church. Cleo describes him as very relaxed; he talked slowly and preached slowly. Phale modeled his preaching after Dr. Hubert's style. Once, when Phale served as the guest preacher for Rev. Ivor Moore (the man whom Mattie Echols, sister of E. J. Echols, married) in Munford, New York, one of the deacons asked Phale if he had ever met C. D. Hubert. Phale told him that he had served as Hubert's assistant when he was a student at Morehouse. The deacon replied that he knew that Phale must have known Hubert because he preached just like him. The deacon remembered Dr. Hubert serving as the pastor of his church while he was matriculating at Colgate Rochester Divinity School.

Dr. Hubert could relate to people of all walks of life. At Morehouse and Spelman, everyone wanted to take his classes because he was an easy grader. He talked to his students about life, taking a scripture and building his entire lecture around it. One did not have to do a lot of research for his classes; they were high on inspiration and low on work. He was a nice, loveable person.

At the time that Phale went to Morehouse, the saying was that there were three Morehouse men who stood alone in their fields: C. D. Hubert was the No. 1 *social* interpreter of the principles of Christ; Mordecai Johnson was the No. 1 *political* interpreter of the principles of Christ (evidenced by his political activity in building Howard University); and Howard Thurman was the No. 1 *mystic* interpreter of the principles of Christ.

Lightfoot writes about her father's impressions of C. D. Hubert: "Charles was 'ready to receive' Dr. Hubert's teachings. His professor's ideas spoke directly to his condition. 'There was an emphasis on *not* being an old-fashioned fundamentalist. . . . For example, I began to see the Genesis story as a "myth of creation." . . . I began to perceive a difference between fact and truth . . . truth spoke to a deeper reality'" (ibid.).

When he arrived at Morehouse, Phale immediately joined a fellowship of preachers on campus. He met Joel King, the brother of Martin Luther King, Sr., who was pastoring Ebeneezer Baptist Church at that time and who had graduated from Morehouse College a few years earlier. Phale was impressed that Joel King pastored a church in south Georgia while pursuing a college degree. This was a transitional period for the African American ministry, in which preachers were just beginning to be trained. Most of the ministers Phale had encountered were not college-educated. It made a deep impression on him that Joel had a church and was still furthering his education.

Phale organized a campus ministerial alliance and became president. When he discovered there was a Baptist ministerial alliance in Atlanta, he began attending those meetings. Joel King introduced Phale to his brother Martin Luther King, Sr., and the other Baptist preachers—with all of whom he developed lifelong friendships. Dr. King eventually introduced Phale to his sons, Martin, Jr., whom Phale called Mike, and A.D. I recall Dr. King, Jr., visiting our home when I was a child, when he preached for my father during the Montgomery bus boycott. I was thrilled to sit next to him at the dinner table. His preaching voice was very much like my father's; however, his speaking voice was a deep baritone. The Hales and the Kings enjoy a warm friendship still. Martin Luther King, Sr., and Mrs. King were like grandparents to me, and I count as one of my closest friends A.D.'s daughter Alveda King Beal.

Through his involvement in the ministerial association in Atlanta, Phale developed a relationship with another Baptist preacher in the city who, because he pastored several churches, often called upon Phale to preach for him. Phale developed a reputation as a dynamic preacher and was given opportunities to preach around the whole state of Georgia. Their relationship broke down when the preacher instructed the deacons not to give Phale the after-offering that was collected for him after he preached. He said that he would personally give it to Phale, but Phale never received the after-offering after this.

When Phale confided his concerns to Dr. Hubert about not receiving the offerings collected for him and that he desperately needed to

Phale *(standing, right)* meeting with Martin Luther King, Jr. *(seated, center)*, in April 1956. Also pictured are Mrs. King, Charles Francis, Jr., president of the Ohio NAACP *(next to Dr. King)*, and J. Maynard Dickerson, general chairman of the Ohio NAACP. (*Columbus* [Ohio] *Dispatch*)

stay in school, Dr. Hubert invited him to work as an assistant to him at Providence. Cleo tells of a deacon at Providence who always slept when Dr. Hubert was preaching but woke up for Phale's sermon. He knew what Dr. Hubert was going to say, he said, but he had to stay awake to see which way Phale was going to go.

Phale remembers the first meeting of the Student Council that he attended. Carl Strickland was the president; as Phale watched Carl conduct the meeting, he thought to himself, "I can do that." Then and there, he decided that he would one day become president of the Student Council of Morehouse College—and he did!

Phale was elected president during his senior year. This opened up a wealth of enrichment for him. He met leading African Americans

Phale as Student Council president, Morehouse, 1940
(Phale is seated at end of table).

who visited Morehouse, among them Jesse Owens, following his Olym-
pic victory. Judge Leo Jackson of Cleveland, Phale's classmate at Morehouse, says that Phale was indeed a "big man on campus." The students respected him so highly that he was not even regarded as a
contemporary but as a member of the faculty. Judge Franklin describes
Phale as a great speaker, who held the other students enthralled when
he spoke.

His friends from that period were mostly second- or third-
generation college-educated people. His friends had fathers with large
churches in the North, like E. J. Echols, Jr., and George Sims, Jr. They
were not up-from-slavery types like Phale. Yet he emerged as their
leader. One of his classmates was the second generation of his family to
attend college; he had graduated in 1940, his father in 1911.

Phale had two setbacks during his years at Morehouse. First, he
was dismissed from school because he had not paid his bills. He went
back to Buffalo and the steel mills to earn enough money to return.
Perhaps he looked so prosperous and carried himself with so much
dignity that college officials did not believe he really did not have the
money.

Phale at Morehouse with the Sphinx Club when he pledged Alpha Phi Alpha fraternity, 1938 *(Phale is standing, second from left)*.

The experience was humiliating for Phale. There were rumors in Buffalo that he had flunked out academically. However, he worked, saved more money, and returned to Morehouse. In addition, Maggie and Allen lent him money. When he graduated from Morehouse, he owed a thousand dollars to Morehouse College and another thousand to Maggie and Allen. He repaid them over time, at a rate of five dollars a month. Needless to say, it was many years afterward that Morehouse released his diploma. When Phale explained his debt to Cleo before they got married, it seemed to her he must owe each of them ten thousand in 1943 dollars.

Second, while he was at Morehouse his mother died. His father had written that he should return to Mississippi quickly if he wanted to see his mother alive. He was pledging the Alpha Phi Alpha fraternity at the time he left to go to his mother's bedside; he never did become a member. His mother died of a heart attack shortly after his return to Morehouse, but he could not afford to return for her funeral. Phale felt that her health had suffered from having too many children too close together. Also, the health care available to her in Mississippi was poor.

LAGRANGE, GEORGIA

In the spring of 1940, Phale was invited to preach at First Baptist Church in LaGrange, Georgia. It happened this way. Mr. Kelly, the principal of what later became the Kelly Grammar School, was also chairman of the deacons' board at First Baptist Church (which was founded in 1828). Mr. Kelly's daughter was married to Dr. Howard Thurman. As chairman of the deacons' board, Mr. Kelly invited Dr. Hubert to speak at their church. Since Dr. Hubert could not accept the invitation because of another commitment, Mr. Kelly then asked him to send his next best man, and Dr. Hubert's next best man was Phale. Dr. Hubert also knew that the pulpit at First Baptist was vacant.

Phale was invited back several times to preach, and the congregation considered calling him to be their pastor. Dr. Hubert spoke with Mr. Kelly and knew that a call was imminent, so he decided to ordain Phale near the end of Phale's senior year at Morehouse so he would be ready when the call came. At the ordination service, Dr. Hubert gave Phale two charges. "Charge number one was [to] search diligently in the New Testament for the footprints of the carpenter from Nazareth. When you find them, walk therein. Nobody has ever gone wrong following Jesus. Charge number two is, Identify with the common people. No one has ever identified with the common people and regretted it."

Rev. E. R. Carter, pastor of Friendship Baptist Church in Atlanta, also participated in the ordination service. It was in the basement of Friendship Baptist Church that Spelman College was founded. (This church was once pastored by Rev. Maynard Jackson, Sr., subsequent to Rev. Carter. I did my student teaching in Atlanta in an elementary school named for Rev. Carter.) At the ordination service, Rev. Carter gave Phale one charge: "If you ever hope to become a great preacher, get in fellowship with and spend some time with great preachers."

In the summer after he graduated from Morehouse, Phale was called to pastor First Baptist. He was in position to follow in the footsteps of such great pulpiteers as Rev. Sandy Ray, Rev. C. T. Walker, and Rev. Morris Allison Trier. When Phale received the call, he agonized with Dr. Hubert over whether he should accept the invitation or pursue his dream of graduate study at Colgate Rochester Divinity School. Dr. Hubert had helped him get a full scholarship to Colgate— it seemed that so many of the great preachers he admired, such as Dr.

Hubert, had studied at Colgate. Dr. Hubert suggested that Phale accept the invitation, pay off his bills at Morehouse, and later go to Colgate Rochester. With that plan in mind, Phale accepted the pastorate of First Baptist Church and moved to LaGrange, Georgia.

The church had been vacant for some time because it was in debt for a new building it had bought. The board had decided to use the pastor's salary to pay off the debt. In the meantime, membership had deteriorated. Mr. Kelly said that they were in a dilemma: if they offered Phale a respectable salary, they wouldn't be able to pay it. If they offered him what they could afford to pay, it would be embarrassing.

Phale's reply was that the Lord had told him to go into the vineyard and work and that He would take care of him. The church did have a parsonage, and the congregation would furnish one room of it, where Phale could stay. He could take his meals at the home of Mr. Kelly, chairman of the deacons' board. Above this room and board, the church would pay him ten dollars a week. Phale accepted the terms.

During the summer of 1940, Phale went to the state Baptist Sunday school convention in Columbus, Georgia. One day he and a friend entered the cafeteria in the school where the classes were being held and looked around for a seat. He noticed a classmate of his from Spelman, Althea Morton, who motioned for him and his friend to join her. Seated with her was Cleo Ingram, a tall, thin, light-skinned, beautiful girl with long dark hair. She had keen facial features and a beautiful warm smile. Cleo had just graduated from high school and was to enroll at Spelman that September. Althea and Cleo had grown up in Mt. Zion Baptist Church in Atlanta and were good friends.

Althea and Cleo had gone to breakfast with the thought of eating something light but discovered that breakfast did not come à la carte. They were served eggs, grits, biscuits, bacon, and all the trimmings. When the two handsome young men joined their table, they offered them their breakfast: it was already paid for, they said, but they were not hungry enough to eat it. Phale and his friend gratefully accepted. The four of them talked while the men ate; then Althea and Cleo excused themselves to attend their classes. At the time, Phale and Cleo did not consider each other as prospective mates. They didn't meet again for a year.

Phale made a big splash in LaGrange. He did not have a car, so he visited the members of his church on foot. (He hadn't done all of that walking in Mississippi for nothing; however, this time he walked with

College days, Phale (1940) and Cleo (1943)

his shoes on!) It was so unusual to see a proud African American man walking down the street in LaGrange wearing a suit and tie in the middle of the day that the police stopped him frequently to ask him who he was.

To build the membership of the church, Phale held a revival and invited Rev. Jordan to preach at it. Mr. Kelly did not approve of Rev. Jordan, because he was not educated, but Phale insisted on inviting Rev. Jordan to serve as an evangelist. Phale invited East Depot High School students to the revival, as well as the students and principals of other schools. And First Baptist had a week-long fire-and-brimstone revival in which the people shouted and testified. The church added over a hundred new members, and Mr. Kelly made a motion that the revival be extended for a second week.

Phale thus completely changed the image of the church, whose reputation before his arrival was as a place where people had special seats and no one could shout. There was a phenomenal growth in the membership during Phale's first year as pastor.

Dr. Otis Moss, Jr., a renowned pulpiteer and currently pastor of Olivet Institutional Baptist Church in Cleveland, was a boy of seven when Phale came to LaGrange. He first heard Phale preach at a Sunday school picnic. Usually, when Otis attended those meetings, the only thing he remembered was what they had to eat, but when he heard Phale Hale speak, it made an indelible impression. Otis Moss, Jr., is counted today as one of the famous sons of Morehouse. Otis Moss's sister Josie tells about the hit Phale made with the women of LaGrange. Josie and her high school girlfriends swarmed to the church to try to get front-row seats when he preached, leading me to believe that a large proportion of the converts who swelled First Baptist's membership rolls were young adoring women.

In the fall of 1941, Phale decided to enroll in Gammon Theological Seminary, since he was not prepared to depart for Colgate. He felt lonely in LaGrange and wanted the stimulation and social outlets that Atlanta had to offer. After two years at Gammon, he phoned Colgate to inquire about transferring; but he needed to spend two of his three years in residency at Colgate to obtain a degree, and he had only one year left. They suggested that he finish his degree at Gammon and enroll at Colgate for advanced study. As it turned out, he never went to Colgate.

During the summer of 1941, Althea Morton and Cleo Ingram were traveling by train to the Georgia Baptist Sunday school convention, which was meeting in Valdosta. As the train was pulling out, they heard a loud commotion: someone was trying to throw his bags on the train as it was moving. Then, he was trying to jump on the train. The porter ran to see what was happening; everyone was watching. Lo and behold, it was Phale Hale, who had nearly missed the train and was climbing on huffing and puffing! Phale hadn't caught all of those freight trains for nothing—a moving train was no obstacle to him.

CHAPTER SIX

The Upward Mobility of Cleo Ingram Hale

Stardust

Sometimes I wonder
why I spend the lonely
night

Dreaming of a song,
the melody

Haunts my reverie,

And I am once again
with you,

When our love was
new,

And each kiss an
inspiration.

But that was long
ago.

Now my consolation

Is in the stardust of
a song.

Beside a garden wall

When stars are
bright,

You are in my arms,

The nightingale

Tells his fairy tale

of paradise where
roses grew.

Tho' I dream in
vain,

In my heart it always
will remain

My stardust melody

The memory of love's
refrain.

MITCHELL
PARISH/HOAGY
CARMICHAEL,
*played by bandleader
Duke Ellington
in the 1940s*

As Phale entered the railcar, he noticed Cleo and her friend Althea Morton and spoke politely. He then took his seat, took his typewriter and some papers out of his briefcase, and pretended to be working. After about fifteen minutes he put the papers aside and went over to talk with them.

When they reached Valdosta, it was pouring rain. Phale went with them to the home where they had registered for housing. As Cleo recalls, "Phale had not registered and did not have anywhere to stay. In those days, you stayed with local families because there were no hotels that admitted us. Phale didn't have me to make his reservations as he did in later years," she laughs, "so he had no reservation."

The irony was that the hostess became so excited that Phale was a pastor that she gave Althea and Cleo's room to him and put them on the sunporch. Dr. James M. Nabrit, Sr., the prominent pastor of Mt. Olive Baptist Church and secretary of the National Baptist Convention, was also staying at that home. Their hostess felt it was wonderful to have Rev. Phale D. Hale, pastor of First Baptist Church, in her home, because he could fellowship with Dr. Nabrit.

Phale, Cleo, and Althea attended the convention together, ate breakfast and dinner together, and got to know one another during that week. Phale told Cleo that he was planning to attend Gammon Theological Seminary (later the Interdenominational Theological Center) in Atlanta in the fall and would look her up.

Cleo began her sophomore year at Spelman College. She also babysat for a white family that employed her aunt in domestic service. When she returned home from work one afternoon, she was greeted by her sister, Dorothy, raving about the handsome, sharply dressed man who had stopped by to see Cleo. Cleo figured it was Phale.

When she saw him again, she told him he couldn't drop by without calling, because she was busy with school, work, and her church activities. Thereafter, he called before coming. Often he would come while other boyfriends were visiting her. Undaunted, he would join them, eating the candy they had brought.

The Yates and Milton drugstore was where Spelman off-campus women met Morehouse men after classes. They had an advantage over the boarding students because they had more flexibility in socializing with the men. For on-campus women, calling hours for dating were five to six in the evening, and they were strictly adhered to. (When I was at Spelman twenty-five years later, a student would be sent to the dean's office for simply talking with a boy on campus outside of calling hours.) Phale often met Cleo and her best friends, Antoinette, Emma Lou, and Rose, at the drugstore. Emma Lou would remind Cleo that Phale was a great catch, what with all the money he made at First Baptist.

THE INGRAM AND MOSLEY FAMILY HISTORIES

A female slave named Millie from Richmond, Virginia, was sold to Benjamin Ingram, a white slaveholder in Georgia. Millie was eight years old at the time of the sale. Her father was Negro and her mother Native American. Benjamin Ingram became the father of her oldest son, Henry, Cleo Marion Ingram's grandfather. Millie eventually married Jack, a slave on Ben Ingram's plantation.

Henry was born in slavery and was nine years old when slavery ended. At that time, he lived with his mother and Jack on a farm on the Oconee River that Jack owned. As soon as Henry was old enough to plow his own plot of land, he married and had seven or eight children.

The Ingram family on the farm, 1905 *(father Henry is seated center, mother Susie is seated on the right, John, who became Cleo's father, is the child standing on the left).*

Henry's wife died when his children were young. He then married Susie Williams, a young woman in her twenties who could read and write and was the teacher in the country school held in the church. Susie, considered an old maid, needed a husband, and Henry, who was much older than Susie, light-skinned and handsome, needed a wife. Their farm was in Buckhead, Georgia, not far from Madison.

Susie's parents were George and Harriet Williams. Susie's brother, Albert Williams, was a prominent leader in the community and chair of the deacons' board of the Jefferson Baptist Church, where they were all members. Susie gave birth to five children. The eldest child, John Young Ingram, Cleo's father, was born in 1900 and died in 1987. The other children were Corine, William Henry, Annie Beatrice, and Julia.

Celie Porter was a slave on a plantation in Eatonton, Georgia. Her slave master impregnated her with a child, whom she named Lucy. Celie never married. She did not feel that the lives most African American women lived was the life for her; she was what would be called today a liberated women. She loved to travel in a time when it was unusual for African Americans to travel. But Celie would move from place to place and get work as a domestic for white families.

Celie's granddaughter, Janist, told Cleo that Celie would pick up books and try to teach herself to read, since when she rode the train she wanted to appear educated. She would buy newspapers and pretend to read them. Once she embarrassed herself by holding her newspaper upside down. After that, she tried to always be sure that, when she was "reading," the paper was positioned the right way. Her granddaughter, Janist, admired her for her spunk. Eventually, Celie moved in with Lucy and lived with her and Lucy's husband, John Mosley, until her death.

Lucy, tall, slender, and light-skinned, had a very different lifestyle from her mother's. She had a child every year and was a farm wife and

Janist Mosley Ingram,
Cleo's mother, 1940.

a farmhand. John Mosley was a hard-working farmer, had a light brown complexion, drank corn whiskey, chewed tobacco, wore overalls all the time, and did not go to church.

Twelve children were born to Lucy and John: Mary Lucy, Rawlin, John Henry, Frank, Celie, Janist, Dan, Luvenia, Anderson, Joe Brown, Johnnie Mae, and Dorothy. Janist, the sixth child, was Cleo's mother. She was born close to the red hills of Putnam County, Georgia, in 1902. She died in 1989. I was named for her. Of the six girls in the family, Janist was the only one to inherit John Mosley's coffee-cream complexion. She was pretty, with coal-black straight hair that fell naturally around her face. Janist was sensitive about her weight. She also seemed to be sensitive about the fact that she was brown-skinned, like her brothers, while her sisters were light-skinned.

JANIST MOSLEY AND JOHN INGRAM

Janist may have married John Young Ingram—one of the young men who came courting from Buckhead, Georgia—in part because of his light skin. John Ingram had blue eyes and was as light-skinned as any white man (perhaps because his grandfather was white). John was also a suitable beau because his family owned their own land. Janist never considered the hired hands as suitable marriage partners.

In those days, the churches in the area would hold what they called the Big Meeting, and the young men would go from one Big Meeting to another to meet the girls. John Ingram went to Eatonton from Buckhead and met Janist. John Ingram's half-brother, Gooden, had married Janist's sister Mary Lucy, so they were a part of the same social circle. Mary Lucy was light-skinned and tall, with beautiful black hair. Her face was not as attractive as Janist's, but she was striking. Mary Lucy looked a lot like her mother, Lucy. Family members later said that Cleo resembled her Aunt Mary Lucy.

Janist and John were married in the early 1920s. Janist was very different in appearance and temperament from John's sisters, and Grandma Susie did not like her. John wanted to leave the stubborn Georgia farmland in search of a better life, but Grandma Susie overprotected her children, especially the boys. A white man, who was the mailman and owned a number of businesses in the community, had once told Grandma Susie that he would send John to school and make a doctor out of him, but Grandma Susie would not let him go. John often spoke

sadly about missing that opportunity. Grandma Susie was very domi-
neering, but Grandpa Henry was very meek and nice.

One year, as soon as the crops were in, John and his brother,
William Henry, left the farm with their wives and went to Orlando,
Florida, to seek their fortune. The only work they could find, however,
was picking crops as migrant workers, which was very hard work and
low-paying. When the weather warmed in the spring they headed to
Atlanta to try the urban life.

Their reasons for migrating to the city are probably similar to
those of other African Americans of that time. Clifford Kuhn, Harlon
Joye, and E. B. West (1991) report that, "at the turn of the century,
[Atlanta's] population was only 89,000, about 40 percent black. By
1920, the number of Atlantans had soared to 150,000, climbing to
200,000 in 1920. Many of these newcomers haled from the hardscrab-
ble farms of the rural South, fleeing failing crop prices, sharecropping
and tenant farming, washed-out land, and the boll weevil" (1). These
authors record the testimony of African Americans who migrated
around the same time as John and Janist:

> Typical of those who left the country was domestic worker Lula
> Daugherty, who came to town in 1920: "We was farmers and the boll
> weevils got there and you couldn't make anything. So my husband
> come up here and went to work at the Atlanta Paper Company. And
> he sent back for me and I come up here."
>
> The same refrain was echoed time and again: "My aunt wanted
> me to come up here and live with her and work, because we wasn't
> making anything on the farm. My father raised food for us to eat but
> at the end of the year you had nothing." "We farmed. We couldn't
> get along. I just quit and came to Atlanta." "I didn't think I could
> stay down there and work, and I decided I'd come to Atlanta."
> "I was like any other country boy, I wanted to go to the big town."
> (1–3)

Three children were born to Janist and John, all of them light-
skinned, as Janist must have wanted it. Cleo Marion was tall and
slender with dark-brown hair, like her grandmother Lucy; Dorothy
Marie, with light-brown hair, resembled her Ingram aunts; and Asa
Calvin, at six feet, six inches, with a heavy build and medium-brown
hair, resembled his mother's brothers.

When the Ingrams arrived in Atlanta, they lived on Butler Place in
a shotgun house off Linden Avenue. Apparently, John had saved some
money from picking crops in Orlando and could immediately secure

Cleo, Dorothy, and Asa, 1931

housing. The house was on an unpaved street. However, they had an indoor toilet, running water in the kitchen, a washbasin, and a large washtub for bathing. There was electricity, a woodstove, and an ice-box. John had a model-T Ford. The house they lived in was near a very nice neighborhood.

John quickly secured a job as a chauffeur for Edgar P. McBurney, a job he held for seventeen years, until Mr. McBurney's death. Even though domestic work is considered low-paying and low-status, at that time this was the work readily available to African Americans. Within the African American community, one's status was drawn from how important and prosperous the white people were for whom one worked. These people did not hire just anyone—there were certain circles they drew their help from. They also liked their domestics to be sharply dressed and look good. Therefore, with John's white look, it was relatively easy for him and, later, his sisters to secure jobs with prominent Atlanta families.

Edgar Poe McBurney was born in 1862 in Tompkins County, near Ithaca, New York. His parents, James C. and Lucina McBurney, maintained homes in Jersey City, New Jersey, and in Atlanta, Georgia, for many years. He spent the greater part of his life in Atlanta, where he was active in the business, social, and cultural life of the city. With his

John Ingram in
chauffeur's uniform, 1932.

father, he organized and managed the extensive West View Cemetery in Atlanta. Edgar McBurney was also the vice president and general manager of the Empire Cotton Oil Company, an organization with ten or twelve large mills in Georgia. Among his other business affiliations were the Georgia, Southern, and Florida Railroad, the Trust Company of Georgia Associates, and the First National Bank of Atlanta.

McBurney was active in the Chamber of Commerce of Atlanta and the Atlanta Presidents' Club, an organization of the presidents of thirty-five civic groups of Atlanta. Another of his interests was the High Museum. Upon his death in 1940, he left a trust fund of over a million dollars to maintain his home as an art museum, part of the High Museum.

During Cleo's childhood, John earned twenty-five dollars a week as Mr. McBurney's chauffeur, providing a comfortable living for his family and allowing his wife to stay home. During the Depression, he was earning more than Atlanta schoolteachers—a dubious honor, because the teachers were paid so little. Arthur Idlett, a Morehouse College graduate, discussed his salary as an educator around that time:

> So I got me a job teaching. And I was teaching biology and algebra. I was going to work at 8:30 and I was off at 12:00 o'clock. I was just teaching three classes a day, you see, making $20 a month. The average salary was about $60 a month then for teaching. And I was making $20. I was selling insurance for the National Benefits Company. The National Benefits Company went out of business.
>
> And then my next year, I got a job as principal of a high school in Greensboro, Georgia, making $80 a month for nine months. Didn't get paid during the summertime. Then the Depression started coming on. They started cutting salary. They cut me down $10 every year, cut me down. I worked one year for $70, then one year for $60, and one year for $50. Then President Roosevelt started the NRA, see, and he set that minimum salary. Now, here I've got my A.B. degree, and some of these fellows around there that just had their elementary school education, they were making $12.50 a week. And I was making $12.50 a week. They were working the year round. I'm working nine months, $12.50 a week. And, boy that thing was disgusting. I said, "I'm going to get me a job doing something else." (ibid., 162–63)

Janist was a good manager and saved every penny she could. They were quickly able to rent a house about three blocks away from Butler Place, on Linden Avenue, a nice house, with three bedrooms, a living room, a kitchen, and a bathroom. All of the houses had front and back porches. In those days, family activities took place on the porches instead of in family rooms; the children played on the back porch, and everyone sat on the front porch on Sundays, when they were dressed up. This house had electricity, running water in the kitchen, a bathtub in the bathroom, an icebox, a coal stove, and fireplaces.

The coal man brought coal every day, because there was no place to store it. The iceman came every other day. Vegetable venders came down the street and sold sweet milk and buttermilk. The chicken man sold live chickens. Everyone grew food in home gardens.

The Ingrams felt very fortunate in their new neighborhood, on the east side of Atlanta in what is today essentially downtown. They were a block from Piedmont Avenue and surrounded by other people who were upwardly mobile. On one side were the Thomases; Mrs. Thomas was a caterer for rich white people, her husband worked "downtown," and their daughter was a schoolteacher. On the other side of them was Mrs. Annabelle and her husband; she was a maid and her husband was a chauffeur. On the other side of the Thomases were the Murdocks. He grew bananas and worked for the post office.

The Ingrams stayed in this house until Cleo was six years old, by which time they had saved enough money to buy a house.

After John and William Henry got established in Atlanta, other members of their family began coming. One sister moved to Atlanta and roomed with someone until she married. Once she was settled, they sent for their parents and two younger sisters. The parents were too old to farm, and with the boys gone they did not have enough manpower. They rented a house not far from Linden Avenue, on Hunt Street. The youngest sister moved out eventually and married a cousin of her sister's husband. Janist's sister Luvenia moved in with them while they lived on Linden Avenue (Cleo couldn't say "Luvenia" as a child and gave her the nickname "Tee Tee," which stuck.)

John's sisters became domestic workers for wealthy white families, one as a cook and the other as an upstairs maid. Kuhn and his colleagues point out that domestic work was the typical occupation for African American women at that time. "In 1930, over 21,000 black women, or 90 percent of all black women employed in Atlanta, worked as domestic workers of some kind. Fifty-seven percent of all black women in Atlanta worked, compared to 20 percent of white women, meaning that *every other black woman in the city labored as a domestic worker*" (ibid., 111).

His sisters were not as fortunate as John in terms of compensation and schedules. The sister who was a cook had to be at work around 7:30 A.M. to prepare breakfast and serve it at the appointed time. She could not leave until dinner was prepared and served and the kitchen cleaned. She served dinner around 5:00 P.M., so she wouldn't get home until about 6:00 in the evening. She worked six days a week, having only Sunday and half a day off on Thursday. She was paid five to seven dollars a week. When her employers had parties, the help would be required to stay as late as 9:00 in the evening, serving and cleaning up. The regular help received no extra compensation for those occasions. As a teenager, Cleo would receive a dollar for helping after school.

Alice Adams's testimony corroborates Cleo's recollection of the working conditions of her aunts. However, Alice described a lower rate of pay:

> I didn't have laundry to do, but I had to cook. Now I enjoyed the cooking because I loved to cook, and I still like to cook. I would serve the parties. Sometimes on Friday I would have to serve a party—make sandwiches and serve about twenty-five or thirty peoples a luncheon, and from that fix dinner. That I enjoyed because I loved entertaining. But you didn't get any extra pay for serving parties. That was in your work. You just had to serve extra peoples.
>
> . . . She'd help me if I needed money for house rent or if I needed money for clothing. The onliest objection was long hours and little pay. She was willing to do anything to help me—but the money. Four dollars a week. Just no money. And everybody was the same. They all was that way.
>
> But still, I wasn't happy at the long hours. I worked from seven to seven. It didn't seem so hard, but the hours was long—just long hours. Now, we was off for half a day on Sunday, the same thing on Thursday. Now, do you know what half a day was? You'd get off at one o'clock, get home around three. Well, I did that for about twenty-some-odd years. I couldn't go to church because I had to work. I wanted to go to church and I wanted to visit friends and take care of my house. And you didn't have time, you just had to work. (ibid., 118, 119)

Such a schedule made it very difficult for African American women to raise their own children, and they could not afford child care on such wages. Consequently, their own children were often raised by grandparents, whom the children virtually lived with.

Cleo was very grateful that Janist did not work and stayed at home to raise them. If she had worked as a domestic, as most African American migrants did, Cleo would have rarely seen her mother. But Janist was committed to raising her children; wherever she went, her children went. Cleo, Dorothy, and Asa never had a babysitter in their entire lives. Cleo says that Janist would have lived on bread and water rather than leave her children to go to work. She was very protective of them and didn't trust anyone to take care of them but her. Janist never spoke against domestic work: she felt that it was fine for women who didn't have children, like her sister Tee Tee and her cousin Annie Mae, both of whom lived with them. Tee Tee worked downtown at city hall; Cleo is not sure whether she was a maid or ran an elevator. Annie Mae was a domestic worker and a cook.

Janist was very thrifty and resourceful: she sewed all of their clothes; she rented rooms to her relatives, first Tee Tee and, later, Annie Mae; she did laundry for the white families her sisters-in-law worked for when the maids were overloaded (the chauffeurs would deliver and pick up the laundry). Janist also did the laundry for Tee Tee and Annie Mae for a dollar each a week. Through such devices, Janist was able to earn money for extras without leaving the house to work.

John enjoyed his work with the McBurneys; he had a lot of freedom, and it was not hard work. He drove Mr. McBurney to the office and Mrs. McBurney wherever she had to go. He did not have to be the butler or do yard work—only drive. The McBurneys spent summers in Atlantic City, New Jersey, and winters in Palm Beach, Florida. John was frequently gone months at a time, chauffeuring them. There were rooming houses in each city where the help stayed, and they had their own fellowship.

When John was on the road, he was given an additional allowance to cover his expenses, so Janist would have his entire salary to maintain the household. Cleo recalls riding the bus with her mother to Mr. McBurney's office to pick up the salary on Fridays from his secretary, Miss Pauline.

Cleo also remembers fondly going with their father several times to meet and visit with the McBurneys. Janist dressed them up in their best clothes and curled their hair in Shirley Temple curls. The McBurneys' house was beautiful. There they met the cook and also Florence, Mrs. McBurney's personal maid, who worked for the McBurneys for fifty years until they died. Florence took them up to Mrs. McBurney's bedroom, where Mrs. McBurney sat at a dressing table putting on her makeup. Cleo thought it the prettiest room in the world and wanted one day to have a room like that. Mrs. McBurney was very nice to them, and Mr. McBurney would talk with them. The McBurneys did not seem to have any children; at least Cleo never saw any or heard them mention having any.

Mr. McBurney did not lose his wealth during the Depression. He often told John that, as long as the Republicans were in office, he would be secure. John seemed to take that to heart, because he voted Republican most of his life, even after Mr. McBurney died, until Barry Goldwater ran for president. It was unusual that Mr. McBurney was a Republican in Atlanta, part of the Democratic South. One explanation might be that Mr. McBurney had been born in New York and raised in New Jersey.

ADJUSTING TO URBAN LIFE

Cleo did not have to make the big push from the country to the city that Phale did. Her parents had borne the weight of figuring out what was needed for upward mobility in the city. They no doubt knew the value of a good education, because their education was so limited and it stood in such contrast to what was valued and needed in the city.

Cleo believes that John experienced no problems in adjusting to urban life. He was immediately able to secure a good job, which he had for seventeen years. When Mr. McBurney died in 1940, John's sister and her husband opened a funeral home, and he worked with them for the rest of his life.

John was tall, handsome, personable, and had a lot of friends. He was dashing, charming, and popular with women. So many African Americans were working in domestic service at that time that he had a satisfying peer group, with its own parties and social affairs. John had his own niche in this society of domestic workers. Janist, because she did not work in domestic service, was left to make her own friends. She did not meet the people John met.

John and other domestic workers also learned a lot from their employers. One of his sisters, who had learned to sew from her mother, Susie, refined her sewing by working for white people. Another sister's cooking was refined by her experiences cooking for the wealthy whites. Janist felt keenly her lack of education and exposure. She continued to cook the way they cooked in the country throughout her life; she taught herself how to sew and made stuffed animals and hats for her friends, but her sewing was never as refined as that of her sisters-in-law. Cleo remembers that, as she was growing up, Janist made their school clothes and that they were comparable to what everyone else was wearing. However, as Janist got older, she didn't upgrade her sewing. Cleo and her sister began making their own clothes when they were teenagers.

Janist always felt that John liked educated women. Catherine, a schoolteacher who lived next door to them, was a terrible threat to Janist. John would give Catherine a ride to school in the morning, because she, like most people, did not have a car. But Janist did not even want John to talk to Catherine. Schoolteachers were unmarried in those days; they would lose their jobs if they married. Also, Catherine lived with her mother and so did no housework, which was Janist's primary occupation. She went to work, came home, sat on the porch, and talked to John. Janist began to talk about sending her daughters to college when she noticed that John admired women who were college-educated.

Janist and John belonged to a social club, whose members played whist and ate food together once or twice a week, in one another's homes. Janist would serve food and her homemade rice wine on card tables in the living room. Occasionally they needed an extra person, and John taught Cleo how to play whist so she could fill in. She became a very good player and looked forward to a chance to play and to listen to adult conversation. She found herself counting people as they came in, hoping to be needed. Otherwise, the children put together jigsaw puzzles or played Chinese checkers and regular checkers.

Janist learned from the members of her social club how to make new dishes—dainty sandwiches, rolls, potato salad, and salmon salad—that she had not made in the country. They made new desserts, like gelatin, that were not made in the country. Annie Mae also shared with Janist new dishes she had learned at her job as a cook.

The Ingrams joined Mt. Zion Baptist Church because it was close to their home. Also, the services were very much like the country services they were accustomed to. The pastor, Rev. J. T. Dorsey, was a "whooper," like country preachers. Cleo remembers how he could "call them in." Rev. Dorsey used to say that "he could call more people in by just putting his hat on the lamppost than most preachers could by preaching."

Most of the members of Mt. Zion were new urban migrants like them, not the old Atlantans. Both Janist and Tee Tee were active in the church. John joined the church, but he did not like it because of its country atmosphere. Cleo doesn't remember her parents ever attending Mt. Zion together. John would often dress Cleo and Dorothy up and take them to Liberty Baptist Church. Rev. Hall, a tall, light-skinned man, was the pastor at Liberty Baptist, which was more urbane and had an educated membership. John wanted to associate with more educated people than he found at Mt. Zion. John would also take the girls to Wheat Street Baptist Church. In later years, he joined Allen Temple A.M.E. Church and became a steward.

Tee Tee would take the girls to Mt. Zion, particularly when Asa was a baby and Janist stayed at home with him. Tee Tee would accompany them to Sunday school and go back with them to the Baptist Young People's Training Union. Cleo and Dorothy loved Mt. Zion, where they made many friends. Cleo remembers crying when her mother would not let her go to Sunday school because it was raining. She argued that they went to regular school when it is raining, why not Sunday school? And her mother let her go. Cleo loved the Bible and found it fascinating. A favorite Sunday school teacher was Emma Pope, who had the children memorize passages from the Bible. Asa, on the other hand, never liked going to church.

Rev. Dorsey preached only on the first and third Sundays of the month. People from the country were not accustomed to going to church every Sunday, because the pastor usually pastored several churches and rotated his visits. Rev. Dorsey preached at a small church in Lithonia one Sunday of the month. On the off Sundays, the associates (whom Janist called "jacklegs") preached.

On the Sundays when Rev. Dorsey preached, you couldn't even get into the church. Cleo and Dorothy, however, always had seats, because they attended Sunday school. They watched their mother come in late and walk straight to the front of the church, the deacons falling all over themselves trying to give her their seats. Janist went to church only when Rev. Dorsey preached. Janist was deeply religious, and Cleo remembers that she always prayed on her knees.

Tee Tee also accompanied the girls to Sunday school conventions. After Cleo had met Phale, Tee Tee heard him preach at a Sunday school convention. Realizing that Phale was interested in Cleo, she commented that he was a "good preacher."

On Sunday afternoon, John might take the children to visit his friends. Sometimes Janist would go, but she didn't seem comfortable with his friends, who were people in domestic service like himself. Sunday afternoon was also a time for the family to be together; they would take long automobile rides and buy ice cream cones.

An important event in Janist's life occurred in 1928 during a visit to Grady Hospital for a checkup after giving birth to Asa. She saw a poster that said, DO YOU HAVE ENOUGH CHILDREN? The poster directed her to a clinic, where she was introduced to birth control techniques. Janist was the first woman in her circle of women to have some knowledge of birth control. African American women always felt white women knew something about limiting the size of their families that African American women did not know. The ability to limit the size of their family in this new urban environment was certainly a key to this family meeting its goals. Janist also shared this information with her sisters who still lived in the country. Cleo recalls her commenting that one sister had had "enough children" and that she needed to talk with her.

INTELLECTUAL STIMULATION

Janist was always busy; she was an immaculate housekeeper. Daily, the house was swept, the furniture dusted, the floors mopped, and the porches and sidewalks swept. There was a schedule for housekeeping, which included washing and ironing clothes and cooking. There was a schedule for everything. You arose by a certain time, combed your hair, washed, dressed, made your bed, did your chores.

Janist also loved to sew; the greatest delight of her life was to make "dress-alike" outfits for her two daughters. She would curl their hair in Shirley Temple curls and put on the ruffled dresses that she had made and send them to a neighborhood Sunday afternoon tea party to play a piano selection or recite a poem. Cleo and Dorothy took piano lessons from Mrs. Manago, a college-educated woman who lived behind them.

Dorothy also liked to sew. Cleo, on the other hand, liked to read. Reading exposed Cleo to a whole new world. They, of course, didn't have television, so their only window on the outside world was the movies. Cleo also had been in the McBurney house and was curious about people who lived in houses like that.

In those days, children did not take part in adult conversations. Janist believed that children who heard too much adult conversation would become "womanish." There were things that adults knew that children should not know. The Ingrams had a radio, but the children could turn it on only at certain times. They also had phonograph records, which they played over and over. John liked to listen to the radio, to Kate Smith. The children listened to Amos and Andy and Fats Waller.

Cleo liked to visit Grandma Susie, who had been a teacher in a country school before she married. She spoke good English and had beautiful penmanship, sewed beautifully and dressed well. Grandma Susie was available to talk to and spend time with. Janist, on the other hand, was always busy. She was also a person of few words; her communications to her children were short and to the point. Grandma Susie would hold Cleo in conversation, reciting poems and quoting from the Bible. Cleo and Grandma Susie also shared a love of meat. Janist often cooked meatless meals and said that Cleo was just like the Ingrams in loving meat. So Grandma Susie would save meat for Cleo when she came to visit.

Cleo never remembers anyone in her family reading anything other than the newspaper. They took the African American newspaper, the *Atlanta Daily World,* which came in the morning. Their paperboy for the *Atlanta Daily World* became a millionaire; he was Nathaniel Bronner, one of the Bronner brothers who owned a company based in Atlanta that sells beauty supplies.

They also took the white paper, the *Atlanta Journal,* which came in the afternoon. They subscribed to the afternoon paper because the stock market figures determined whether they had hit the "number." The numbers lady, who lived on Woodrow Place, came to their door every day to take their bets. She was as regular as the mailman, the iceman, and the coal man. Everyone played the "number." Cleo did not realize it was illegal to play the number until years later, when she married Phale. In those days, white people did not pay any attention to what African Americans did as long as it did not affect them. Kuhn and his colleagues point out the disrespect and neglect whites showed for African American Atlantans:

> "For years my husband was news editor for WSB radio," relates white liberal Eliza Paschall, "but before that he was a reporter for the *Journal.* I remember so well his description of the first time that he ever really thought about race relations. When he went out on the police beat, as they all started out in those days, he phoned the paper and said, 'We've got three murders.' 'Wow, where are they?' So he gave the addresses, and all of a sudden the man said, 'They all niggers?' And Walter said, well, he really didn't know, but did that make any difference? They were all murders. And the man said, 'Look,

anytime there's this address or this section of town, just don't bother us. That's not news.'" (12)

Other reading material in Cleo's home were calendars distributed by undertakers, the Yates and Milton drugstore, and the Atlanta Life Insurance Company; cards with Jesus' picture distributed to the children in their Sunday school class; and dream books for figuring out which number to play. They also had the Bible, which they used in the Baptist Young People's Training Union and which Tee Tee would read. They also had hymn books; Tee Tee played the hymns on the piano. Cleo also frequented the public library, spending long hours with the treasures she found there.

The literature in the field indicates that the elder child is usually the highest achiever in families. Even though her siblings did quite well (Dorothy is a college graduate and was a teacher for many years, and Asa finished high school and was a television and movie film technician), Cleo achieved the highest academic level, having completed a master's degree. I asked Cleo whether there were things in her background she could point to that caused her to achieve the highest academic level in her family. She says, for one thing, she was given the responsibility of taking care of the younger children. Often her mother would call her to leave her own play and care for the baby. She believes this made her feel responsible for everyone, even as an adult. Dorothy was more of an extrovert than Cleo. She would rather play with other children than spend hours reading. Cleo loved to read; Dorothy and Janist considered it odd that she read every word of the thousand-page novel *Gone with the Wind*.

Cleo believes that Janist's philosophy of upward mobility was that you should be clean and well-groomed and you should have a clean house; and that you should go to school, to church, and to teas, where you would recite poems and play piano solos. She didn't apply any pressure on her children to perform well in school. She also didn't believe in complimenting children, which she believed would make them bigheaded, or "womanish." Cleo always made good grades in school, and though her mother seemed pleasantly surprised, she never praised Cleo directly. But Cleo did overhear her bragging to her friends about Cleo's grades.

Cleo also never heard Janist encourage the younger children to try to approximate Cleo's school performance. Janist loved Dorothy and Asa so much that whatever they did was all right. There was a great deal of competition between the girls, and Janist saw Dorothy as doing better in the arenas she was interested in—sewing, housecleaning, and playing the piano. But Cleo excelled in school, an arena Janist had little interest in.

I wondered whether Janist felt threatened by Cleo as she began to deviate from her mother's way of doing things. Cleo believes that Janist wanted her to be successful but only by doing the things Janist did in the way she did them. Janist favored Dorothy because she was willing to follow in her mother's footsteps. Janist liked to sew, and Dorothy like to sew, but I have never seen my mother sew, other than mending. Janist was not a good cook; Cleo majored in home economics in college with the intention of becoming a dietition.

I asked Cleo why she was willing to deviate from her mother. "Because I didn't like the way she did things," she answered. "There were many areas that could stand improving in the way she prepared food. As I became older, I began to see how other people were doing things. However, I understood Mother and loved her dearly. I just got used to her reaction and didn't let it bother me that she did not approve of my deviating from the way she did things."

SOCIAL ISSUES

There was no discussion of politics or social or racial issues in Cleo's home. There was no discussion of the fact that African Americans had to sit at the back of the bus. Janist did not want her children to ride the buses, but she never said why. Did Cleo know that African Americans were required to ride at the back of the bus? "Did I! You knew that you had *better get back there*! You were drilled on that. I also knew how to read COLORED when I saw a sign at the restrooms." But her parents never discussed the morality of it or their feelings about it.

Janist simply avoided public restrooms or any public situations where she would confront the color line. Over time, she conveyed to her children that eating in a restaurant was almost a sin. In later life, she refused to eat outside of her home at all and would feed her family before they left home. If they went to a picnic, they would go only to socialize. They did not often encounter white people, other than working for them, and once they moved to the west side of town, they lived almost totally in an African American world.

At Washington High School, C. L. Harper, the principal, would bring outstanding African Americans of that time to speak—Ralph Bunche, Mary McLeod Bethune, and others. They provided role models to motivate the students, but the race problem was not discussed. Cleo assumes that the issue was avoided because Harper, as principal of the first African American high school in Atlanta, had to satisfy his white supervisors. "They taught black history by building black people up, not by tearing the white people down." Cleo read *Native Son* in the eleventh grade and slowly began to realize what was going on between the black and white people. It wasn't until Cleo got to college that she learned what white people were like, because at Spelman the race problem was discussed in class. However, the Morehouse men received a more realistic picture than the women at Spelman because Florence Matilda Read, the president of Spelman, was white and because white people ran Spelman.

When Cleo was six years old, Janist had saved enough money to buy their own home. It was during the Depression, but John had a secure job and housing prices were down. The house on Nutting Street had larger rooms than the house on Linden Avenue and, in addition, had a dining room. It was all on one floor, like the house on Nutting Street. Very few Atlanta houses in those days had more than one story. One had to be almost wealthy to have a house with two stories. There was a living room, a dining room, an area for the icebox separate from the kitchen, a kitchen, and a bathroom on one side of the house; on the other side were three bedrooms. This was in the South, where there was plenty of room, so the houses were spread out. They had huge porches.

The wash was done on the back porch in stationary tubs. There was a charcoal bucket for the fire and a large galvanized tub for boiling the clothes. They were then rinsed and hung on the clothesline in the yard. At the other end of the porch were chairs and seats where the family sat and talked.

There was also a one-car garage and two beautiful weeping willow trees, one between the house and the garage and one at the far end of the yard, which the children would lie under. There was a swing on the front porch, where one could sit on special occasions. The back porch was high enough to allow play space under the porch. Here, the children would make mud pies and play all day with the neighborhood children.

A HETEROGENEOUS NEIGHBORHOOD

There was an alley called Woodrow Place that ran perpendicular to
Nutting Street across from the Ingrams. Janist did not allow her children to venture onto Woodrow Place or to play with the children who
lived there. The residents on Woodrow Place lived crowded together
in shotgun houses, since many people moving into the city from the
country lived together until they found jobs. This seemed to be the
first stop for some upwardly mobile families, because Cleo recalls that
there were always families moving in and out; the progressive ones did
not stay there long.

Janist felt that these people's standards were low. They had shoot-
outs, knife fights, and drinking parties. Janist was also critical of how
their children looked. She believed that children should be bathed
daily and dressed in clean clothes. These children's hair was not combed
and their braids were tangled and filled with lint.

Janist did allow her children to play with the children on Nutting
Street and Linden Avenue. On Irene Street, which was directly behind
Nutting Street, most of the people were professionals and did not have
many children. In those days, people picked their children's playmates.
Cleo was invited to play with Mary Emma, who was from Columbus,
Ohio, and would visit her grandmother, a school principal, in the
summer. Years later when Cleo lived in Columbus, she again saw Mary
Emma.

Thus the qualification for being in Janist's social group was not
educational achievement; it seemed to be home ownership and a nice
car. Most of her friends worked for wealthy white people and were paid
relatively well. They were two-income families who owned their own
homes. Most of them had no children. Janist was comfortable among
these friends. Most of the neighborhood women were in Janist's circle.
These women did not go to Mt. Zion Church but to Wheat Street, Big
Bethel, or Allen Temple.

John went so far as to have tall hedges planted in front of the house
so that no one from Woodrow Place could see their front porch. This
attitude is typical of what William Julius Wilson (1987) describes as
subgroup residential isolation, in which higher-status residents of a
neighborhood try to prevent the deterioration of their neighborhood,
school, and the like when migrants arrive. However, he also notes the
strengths implicit in such segregated neighborhoods in providing so-

cial stability and a diversity of role models for children, strengths that are not present today. "Indeed," says Wilson, "in the 1940s, 1950s, and as late as the 1960s such communities featured a vertical integration of different segments of the urban black population. Lower-class, working-class, and middle-class black families all lived more or less in the same communities (albeit in different neighborhoods), sent their children to the same schools, availed themselves of the same recreational facilities, and shopped at the same stores" (7).

In those days, African American professionals (doctors, teachers, lawyers, social workers, ministers) lived in higher-income neighborhoods *within* the African American community and serviced that community. Such communities no longer exist. African American middle-class professionals have moved out of inner-city neighborhoods and also work outside the African American community.

> Accompanying the black middle-class exodus has been a growing movement of stable working-class blacks from ghetto neighborhoods to higher-income neighborhoods in other parts of the city and to the suburbs. In the earlier years, the black middle and working classes were confined by restrictive covenants to communities also inhabited by the lower class; their very presence provided stability to inner-city neighborhoods and reinforced and perpetuated mainstream patterns of norms and behaviors. (ibid.)

Janist and John tried to position their children to create friendships with children whose families were of a higher social status in order to fulfill their dreams of upward mobility. However, because John had a secure income, they also contributed to their community through the church and charitable causes. For example, during the Depression, Janist set aside food for the homeless and the hungry who would come to their back porch.

Even though Cleo, Dorothy, and Asa did not play with the children on Woodrow Place, they did go to school with them. Cleo also thinks that some of these children attended Mt. Zion. A child growing up on Woodrow Place lived in a crowded household, whose adults might have started their families without being married and were likely to be either unemployed, selling illegal homemade corn whiskey, or running numbers. However, that child could look across the street and see families that were intact, where the grown-ups were domestic workers, caterers, hair dressers—honest, hard-working people who owned their own homes. These were that child's role models.

By the same token, by living in a heterogeneous neighborhood,

Cleo became friends with children of higher social status, like Antoinette Brown, who lived with her grandparents, her two sisters, and her mother. Her mother was divorced. Her grandfather, Mr. Graves, was a real estate entrepreneur and one of the pioneers of Atlanta. He had educated all of his children: Antoinette's mother was a teacher, another of his daughters was a social worker, and a third was a doctor's wife and civic leader.

Cleo's friendship with Antoinette opened a whole new world to her. Antoinette lived across the street from Emmett Proctor, grandson of C. L. Harper, the first principal of Washington High School. Martin Luther King, Jr., often played with Emmett. Cleo remembers that on many occasions she and Antoinette watched Emmett and Martin playing ball together. W. J. Wilson laments that this intermixing of social classes is not true of inner-city neighborhoods today.

> Today's ghetto neighborhoods are populated almost exclusively by the most disadvantaged segments of the black urban community, that heterogeneous grouping of families and individuals who are outside the mainstream of the American occupational system. Included in this group are individuals who lack training and skills and either experience long-term unemployment or are not members of the labor force, individuals who are engaged in street crime and other forms of aberrant behavior, and families that experience long-term spells of poverty and/or welfare dependency. (8)

EDUCATION

My mother realized that she had to improve herself if she was to move ahead. One of the ways to learn how to improve was at the Sunday teas held in the community. After one tea, Janist and Annie Mae visited Mrs. Manago. Mrs. Hanley, who lived next door to Mrs. Manago, was also present. Both of these women were college-educated. They criticized the woman who had presided over that afternoon's tea because she had "split verbs." They felt she should not have presided if she could not speak correctly.

This conversation affected Janist. When she came home, she recounted the conversation to Tee Tee and asked Tee Tee what a verb was. Neither of them knew. Fortunately for Janist, the friends in her social circle were, for the most part, in her situation, so she felt comfortable speaking the way she was accustomed to. But Cleo, listening to her aunt and her mother, gathered that there was something wrong with the way they talked. After that tea, she paid special attention in school when the teacher covered verbs.

Cleo attended David T. Howard Elementary School, named for an African American undertaker and real estate entrepreneur. The state of education for African American children in Atlanta was deplorable during World War I, prior to the Ingrams' arrival in Atlanta, and it had not improved much by the time Cleo finished Washington High School in 1940.

> "Things were at a low ebb during World War I . . ." states Bazoline Usher, principal of David T. Howard Junior-Senior High. Only about half of Atlanta's student-age population of around 40,000 attended school in 1910. Black children were far less likely to attend school than white children. While Atlanta's black colleges sponsored private high schools, there existed no public high school for black students in the city until Washington High opened in 1924. In fact, in 1913, the Board of Education tried unsuccessfully to abolish the seventh and eighth grades in the city's black schools, on the grounds that those grades were unnecessary for future manual laborers. (Kuhn et al., 130–31)

These authors also quote Walter Bell: "Back in that day and time, a good-sized group of blacks may have started in the first grade but by the time they had gotten to the seventh grade, the vast majority of them had dropped out. It was necessary in order to live for both the black girls and boys to go to work. The boys went to work as delivery boys, the girls as domestics, and so they dropped out, one by one" (ibid., 131).

Further, black schools were dilapidated and unsanitary, with meager facilities and no cafeterias. The buildings for blacks around 1918–20 were deplorable. At that time, because of overcrowding, all Atlanta public schoolchildren attended schools in double sessions, each lasting only a part of the day. In 1914, the Board of Education, responding to pressure from white middle-class parents, eliminated double sessions and restricted class size to forty-five students—*but for white schools only* (ibid.).

The African American community provided critical support for a four-million-dollar bond referendum with its insistence that the city build its first black public high school. They had long struggled for better public education; in 1902 and 1909 African Americans had supported bond issues in the hopes of gaining school improvements, only

to be left out when the final allocations were made. In 1923, 11,469
African American children were enrolled in the system, but only 4,877
seats were assigned to them (ibid., 138).

The testimony cited in Kuhn et al. speaks of the climate in which
Cleo was educated. E. T. Lewis recalled,

> You had a large reservoir of black children who were eligible for high
> school because they had finished elementary school, but some of
> them hadn't been in school in five, six, seven years. When I started
> teaching, one of my first twelfth-grade classes consisted of several
> people that I had finished elementary school with myself. We finished
> elementary school, they couldn't go to high school, they stayed out
> and did various things the four years that I was in college. Washing-
> ton High School opened in 1924 and they started in junior high
> school. So, when I started teaching in 1929, they were in the graduat-
> ing class of that year. I had some boys in the eighth grade eighteen,
> nineteen years old.
>
> It wasn't but a few years later that the school was overrun. I know
> by 1935 we had almost 6,000 students in a school that was built for
> 2,000. And we overflowed the main building. We built wooden
> structures in the back; we called them portables. And we taught over
> 2,000 people in portables at one time on that campus. (140–41)

"Some of the students came to school on double sessions," said Bazoline Usher. "Some teachers would have the group of students come in
the morning; they might have sixty-five in the morning, and they
might have seventy-two in the afternoon session, coming in at 11:30"
(ibid., 141).

"I taught there for ten years, from '37 to '47," related Estelle
Clemmons,

> and I don't think I ever had a class with less than fifty children in it.
> I had one math class with seventy-five students in it. There was
> actually no space for me, hardly, inside of the room because students
> were all doubled up two to a seat. And this was a small room. I
> remember I actually prayed every day, and I would say, "Lord, help
> me to get out of a situation like this," because I wanted to do my best
> and I didn't feel that I could do my best by my students in such
> crowded conditions.
>
> We didn't have enough books. During those ten years that I
> taught there I never had enough books to go around in a single class.
> And the books that we did have were usually old books that had
> come from other schools, the white schools, predominantly. I re-
> member one day in March—you know how windy it is in March—a

big truck drove up behind the main building piled up with a lot of books. And because of the wind, some of the pages blew out of the books all over the campus. And I said to myself, "This is what is being sent out here for our students to use." And it hurt, it really did hurt. (ibid.)

African American schools lagged considerably behind the white schools during that period. "As late as 1940, the average per pupil cost for white students was $95.20, more than three times the amount expended per black student. In 1942, there were over ten times more books in the white junior and senior high schools as in the black junior and senior highs" (ibid.). Walter Bell remembered that "some of the people on the Board of Education back in the twenties stated very clearly that as far as providing facilities and supplies and material in the schools that what they should do is take care of the whites first, and if there was anything left, they'd give it to the blacks. And that's about what happened. In many, many cases, the whites had more supplies, more books, more of everything than the blacks had" (ibid.).

Even with such underfinancing, black teachers in those schools were hardworking and committed. "They made a good showing for themselves, with the meager materials they had to work with," according to Bazoline Usher. Washington High School certainly attracted a select group of committed teachers. E. T. Lewis told Kuhn and his colleagues,

> We had one of the best faculties of any high school in this city, white or black. They got some teachers from the private high schools (affiliated with Atlanta's black colleges). Also, we got teachers from the graduating classes of all of the colleges here in the city. And since teaching was one of the best fields open to the Negro at that time, we were able to get top graduates from all of these schools.
>
> You didn't have the turnover like you did in the white schools. For example, when I was teaching at Washington High, there were at least six people in the math department who had between twenty-five and thirty years' experience. When it comes to Negroes, we had the tendency to stick to teaching for two reasons: one, we couldn't find anything better, and two, we loved it. (141–42)

"The faculty was a very resourceful group of people," remembered J. Y. Moreland. "They would go out and get things that they needed to teach us with. All our teachers worked closely with Morehouse and the other schools in the Atlanta University system and they got things there that they needed" (ibid., 142).

There were double sessions throughout Cleo's elementary school years. She then attended David T. Howard Junior High School, which had portable classrooms outside the main building, so she went to school full time. In addition, a large proportion of African Americans had dropped out of school by junior high, and more and more African American families were moving to the west side by that time. The only high school Cleo could attend was Washington High School, which meant she had to ride city buses across town, transferring downtown.

Janist and John were very concerned about Cleo's long journey, aware of the prejudice their daughter would encounter on the buses and downtown. They also realized that Dorothy and Asa would have to go the same route in the near future. So they sold the house on Nutting Street and bought a house right behind Washington High School on the west side of town, as close to the school as they could. The new house was not as nice as the one on Nutting Street, but it provided the protection they sought for their children by reducing the commute to school. While housing conditions improved during the period, most dwelling units in the city still were considered substandard as late as 1940 (ibid., 33).

The Ingrams thus became a part of a migration of African American Atlantans from east of downtown to the west side.

Various factors helped bring on this migration. Depressed cotton prices precipitated a local housing crisis between 1915 and 1920, as new housing starts came to a near halt. Housing was further tightened by the Great Fire of 1917. "Several interrelated developments attracted black Atlantans to the area west of Ashby Street, previously off-limits to blacks. After World War I, a number of Auburn Avenue businesses started branch offices on Hunter Street (now Martin Luther King, Jr., Drive). The formation of the Atlanta University Center in 1929–30 consolidated all of the city's black colleges on the west side" (ibid., 42). Also, Booker T. Washington High School, the city's first African American high school, and Washington Park, Atlanta's first public park for black citizens, were located west of Ashby Street.

> Despite violence, intimidation and other efforts to control where they lived, thousands of black Atlantans moved westward and broke the residential color line after 1920. By 1940, fully 40 percent of the city's black population was on the west side. Yet both *de jure* and *de facto* housing segregation persisted for decades. . . . Despite the emergence of a large black middle class, black residents continued to reside in comparatively poor housing, and to be discriminated against

by lending institutions. And black and white Atlantans today tend to live farther apart from each other than they ever did. (ibid., 45)

In those days, Cleo says, her parents had no way of evaluating the quality of the education she was receiving. They had no sense of what the white children were getting compared to them. They didn't know where the school's books were coming from. Her parents just knew that the children needed an education and that the education they were receiving was much better than what they themselves had received. Janist and John just wanted the children to go to school and stay in school. They realized their own limitations in negotiating the urban environment with their country education. They did not feel accepted by people in the higher social stratas, but they had enough contact with educated people to know that education was the ticket to success. They felt their children had the "look," in terms of light skin and Anglo facial features, to be upwardly mobile. All they needed was the polish and credentials, which education would provide.

ASPIRATIONS

On Sundays, John would take the children on automobile rides through the Spelman College campus, saying that he wanted Cleo and Dorothy to go there someday. Both parents wanted the children to be schoolteachers. Janist always upheld Catherine, the schoolteacher next door, as a model for her daughters; she admired the fact that Catherine's hair was done and her nails polished. She wanted her daughters to be "ladies" and not have to work hard. There was not much for an African American to aspire toward other than being a teacher or getting a job in the post office; a few became doctors. Janist did not promote marriage as a ticket to her daughters' success.

One incident signaled who Janist and John did *not* want Cleo to marry. Throughout their childhood, Cleo and Dorothy would go to the country to visit Aunt Mary Lucy and Uncle Gooden. When Cleo was fourteen, the boys started looking at her and she started looking at them. A boy called Gummy, whose real name was Ed, liked her, and she thought Gummy was sharp, even in overalls. He came to Aunt Mary Lucy's house to see her. When the girls returned to Atlanta, somehow the word got back to their parents about how pretty they were and how the boys were looking at them. John said, no, no, no, he did not want them courted by country boys. And that was the end of summer visits to the country.

I asked Cleo whether her mother gave the girls any instructions about avoiding premarital sexual activity. Cleo says that her mother's constant refrain was that if they became pregnant out of wedlock, or married a man who couldn't support them, they would end up "working in the white folks' kitchens."

Unlike Phale, she was pushed and positioned by her parents, who had experienced urban living and knew what she needed to function in the future. Phale had to ferret that information out for himself with no assistance from his parents. But Cleo did have goals and aspirations for herself and was not simply following her parents' plan. She was very impressed, for example, by the McBurney house, and she wanted to learn how to live in such a beautiful house. She wanted very much to attend the Atlanta University Lab School, a private high school operated by Atlanta University. The children of professional families attended that school. "With all my heart," she says, "I wanted to go to Lab High."

Cleo feels that her friendship with Antoinette Brown opened up the world of Atlanta's African American elite to her. Her friends went to Lab High, Antoinette wanted to go, and also their friend Rose Lee. The three girls agreed that, since their families could not afford to send them to Lab High, they would work hard, make good grades, and win scholarships to Spelman. And they did.

THE ATLANTA AFRICAN AMERICAN ELITE

When I went to Spelman from Columbus, Ohio, I felt that I was part of the African American middle class by virtue of having a father who was a professional. But status among native Atlantans was based on family lineage. They wanted to know what your great-grandfather died of. They wanted to know what your people did during slavery. I was curious about what experiences my mother had had with the African American elite when she was a young woman, because she had less armor than I did.

Antoinette's family was part of the elite, and occasionally Cleo would attend the Congregational church with Antoinette. Rumor had it that one had to be light-skinned to attend that church. Cleo was so light-skinned she almost looked white. Her friends' parents would ask

Cleo,
Antoinette Brown,
and Rose Lee, 1938.

her who her parents were and what they did. It didn't take her long to figure out that, once she revealed that her father was a chauffeur and that her mother was at home, she would be excluded from social events.

Cleo would go swimming with Dorothy, her sister, at the home of L. D. Milton, a professor at Morehouse College and, eventually, president of the Citizens and Southern Bank; the two girls were friends of his daughters, Eleanor and Betty. When Mrs. Milton found out who her parents were, Cleo noticed that she was invited over to swim but was not included on the "list" for invitations to birthday parties and other such formal affairs.

Thus Cleo began to figure out who was who and what was what. The *Atlanta Daily World* had a social column, which she read. You had to be in the in-crowd, she noticed, to be mentioned.

Whenever my parents discussed social snobbery when I was a child, my father would always end the discussion by declaring that their focus was not on the families they came from, it was on building their own family.

SPELMAN COLLEGE

Cleo was awarded a full-tuition, one-year scholarship to Spelman. Delta Sigma Theta sorority gave her a half-year scholarship for an additional year. Cleo needed that scholarship so much and appreciated it so deeply that she joined this sorority later in life. Cleo got a job as a clerk in the college bookstore; her earnings were applied to her tuition and paid the remaining amount she owed. She lived at home and walked to school, so she did not need money for room and board.

Did Spelman turn out to be everything she thought it would be? "Everything I thought and more. Going to Spelman was an important step in my life," she replied. At Spelman, Cleo had the opportunity to be in school with girls she had met through Antoinette and who had attended Lab High: Doris Cooper, Edith Reid, Antoinette's cousin Harriet Nash, and Virginia Tillman, who were all from professional families. Cleo was keenly aware that she was not from a professional family, but Spelman gave her the opportunity to be on a par with them. Undoubtedly, Cleo's light skin and beauty were also tickets to acceptance by her higher-status peers. Cleo, Antoinette, and Rose all decided to major in home economics. It was a group decision, and they were able to provide support for each other.

Cleo describes her days at Spelman as a beautiful experience. Each of the girls met the others' Morehouse friends, so they had a lively social group. They would hang out at Yates and Milton drugstore, eating tuna sandwiches and drinking Coke.

L. D. Milton described his and Clayton R. Yates's drug store: "We developed crowds of people coming to that drugstore. On Sunday, my Lord, you couldn't get in the drugstore for the people piled in there. After one year, we were opening our second drugstore, on the west side. In subsequent years we opened three more stores until we had five drugstores in the city of Atlanta. No white chain in this town had as many drugstores as we had" (ibid., 106). This time between the world wars "was a time when young people often assembled at local soda fountains and ice cream shops" (ibid., 206). Barber Dan Stephens said, "That's when the boys and girls would gather at the drugstore [of] Mr. Yates and Mr. Milton, and the boys would set the girls up to a banana split and a chocolate ice cream and all those things" (ibid.). Also, through her job at the bookstore, Cleo was able to meet everyone on the campus. Socially and emotionally, her experience at Spelman was happy.

There was an insular quality about the Atlanta University Center colleges that transcended the racial realities in Atlanta. A leading professor at that time, Clarence Bacote, remembered Atlanta University Center as "an oasis. You could live here, at any of these schools, and not suffer the injustices that the person who had to make his living in the city did. You didn't have to face Jim Crow, you had your own group right out here. And indeed, all of the many activities at the black colleges were integrated, about the only place in town where that was the case" (ibid., 158).

Cleo accepted the fact that Spelman had a white president and was essentially run by white people (in contrast to Morehouse, where there was an African American president). In the early 1940s, only a limited number of African Americans had reached the educational level to be professors.

Florence Matilda Read is a legendary figure in Atlanta University Center folklore. Not only was she president of Spelman College, she was on the board of trustees of Morehouse and treasurer of Atlanta University. She was the premiere representative of white northern philanthropists who contributed to those schools. That was the source of her immense power. All my life I heard Miss Read stories. However, even I was shocked when I read Taylor Branch's *Parting the Waters* and discovered that Miss Read had fired W.E.B. DuBois (the legendary African American scholar and chairman of the sociology department at Atlanta University) by simply refusing to issue him a paycheck.

What did Cleo think about Miss Read? She says that, at that time, women at Spelman were not groomed to be aggressive or to be leaders. They were to do what Miss Read and Mrs. Lyons said to do. Mrs. Lyons was the dean of students and the sister of John Hope, who had been the president of Morehouse College and of Atlanta University prior to his death. Cleo doesn't think she ever saw Mrs. Lyons smile; the girls called her "Stone Face." If they were ever called into her office, they felt she was about to execute them. Miss Read and Mrs. Lyons believed an appropriate vocation for a Spelman graduate was to be a teacher and that she should go to a rural area of the South and teach or to Africa as a missionary. She was groomed to serve mankind, to follow the rules, and to not question authority.

In contrast to Morehouse men, who were stimulated to be leaders, to be movers and shakers, Spelman women were taught to be ladies, even to the wearing of gloves and hats when they ventured off campus. Marrying and starting families were not encouraged. If a Spelman woman did marry, she was expected to marry a Morehouse man. But she was expected to delay marrying until she had made her contribution to mankind.

Spelman women were required to attend chapel every morning at 8:00 o'clock. Even if they lived off campus, they had to be there on time. They had assigned seats, and row monitors quietly recorded the names of those who were absent. After they accumulated a certain number of absences, they were called in by the unsmiling dean.

In spite of compulsory attendance, Cleo loved chapel and feels that Miss Read conducted it well. The music and scripture were very moving; in fact, Cleo still uses some of Miss Read's passages to this day. Also, her freshman year at Spelman was Dr. Benjamin E. Mays's first year as president of Morehouse, and Miss Read often invited him to speak at Spelman's chapel services. Cleo found his messages extremely enriching. Miss Read also invited other notable African American and white speakers to speak.

Basically, Miss Read cuts a pretty formidable figure in Cleo's memory. There were girls she singled out to whom she related personally, but Cleo was not one of them. Rather than love, Cleo felt a fear of Miss Read. Spelman in those days was not the way it is now, with a youthful African American female president, Dr. Johnetta Cole. Dr. Cole is helpful toward students, who are encouraged to get to know her. When Dr. Cole is jogging on campus, the students join her and jog with her. Miss Read, in contrast, wore conservative dark clothes and matronly shoes.

In spite of these memories of Miss Read and Mrs. Lyons, Cleo sent me and my sister to Spelman. She contributes financially to Spelman and is very active in the Columbus, Ohio, Spelman Club.

Two African American professors joined the faculty while Cleo was at Spelman. Owen Dodson was professor of theater, and Anne Cook professor of speech and theater. They worked with the Spelman-Morehouse-Atlanta University Players, a theater group that Cleo was a member of. These professors helped Cleo improve her speech and broaden her southern accent. Her brother, Asa, ultimately went to a speech therapist when he moved to New York City to help him broaden his southern accent. Cleo believes the changes in her speech helped her move beyond her working-class southern background.

Cleo also feels she received an excellent education at Spelman. Her goal was to be a dietitian, and she had to take a heavy load of science courses to prepare her to take the additional training she would need. Even though marriage changed Cleo's plans to go to Washington, D.C., and do advanced study at Howard University's Freedmen's Hospital, her friend Louise did follow that course and found that Spelman had prepared her very well. Cleo was a teacher before her children were born. Before she reentered the workforce, when I was in high school, she earned a master's degree in early childhood education from Ohio State University.

Cleo did very well academically at Spelman. In the senior yearbook, the *Campus Mirror*, a prophecy and a superlative were written for each person. Cleo was called the "most ladylike," and was imagined as "living in Buffalo, New York, where her husband is the pastor of a large church. It is rumored that when he is absent, she substitutes. Oh, those hidden qualities!"

The prophecy was written by Norma Payton Reid, a classmate of my mother's whom I have gotten to know because she is an early childhood professional. I met her when my mother and I attended a meeting of the National Association for the Education of Young Children. Norma married a dentist and lives today in Los Angeles. Her prediction that Cleo would live in Buffalo was easy, because that was where Phale was from. The insightful part of her prediction is that Cleo would become a moving and effective public speaker, because as it turned out she is invited to speak at churches throughout the country on Women's Days. It gladdens me that her classmates saw her spiritual qualities and public speaking talents even then.

DUAL SOCIALIZATION

Having had the opportunity to know my grandmother Janist well into my adult life, I am struck by how different my mother is from her mother. In fact, I experienced cultural dissonance in trying to relate to my grandmother. It was not until her funeral, when family members from the country assembled, that I fully understood her context. The big leap forward in education and exposure between my mother and her mother made my mother's child-rearing strategies quite different from my grandmother's. And I became a person my grandmother couldn't understand.

I was curious how my mother had created herself out of the raw material available to her. How had she maintained her love for her mother, which was apparent, while learning what she needed from others for her upward mobility? This is a significant issue: inner-city African American children are confronted with the same dilemma— learning to speak and behave differently from the people who love them and are raising them. What a tremendous task this is for a child! As members of the helping professions, we need to elevate to the level of science the study of the challenges children face in achieving upward mobility when there is discontinuity between their home environment and the mainstream.

Cleo reminded me that her friend Antoinette was a part of Atlanta's African American elite and that knowing her and her family had influenced Cleo a great deal. She saw them as living in a different world from Janist's world. However, this did not make her love Janist any less. Janist had many strengths: she was a strong, independent woman.

> I wanted her to be my mother. I wanted to go beyond some of the things she was doing and the way she did things. However, there was so much happiness in our home. We didn't necessarily kiss and hug all of the time, but there was so much security. It was a good feeling to come home. She always had a hot meal ready, clean clothes, a clean house. I appreciated that. Mother made us comfortable and happy. Also, wanted us to have friends in the upper class. She didn't want us to play with the children on Woodrow Place. Dorothy's best friend, Frances, lived two doors from Antoinette. Her mother was a social worker. She liked the fact that we had friends whose parents were professionals.

Even though her childhood friends did not go to Mt. Zion, Cleo loved Mt. Zion. She liked the people, who were real Christian people. Tee Tee worked in the church auxiliaries and strongly supported Cleo's involvement in the church. Cleo could have changed her church membership if she had wanted to. However, the people in Mt. Zion made her and Dorothy feel good about themselves, just as Janist made them feel good about themselves. Janist and John and her church gave her a secure base for becoming upwardly mobile, so Cleo could branch out and incorporate other ways of doing things without alienating her family or her church friends.

JULIA PATE BORDERS

When Cleo was at Spelman, she made a friend of Della, a fellow student, from rural Georgia. Julia Pate Borders, a Spelman graduate and the wife of Rev. William Holmes Borders, the pastor of Wheat Street Baptist Church and a faculty member at Morehouse, contacted Spelman for a student to live with the family and assist with housework and child care. Della moved in with the Borderses, who helped pay her expenses at Spelman.

Mrs. Borders taught English at the Atlanta University Lab School. She was an excellent speaker, gracious, and popular. As teenagers, Cleo and Dorothy had sometimes gone from Mt. Zion Sunday school to Wheat Street Baptist Church for church services and so had seen Mrs. Borders before. Now, through her friendship with Della, Cleo had the opportunity to visit the Borders' home and to get to know Mrs. Borders. Cleo never thought then that she would also become a minister's wife, but when she did, Mrs. Borders was her role model:

> Mrs. Borders was a different type of minister's wife than the types that I had had the opportunity to observe around Atlanta. Most of the minister's wives wore nothing but black clothes and no makeup. They also were at church for every activity, morning, noon, and night. They never smiled; they made no contribution to anything. They were just a part of the woodwork—an invisible supporter of their husbands. At home, they got up in the morning and dressed up. The people in the church brought food from their houses. The minister's wife didn't cook. The members helped them with their children. They were on duty all of the time. Some were in charge of the music at the church. That was almost a requirement for a minister to marry someone who had a musical background.

But Mrs. Borders was an extremely intelligent woman who had come from a rural background to Spelman College. She had a tall, queenly stature. Her speech was articulate and without fault. She was a hard worker, a teacher, and a leader in the Wheat Street Baptist Church. She was an excellent speaker, who was involved in the community activities of Atlanta. She was loved by African Americans in Atlanta. Many would introduce her to audiences by comparing her to Eleanor Roosevelt. She was the mother of a son and daughter, who both became physicians.

MARRIAGE

One favorite Miss Read story in our family was in regard to her unwritten rule that Spelman students who married would be expelled. While Phale was a senior at Morehouse and president of the student body, he performed the wedding ceremony for two of his friends, students at Spelman and Morehouse. The event was reported in the society column of the *Atlanta Daily World* and, in this way, came to Miss Read's attention.

Miss Read contacted C. D. Hubert, acting president of Morehouse, and expressed her intention of expelling the Spelman bride involved and demanded that the groom and Phale be suspended from Morehouse as well. Dr. Hubert, who was also a mentor to Phale, retorted that this was an "unwritten rule" and she could not expel students for a rule that had not been formally made. Reluctantly, she accepted this reasoning. She then formalized the rule.

Subsequently, Cleo and five of her friends broke the rule. In August, the summer before her senior year, Cleo and Phale were married—by Dr. Hubert, no less, in his study, in a ceremony attended by her sister and parents. They obtained their marriage license secretly, in

Phale and Cleo, just married, 1943

The Hale Family, 1952 (*Inset:* Hilton, 1959)

Milledgeville, Georgia. There was a rumor that Mrs. Lyons had a list of girls rumored to be married but whom she couldn't prove were married, since most of them obtained their marriage licenses in small towns outside of Atlanta. One of Cleo's friends, the daughter of a prominent physician in Atlanta, married in a large church wedding, possibly as a test of the rule. She finished her degree at Morris Brown College.

Spelman students were required to spend their senior year on campus, so during this first year of marriage Phale commuted between LaGrange and Gammon, and Cleo visited him in LaGrange every six weeks.

After her graduation, Cleo moved to LaGrange, where Phale pastored for another year and a half before accepting the call of the Mt. Olive Baptist Church in Fort Wayne, Indiana. After a merger, this church became Union Baptist Church. Their first two children, Phale D., Jr., and I, were born in that city. Four years later Phale accepted the call to pastor the Union Grove Baptist church and moved to Columbus, Ohio, where they have lived for forty-four years. Their two younger children, Marna Amoretti and Hilton Ingram, were born in Columbus.

THE PRICE OF UPWARD MOBILITY

It is likely that Cleo paid a price for upward mobility in terms of closeness to her family of origin, a price that was not exacted from Phale, whose family holds him almost in awe and with whom he has a warm and loving relationship. Once Cleo moved away and became a public figure in her role as a pastor's wife and, ultimately, a politician's wife, Janist did not feel a part of Cleo's life.

Cleo's family did not seem to understand her need for closeness with them; basically, all they wanted to know was that she was well. They seemed to feel that she visited too often, stayed too long, and brought too many children with her. Her four children exceeded the norm for members of her extended family, who had only one or two. They believed one should stay at home with one's children.

But Maggie, Phale's sister, empathized with Cleo and offered her the love and support she needed. Maggie annually opened her home in Buffalo for month-long visits by our entire family of six. However, psychological distance was created between Cleo and her family by living so far apart.

CHAPTER SEVEN

Unbank the Fire: Toward Upward Mobility

What do you do with a former slave, when you no longer need his labor?

CONGRESSMAN
AUGUSTUS
HAWKINS

Despite the pious rhetoric about equality of opportunity, most parents want their children to have a more than equal chance of success— which means, inevitably, that they want others, not all others but some others, to have less than equal chances.

CHRISTOPHER
JENCKS

When my father was a boy, his daddy, Church Hale, would throw ashes on the fire in the woodstove to put it out at night before they went to bed. This was called banking the fire. In the morning, there would still be live sparks under the ashes. Church would remove the ashes and let the sparks reignite the wood. This removal of the ashes was called unbanking the fire.

The idea for the title of this book came from the interview with my mother about my father's family. She says that Aunt Maggie felt that Smith Hale had "the spark" in my grandfather's generation and that Phale had "the spark" in their generation. It seemed to Cleo that Clem had taken "the spark" from Phale.

This notion of the spark intrigued me. I considered naming the book *Ignite the Spark*. However, upon reflection, I did not want the message of the biographies I have written to be that every now and then a worthy African American comes along who should be given a helping hand. I also do not want these biographies to be used as an example of what one or two individuals can achieve through extraordinary hard work and perseverence.

Masses of African Americans, faceless to policymakers, are really live embers upon whom ashes have been thrown. Extraordinary effort and money are not needed to enable them to reach their potential. All that has to be done is to remove the ashes—the oppression and the inequality—so that what is there can come forth.

TOWARD UPWARD MOBILITY

The biographies of my mother and father are meant to give faces, hopes, and aspirations to sharecroppers and domestic workers and others who are invisible to those who exploit their labor. The accomplishments of those who won out in spite of the stacked deck speak about the importance of investing in the potential of all of our citizens.

One example of raw brilliance I uncovered as I engaged in research for this book was an uncle of Phale's, William R. Hale, who filed patents in 1923 and 1925 for a motor vehicle that laid the foundation for the modern helicopter. William Hale was born William Roberts in 1868 and was, I believe, related to Phale on his mother's side. He received about three years of education in a sharecroppers' school in Mississippi.

As a young adult in Mississippi, he came into conflict with a group of whites. He sought refuge with the whites he worked for, who helped him leave the state. He went to Birmingham, Alabama, and because of fear of discovery, changed his last name from Roberts to Hale. There must have been some closeness between the two families and he must have felt admiration for the Hales to have taken their name. He finally moved to West Virginia, where he worked in the coal mines. In West Virginia, he identified so strongly with the Hale family that, as I sought to document his relationship with Phale, it was with some difficulty that I determined that he was not a Hale by birth.

According to his son, he loved to tinker with things and to work on his inventions. He tried to get funding to manufacture his inventions himself by selling stock in them. However, he must not have been able to raise the necessary money, so around 1933 he sold his invention to a white man for sixteen thousand dollars. Although we traced the path from his invention to the helicopter, the World Book Encyclopedia credits a white man with the discovery in 1939. It is dazzling to think of what William Hale could have accomplished in his lifetime if this society had unbanked the fire.

Phale and Cleo's four children are all college graduates. Among us, we have earned eight college and graduate degrees. There were twelve children in Phale's family of origin. All of his siblings established working-class families and were God-fearing and tax-paying citizens. However, of all of the children born to those eleven, only one—Fred Hale, Jr.—achieved the baccalaureate degree. Clem Hodges, who followed Phale to Morehouse College, and his wife, Leah, have two sons, both of whom are college graduates; one is an attorney. It is clear that a spark that is nurtured in one generation has a multiplier effect in subsequent generations. My maternal grandmother, Janist, once noted with pride that every one of her grandchildren is a college graduate.

These biographies unveil the process through which each family tried to meet its goals in spite of the hardships inflicted by society. I have tried to give a slice of African American life—the values, the love, the cultural styles of this historical period. (Note the pervasive nicknames among the Hales.) I also have woven in commentary on values germane to education and upward mobility. In each biography, I have tried to unearth the hidden treasures my parents built upon to achieve upward mobility, even though all four of their parents were poorly educated and the school systems, designed by whites, did not prepare them for upward mobility but prepared them only to inherit their parents' social status.

I have highlighted the influence of role models in their lives. Members of the helping professions labor under great stress, and the rewards from touching lives are often deferred. I wanted to reveal the influence of significant others both inside and outside their families on my parents' upward mobility. For example, the partial scholarship that Delta Sigma Theta sorority gave my mother played a large part in enabling her to go to Spelman. Groups that provide scholarships need to know what a big difference a small amount of money can make.

When I first conceptualized this book, I intended to write my father's story only. However, as I talked with my parents and thought about it, I began to see important themes emerge from my mother's life as well. Phale's task of creating himself out of the Mississippi mud was more difficult, because his was essentially an up-from-slavery experience; Cleo's parents had made that first big push from the country and knew what was needed to survive in twentieth-century urban America. They were able to position her to take advantage of the opportunities in Atlanta, limited though they were.

African Americans in general have had to achieve upward mobility in one generation, standing on the shoulders of uneducated parents. White immigrants have been able to utilize a gradual, three-generation process to move from uneducated, unskilled immigrant to the holder of the baccalaureate degree. Further, even middle-class parents, such as mine, have had to bear a heavy burden delivering their children through de facto segregated schools to middle-class status. For example, when I attended high school in Columbus, Ohio, the local newspaper equated a diploma from my high school (almost totally African American) as equivalent to the completion of the ninth grade.

My siblings and I have achieved our educational levels because we have extraordinary parents, who compensated for below-average schools. I shall never forget an instance when my older brother, then in junior high school, brought his tentative class schedule home and asked my father what course of study he should take. Daddy was amazed; he asked, "Does the school assume that all of the children have someone at home well enough educated that they can advise their children on a course of study?" As a pastor in that community, he knew that all of the children did not. Why had that information escaped school officials? At least my parents could draw some small comfort from the fact that the education we received in our Columbus schools was better than what they had received in Mississippi and Georgia. But education in inner-city schools today has deteriorated far below what it was for me two decades ago.

UNEQUAL SCHOOLS

Jonathan Kozol (1991) points out that, when you speak of educational equity, you have to take into account the weak skills of the students' parents, who were victims of segregated schools in states like Mississippi and Georgia, where the vast majority of African Americans migrated from.

Kozol points out further that "critics also willfully ignore the health conditions and the psychological disarray of children growing up in burnt-out housing, playing on contaminated land, and walking past acres of smoldering garbage on their way to school" (37).

The stories of my parents are typical in the sense that the situations they had to deal with were the same as those of millions of other African Americans. All of those who have achieved middle-class status have had to overcome such hardships; those who have not achieved middle-class status either did not have the extraordinary intelligence or the extraordinary support systems that my parents had, which enabled them to overcome incredible odds. The decks are stacked in this society such that whites of average ability are able to reach extraordinary heights while African Americans must have extraordinary ability or support systems to escape poverty and despair.

John Coons (1970) writes:

> The reliance of our public schools on property taxes and the localization of the uses of those taxes have been combined to make the public school into an educator for the educated rich and a keeper for the uneducated poor. There exists no more powerful force for rigidity of social class and the frustration of natural potential. . . .
>
> The freedom claimed by a rich man, to give his child a preferential education, and thereby achieve the transmission of advantage by inheritance, denies the children of others the freedom inherent in the notion of free enterprise. Democracy can stand certain kinds and amounts of inherited advantage. What democracy cannot tolerate is an aristocracy padded and protected by the state itself from competition from below. (5, 207)

Kozol documents the disparity in funding of wealthy suburban school districts in comparison to poor city school districts. He also asserts that one has to factor in student needs in any discussion of equity. "Equity," he states, "does not mean simply equal funding. Equal funding for unequal needs is not equality" (54). Also, efforts to create national tests and standard achievement indexes do not take into account the fact that many city children have to earn money after school. Then there is their lack of adequate health care and the effects of intergenerational poverty. Yet the inner-city child takes the same tests as the child in the suburbs.

Though loath to spend money to equalize education, Americans are ready, willing, and able to spend money on incarceration. Kozol points out that, according to the New York State Department of Corrections, 90 percent of the male inmates of New York City's prisons are dropouts from the city's public schools. Incarceration of each inmate costs the city nearly sixty thousand dollars a year. The annual cost of maintaining an African American male child in Head Start or Morehouse College is miniscule compared to that figure.

The inequality is so great because of the way schools are funded; most public schools depend on property taxes for their initial funding, and this is the foundation for school financing inequality. The property tax depends upon the taxable value of the homes and industries in an area. A wealthy suburb has a larger tax base in proportion to its student population than a city of thousands of poor people. Even though, in the United States, very poor communities tax themselves at a higher rate than do affluent communities, they still end up with less money for each child in their schools.

In addition, the federal government allows homeowners a tax deduction for the property taxes that they spend to fund their children's schools, which constitutes a federal subsidy for an unequal education, since the value of property in the inner city is lower than in wealthy suburbs. Furthermore, the mortgage interest that homeowners pay is also tax deductible and so is, in effect, a second subsidy. These subsidies are considerably larger than most people think. "In 1984, for instance, property-tax deductions granted by the federal government were $9 billion. An additional $23 billion in mortgage-interest deductions were provided to home-owners: a total of some $32 billion. Federal grants to local schools, in contrast, totaled only $7 billion, and only part of this was earmarked for low-income districts. Federal policy, in this respect, increases the existing gulf between the richest and poorest schools" (ibid., 55).

This disparity is heightened by the disproportionate number of tax-free institutions—colleges, hospitals, museums—located in the cities: "30 percent or more of the potential tax base is exempt from taxes, compared to as little as 3 percent in the adjacent suburbs. Suburbanites, of course, enjoy the use of these nonprofit, tax-free institutions; and in the case of private colleges and universities, they are far *more* likely to enjoy their use than are the residents of inner cities" (ibid.).

Kozol explores the argument of people who, on other issues, are liberal but who, on the subject of education, point out that "life isn't fair." Should the government try to equalize access to summer camp, private schools, Europe, libraries, computers, better doctors, nice homes? they ask. To this Kozol responds that the government does not assign us to our homes, summer camps, and doctors; it does assign us to public schools. In fact, the government forces us to go to them. If we do not have the wealth to pay for private education, we are compelled to attend the public school in our district. "Thus, the state, by requiring attendance but refusing to require equity, effectively requires inequality. Compulsory inequity, perpetuated by state law, too frequently condemns our children to unequal lives" (56).

State and federal contributions are intended to supplement property taxes. However, the federal contribution constitutes only 6 percent of total school expenditures and state contributions approximately half of local school expenditures. Thus these contributions are seldom large enough to make up for local wealth disparities. Also, when state allocations are cut back during lean times, those school districts with stable local funding are not as hard hit. A circular phenomenon evolves from the funding formula:

> The richer districts—those in which the property lots and houses are more highly valued—have more revenue, derived from taxing land and homes, to fund their public schools. The reputation of the schools, in turn, adds to the value of their homes, and this, in turn, expands the tax base for their public schools. The fact that they can levy lower taxes than the poorer districts, but exact more money, raises values even more; and this, again, means further funds for smaller classes and for higher teacher salaries within the public schools. (ibid., 121)

UNEQUAL ACCESS

Magnet, or selective, schools—increasingly offered in urban school systems to hold white children in public schools by offering them "choices"—really constitute private schools operated within the public school system. These choices are highly attractive to the more sophisticated parents, who are disproportionately white and middle-class. They are parents who have the ingenuity and often the political connections to obtain admission for their children. Even though the selection criteria for these schools seem to reflect a meritocracy, the merit is largely predetermined by conditions closely tied to class and race.

> Children who have had the benefits of preschool and one of the better elementary schools are at a great advantage in achieving entrance to selective high schools; but an even more important factor seems to be the social class and education level of their parents. This is the case because the system rests on the initiative of parents. The poorest parents, often the products of inferior education, lack the information access and the skills of navigation in an often hostile and intimidating situation to channel their children to the better schools, obtain the applications, and (perhaps a little more important) help them to get ready for the necessary tests and then persuade their elementary schools to recommend them. So, even in poor black

neighborhoods, it tends to be children of the less poor and the better educated who are likely to break through the obstacles and win admission. (ibid., 60)

School choice plans are very attractive to political conservatives, because it places the burden on the individual to break down the doors to a better education for their children. It meshes well with their faith in individual ambition and autonomy. "But to ask an individual to break down doors that we have chained and bolted in advance of his arrival is unfair" (ibid., 62).

One of the greatest drawbacks of magnet schools is that the better teachers and more motivated and successful students are attracted to them, and so neighborhood schools and students must settle for what is left.

UNEQUAL OUTCOMES

Unequal school financing creates a continuity between today's inner-city schools and the segregated schools provided for the grandparents and great-grandparents of these children. Kozol foreshadows the point I make in chapter 11 about the qualitative differences in outcome between inner-city schools and the schools of the suburban middle-class:

> The children in one set of schools are educated to be governors; children in the other set of schools are trained for being governed. The former are given the imaginative range to mobilize ideas for economic growth; the latter are provided with the discipline to do the narrow tasks the first group will prescribe.
>
> Societies cannot all be generals, no soldiers. But, by our schooling patterns, we assure that soldiers' children are more likely to be soldiers and that the offspring of the generals will have at least the option to be generals. (176)

Kozol is amazed that there is an unspoken acceptance of this rigged game among the wealthy, since it conveys a sense that other people's children are of less inherent value than theirs. Worse still, these parents give their children a sense that they deserve their victories. Their children learn to shut from their minds the possibility that they are winners in an unfair race. And the poor children in the inner city are made to feel that they do not much matter. The message they receive is that they are ugly, so it is appropriate that they be crowded into an ugly place; that they are dirty, so it won't hurt them to be crowded into a dirty place.

Wealthy students often retort that they are not responsible for injustices that occurred during slavery or earlier in the twentieth century and that African American children today should not be entitled to preferential treatment because of what has happened in the past. Part 1 of this book was written to document the cumulative effects of past injustices. Kozol's book reveals the extent to which those injustices are institutionalized in the present so that they will go on forever.

This is the point that William Julius Wilson (1987) makes. Racism and social class discrimination have been so finely institutionalized in this society that direct racism is not necessary. A system has been created that effectively sorts people by race and class so that disadvantage is reproduced on its own, generation after generation.

Kozol distinguishes a trend toward designating an urban school curriculum that focuses on "realistic" goals for low-income children. Many corporate leaders speak of "training" these children for nothing better than entry-level jobs that their corporations have available. But the curriculum in suburban schools should be more expansive, with a focus on college preparation. According to this view, investment strategies should be matched to the economic potential of each person. Early testing to assign each child to a "realistic" course of study, tracking children by ability determined by the tests, and expansion of a gifted and talented educational system for the children who show the most promise are also favored.

Kozol points out that first we circumscribe the destinies of poor children and then we look at the diminished product and say, "Let's be pragmatic and do with them what we can" (75). Many urban high school students, for example, do not study math but rather "business math," which is nothing more than elemental bookkeeping. Courses such as hairdressing and manicuring, which would be viewed as insults by suburban parents, are common in inner-city high schools because they reflect the adult roles that African American girls are expected to fill. These bottom-level jobs exist, and someone has got to do them, goes the reasoning. However, it is evident who that someone will be. "No corporate CEO is likely to confess a secret wish to see his children trained as cosmetologists or clerical assistants. So the prerogatives of class and caste are clear" (ibid., 76). Such thinking by wealthy parents regarding the education of other people's children is not far from that in Mississippi in 1933 that limited my father's prospects.

> A lot of wealthy folks . . . think the schools are doing a sufficiently
> good job if the kids of poor folks learn enough to cast a vote—just
> not enough to cast it in their own self-interest. They might think it
> fine if kids could write and speak—just not enough to speak in ways
> that make a dent in public policy. In economic terms, a lot of folks (in
> the suburbs) would think that (poor) kids were educated fine if they
> had all the necessary skills to do their kitchen work and tend their
> lawns. (ibid., 216)

In 1981 the state of New Jersey was brought to court for operating two
separate and unequal public education systems. The state argued that
"education currently offered in these poorer . . . districts is tailored to
the students' present need and that these students simply cannot now
benefit from the kind of vastly superior course offerings found in the
richer districts" (ibid., 170).

MONEY TRANSFER

If wealthier school systems have extra money, what is the harm in
using it for their children? But Kozol points out that every school
district is competing for the same restricted pool of gifted teachers.
When wealthier systems are able to add additional resources, teachers
raise their salary horizons; school suppliers, textbook publishers, and
computer manufacturers adjust their price horizons. The result is that
the poorest districts slip into a less-competitive position. Kozol maintains that the only thing that will fix this is a money transfer; the
population that has the most money is going to have to transfer some
of that money to those who have the least.

Even if genuine equality of schooling were produced for poor
children, other forces would militate against equal school performance.
"Cultural and economic factors and the flight of middle-income blacks
from inner cities still would have their consequences in the heightened
concentration of the poorest children in the poorest neighborhoods.
Teenage pregnancy, drug use and other problems still would render
many families in those neighborhoods all but dysfunctional" (ibid., 123).

Kozol notes that there is a great debate over the primacy of the
school versus the primacy of the family and neighborhood in educational outcomes. Although he maintains that both are clearly elemental forces in the lives of children, "the family differs from the school in
the significant respect that government is not responsible, or at least

not directly, for the inequalities of family background. It *is* responsible for inequalities in public education. The school is the creature of the state; the family is not." (ibid., 123)

THE JOE CLARK APPROACH
TO AFRICAN AMERICAN EDUCATION

U.S. Education Secretary William Bennett once called East Side High School in Paterson, New Jersey, a model for inner-city education and paid tribute to Principal Joe Clark for throwing out three hundred students he thought were involved with violence or drugs. Bennett described Joe Clark as a hero "for an age in which the ethos was to cut down on the carrots and increase the sticks. The day that Bennett made his visit, Clark came out and walked the hallways with a bull-horn and a bat. If you didn't know he was a principal, you would have thought he was a warden of a jail. Bennett created Joe Clark as a hero for white people. He was on the cover of *Time Magazine*" (Kozol, 162).

According to a school official who spoke to Kozol, this lionizing of Clark set the national agenda: whip African American children into line. "Throw out the kids who cause you trouble. It's an easy way to raise the average scores. Where do you put the kids once they're expelled? You build more prisons. Two-thirds of the kids that Clark threw out are in Passaic County jail" (ibid., 163).

> This is a very popular approach in the United States today. Don't provide the kids with a new building. Don't provide them with more teachers or more books or more computers. Don't even breathe a whisper of desegregation. Keep them in confinement so they can't subvert the education of the suburbs. Don't permit them "frills" like art or poetry or theater. Carry a bat and tell them they're no good if they can't pass a state exam. Then, when they are ruined, throw them into prison. Will it surprise you to be told that Paterson destroyed a library because it needed space to build a jail? (ibid.)

While public officials question whether money will solve the problems of educating inner-city children, Kozol points out what it buys for children in the suburbs: "truly scholarly instruction from remarkable and well-rewarded teachers, and . . . a great deal of thoughtful counseling from well-prepared advisers" (76). Kozol contrasts the advantages children enjoy in the suburbs with the dreary pedagogy in inner-city schools. For many of these children, the odds of learning math and reading on the street are probably as good or even better than learning them in the schools. "The odds of finding a few moments of delight or maybe even happiness outside these dreary schools are better still" (59).

Kozol's observations of how pedagogy proceeds in inner-city classrooms parallel the observations I have made while supervising student teachers in similar settings, which I detail in chapter 11. Kozol describes children who are treated like robots; children who learn exclusively through rote; children who are given no conceptual framework; children who do not learn to think, because their teachers are bound to tests that measure only isolated skills. He quotes a school official who complained that "as a result, they can be given no electives, nothing wonderful or fanciful or beautiful, nothing that touches the spirit or the soul. Is this what the country wants for its black children?" (143).

Kozol describes a "test-curriculum that strips the child's school day down to meaningless small particles of unrelated rote instruction. . . . Literature gets lost. The driving notion here is that skills learned in isolation are more useful than skills learned in context" (161).

Kozol concurs with a point I make in the last chapter of this book, that drugs are an attractive alternative to a person living in a world so bare of richness or amenities (73). He describes crack addiction as a kind of "covert" suicide, which is practiced by many people in neighborhoods where the savor has gone out of life (193).

In conclusion, Kozol advocates that psychological studies be conducted on white families to determine why they are afraid for their children to compete on a level playing field. Would it really harm their children to compete in a fair race?

> There is a deep-seated reverence for fair play in the United States, and in many areas of life we see the consequences in a genuine distaste for loaded dice; but this is not the case in education, health care, or inheritance of wealth. In these elemental areas we want the game to be unfair and we have made it so; and it will likely so remain. . . .
>
> Surely there is enough for everyone in this country. It is a tragedy that these good things are not more widely shared. All our children ought to be allowed a stake in the enormous richness of America. (ibid., 223, 233)

SUMMARY

This chapter is meant to bring the analysis of inequality out of the past and into the present. We all delight in exposing the racism of the Deep South in the early twentieth century and in assigning guilt. We need to get past that and take a look at present-day institutionalized injustice so we can develop an agenda for action. I hope that we will all redouble our efforts to achieve equity in school financing and that we will have a deeper insight into true equity of outcome.

The question considered in part 2 is equally important: How can we more effectively use the available resources to create a better fit between the characteristics of African American children and their schooling?

PART TWO

*Educating
African American
Children in
the Context of
Their Culture*

CHAPTER EIGHT

The Transmission of Cultural Values to African American Children

Faith can give you the courage to face the uncertainties of the future.

MARTIN LUTHER KING, JR.

The purpose of this chapter is to describe the values in African American culture that are derived from both traditional African religions and American Christianity. The uniqueness of the American slavery experience and the challenge of living thereafter as an African American created a distinctive folklore, which served as a prism for the development and transmission of African American cultural values.

These values have been transmitted intergenerationally through the oral tradition, a key feature of West African life and culture. It is critical that parents and teachers of African American children understand these cultural values and continue the tradition of transmitting them, because they have played a key role in the survival and sense of self of African American children.

James Fowler (1981) defines faith as a coat against the nakedness of a soul alone.

> For most of us, most of the time, faith functions so as to screen off the abyss of mystery that surrounds us. But we all at certain times call upon faith to provide nerve to stand in the presence of the abyss—naked, stripped of life supports, trusting only in the being,

Proverbs, songs, stories, and fables constitute a rich oral tradition.
(Nancy P. Alexander)

the mercy and the power of the Other in the darkness. Faith helps us
form a dependable "life space," an ultimate environment. At a
deeper level, faith undergirds us when our life space is punctured and
collapses, when the felt reality of our ultimate environment proves to
be less than ultimate. (xii)

Fowler states further that faith is a human universal and that mankind
is endowed at birth with the capacity for faith (xiii). The ways in which
these capacities are activated depend on the kind of environment we
grow in. Faith is social and is shaped by one's community, ritual, and
nurture. However, faith is also shaped by divine initiatives that transcend those of the individual and other people. The manner in which
these initiatives of spirit or grace are recognized and imaged, or are
unperceived and ignored, powerfully affects the shape of faith in our
lives. The Bible also links hope and faith: "Faith is the substance of
things hoped for, the evidence of things not seen" (Hebrews 11:1).
    The study of the cultural values of African American children must
flow from a study of the values of African American culture. In order

to understand these values, we must explore the roots of African American culture, in particular, its religious roots.

Any consideration of the culture and religious experience of African Americans must begin with Africa, because the core of values of the African American religious tradition had their genesis in Africa even though they were shaped by the common experience of American slavery. This perspective on faith has been transmitted to African American children generation after generation through the oral tradition and is part of the cosmology of contemporary African Americans.

Jack Daniel and Geneva Smitherman (1976) point out that there is a traditional African worldview that colors the culture of African Americans. Even though they acknowledge differences among the many ethnic groups, languages, customs, physiognomies, spirits, and deities throughout Africa, these are only surface variations on the deep themes that characterize traditional African culture.

C. Eric Lincoln (1974) states that "it was mainly their dynamic and pragmatic religion which helped the slaves survive in their new environment" (311). According to Leonard Barrett (1974), there is documentation that West Africa in the fifteenth century, before the entrance of the Europeans, had already passed through several centuries of cultural development and had reached a stage comparable to the most developed countries of Europe of that period. This development was evident in all areas of human expression, but mostly in the religious system of Africa. Barrett maintains that the African traditional religion was the motivating force of all African peoples, and it continued to be expressed by Africans in bondage. "The slave master was able to claim the body of the slave, but the worldview of the African was nurtured in his soul, and his soul was impregnable" (313). This was expressed in the spiritual, "Jordan River, chilly and cold, chills the body, not the soul."

The African universe "is a vast system consisting of God, the supreme power who created it, spirits and powers who rule over every aspect of this creation, and at the center, man. All things below man, all lower biological life, was created for man, and the inanimate things serve him also" (ibid.). The whole system is alive because it is energized by a spiritual force emanating from the Supreme Being. One's being depends upon maintaining a harmonious relationship between oneself, one's God, and nature.

However, Africans do not conceive of the world as a place in which to contemplate life; they see it as an arena for activity. Their aim is to live strongly; they pray for long life, health, and prosperity and the strengthening of family, clan, and ethnic group, because they live through them. The ancestors are the guardians of posterity, and people are heavily dependent upon them for all aspects of life.

The pragmatism in the African worldview finds its greatest expression in African folklore and proverbs. "The main theme of the folk tales is the will to survive in adverse conditions. Here we find the ever-recurring theme of the weak against the strong, and here the stress is on cunning, craftiness, and speed. These folk tales gained new significance in the slavery of the New World" (ibid., 314). The folktales contain the collective wisdom of the African people. "In them we find instructions for the preservation of life, leading a moral life, living cautiously, loving God, and holding respect for the aged, as well as the wisdom of gratitude and the beauty of temperance. . . . This worldview found expression in the spirituals, music, dance, and the general life-style of later generations who came to be known as Afro-Americans" (ibid.).

Lawrence Levine (1977) points out that retention of traditional African beliefs and practices was facilitated by the delay that occurred in the conversion of the African slaves to Christianity. There was considerable debate among whites, which lasted for two hundred years, as to whether to give their religion to their bondsmen. They were afraid that baptism would lead to freedom and that labor would be lost, given the fact that work on Sunday was prohibited in the Christian tradition. They also feared that the slaves would develop notions of religious equality.

This vacillation on the part of the slaveholders allowed the slaves the time to accommodate their African religious beliefs and practices to the harsh economic and social system they found themselves in, with its suppression of their freedom to worship in traditional ways (an example of which is the prohibition against using the drum). When conversion to Christianity did come, therefore, it was not at the expense of the slave's folk beliefs.

In fact, there were numerous points of intersection between African beliefs and European beliefs. "The African practices and beliefs which had the best chance of survival in the New World were those that had European analogues, as so many of the folk beliefs did" (ibid., 60). The concept of faith is particularly germane, because there is an ineluctable relationship between magic, medicine, religion, and faith. Faith is particularly strong when a people feel a lack of control over their lives. The absence of power helped to perpetuate the slaves' sacred universe and to intensify their search for supernatural aid and solutions.

Bronislaw Malinowski (1954) points out that "we find magic wherever the elements of chance and accident, and the emotional play between hope and fear, have a wide and extensive range. We do not find magic wherever the pursuit is certain, reliable, and well under the control of rational methods and technological processes. Further, we find magic where the element of danger is conspicuous" (17). In Levine's view, the slaves' magical folk beliefs were a central and necessary part of existence. They stood beside their Christian myths and supplemented and fortified them. Both were sources of strength and release; both served to preserve their sanity. Christianity assured them that the present condition eventually would change and that retribution would come in this world and in the next. It also reinforced their feelings of dignity and self-worth. Their folk beliefs provided hope and a sense of group identification. They also provided the slaves sources of power and knowledge that were alternative to those existing in the master class.

The beliefs in magic and faith were also expressed in medical practices. "While slaves acknowledged the medical care extended to them by their masters—'Our white folks was good as dey knowed how to be when us got sick,' Callie Elder testified—there is evidence that in doctoring as in preaching slaves frequently distrusted the whites and preferred their own doctors and remedies" (Levine, 63).

V. P. Franklin (1984) argues that the shared experience of slavery served as the foundation for the "cultural value system" handed down from the Africans to their American-born offspring, the African Americans. In his book, which is a history of the experiences that formed the African American culture, he uses "the testimony and narratives of enslaved and free Afro-Americans from the end of the eighteenth century to the beginning of the twentieth, as well as Afro-American folk songs, beliefs, and religious practices, in an attempt to provide a viable explanation of the meaning and significance of self-determination, freedom, resistance and education in the lives and experiences of the masses of Afro-Americans in this society" (4).

Scholars (Cone, 1972; Lincoln, 1974; Levine, 1977; Franklin, 1984) agree that constructs such as religious faith as expressed in the African American culture can be properly understood only when their genesis is studied in the context of slavery. The spirituals, for example, were central to the religious expression of the slaves. C. Eric Lincoln (1974) writes, "Blacks feel more deeply than do others, and it is that broader, deeper spirituality which has enabled black people to endure. The spirituals are songs, prayers, praises and sermons. They have been mistakenly derided by those who cannot distinguish between the experience of slavery and the creative genius of a people *in spite* of slavery" (44). John Wesley Work, writing in 1915, summarizes the essence of the spiritual in the culture of the slave:

> In the Negro's own mind his music has held, and still holds, positions of variable importance. In the darkness of bondage, it was his light; in the morn of his freedom, it was his darkness; but as the day advances, and he is being gradually lifted up into a higher life, it is becoming not only his proud heritage, but a support and powerful inspiration. The songs of the slave were his sweet consolation and his messages to Heaven, bearing sorrow, pain, joy, prayer, and adoration. Undisturbed and unafraid, he could always unburden his heart in these simple songs, pregnant with faith, hope, and love (110).

African Americans created their own version of Christianity. The southern plantation encompassed two worlds, one the master's and one the slave's. "The gospel of the oppressor taught obedience and submission, and it was rejected by the enslaved. The gospel of the oppressed spoke of freedom, the ultimate justice of God, and His support for His chosen people" (Franklin, 67). Not only did slaves believe they were the chosen people of God, but there is evidence that many felt that their owners would be denied salvation. Levine cites the story of a slave's reaction to the news that he would be buried in the same vault with his master: "Well massa, one way I am satisfied, and one way I am not. I like to have good coffin when I die [but] I 'fraid, massa, when the debbil come take you body, he make mistake, and get mine" (35).

FEATURES OF THE SLAVE RELIGION

Levine identifies certain themes that characterize the religion of the slaves and that inform our study of the faith of contemporary African Americans. First, the God the slaves sang of was neither remote nor abstract but as intimate, personal, and immediate as the gods of Africa had been: "O when I talk with God," "Mass' Jesus is my bosum friend," "I'm goin' to walk with (talk with, live with, see) King Jesus by myself, by myself" (Levine, 35).

Second, descriptions of the Crucifixion communicated a sense of the actual presence of the singers: "Dey pierced Him in the side . . . Dey nail Him to the cross . . . Dey rivet His feet . . . Dey hanged Him high . . . Dey stretched Him wide"; "Oh sometimes it causes me to tremble, tremble, tremble, Were you there when they crucified my Lord" (Levine, 37).

Third, the slave's Bible was primarily the books of Moses in the Old Testament and Revelations in the New Testament. "All that lay between, even the life of Jesus, they rarely cared to read or hear." Levine continues,

> The lives of Daniel, David, Joshua, Jonah, Moses, and Noah struck the imagination of the slaves because they experienced deliverance in *this* world. Over and over, their songs dwelt upon the spectacle of the Red Sea opening to allow the Hebrew slaves past before inundating the mighty armies of Pharoah. They lingered delightedly upon the image of little David humbling great Goliath with a stone, a pre-technological victory which postbellum Negroes were to expand upon in their songs of John Henry. . . .
>
> They retold in endless variation the stories of the blind and humbled Samson bringing down the mansions of his conquerors; of the ridiculed Noah patiently building the ark which would deliver him from the doom of a mocking world; of the timid Jonah attaining freedom from his confinement through faith (50).

Levine makes clear the parallels between these Old Testament figures and their plight as slaves (51): "O my Lord delivered Daniel," the slaves observed—and responded logically, "O why not deliver me, too?"

> He delivered Daniel from de lion's den,
> Jonah from de belly ob de whale,
> And de Hebrew children from de fiery furnace,
> And why not every man?

Fourth, although Jesus was omnipresent in the spirituals, it was not the Jesus of the New Testament whom the slaves sang about. He was Jesus transformed into an Old Testament warrior: "'Mass' Jesus' who engaged in personal combat with the devil; 'King Jesus' seated on a milk-white horse with sword and shield in hand, 'Ride on, King Jesus'; 'Ride on conquering King'; 'The God I serve is a man of war'" (Levine, 43).

This Old Testament Jesus and the New Testament Jesus were eventually merged with the advent of black theology in the 1960s. James Cone (1969) declares that "Jesus is God Himself coming into the very depths of human existence for the sole purpose of striking off the chains of slavery, thereby freeing man from ungodly principalities and powers that hinder his relationship with God." He quotes Jesus' definition of his ministry: "The Spirit of the Lord is upon me, because he has anointed me to preach the good news to the poor. He has sent me to proclaim release to the captives and recovering of sight to the blind, to set at liberty those who are oppressed, to proclaim the acceptable year of the Lord" (Luke 4:18–19, RSV).

FAITH AND SUFFERING

James Cone (1972) raises a central question in the theology of the slave: "If God is omnipotent and in control of human history, how can his goodness be reconciled with human servitude? If God has the power to deliver black people from the evil of slavery as he delivered Moses from Pharoah's army, Daniel from the lion's den, and the Hebrew children from the fiery furnace, why then are black slaves still subject to the rule of white masters?" (58).

But, Cone argues, the slaves did not question the justice and goodness of God. Their God was righteous and would vindicate the poor and the weak. The singers of the spirituals were concerned about faithfulness in a world full of trouble, about whether the sadness and pain of the world would cause them to lose faith in the gospel of God.

The slaves faced the reality of the world "ladened wid trouble, an' burden'd wid grief," but they believed that they could go to Jesus and get relief. They appealed to Jesus not so much to remove the trouble (although they wanted it removed) as to keep them from "sinkin' down."

> Oh Lord, Oh, My Lord!
> Oh, My Good Lord! Keep me from sinkin' down.
> Oh, Lord, Oh, My Lord!
> Oh, My Good Lord! Keep me from sinkin' down.

The songs of the slaves affirmed that "trouble don't last always." Although they sang, "Sometimes I feel like a motherless child / A long way from home," Cone notes that they were confident that Jesus had not left them completely alone (63).

A preoccupation of the spirituals seems to be that despair and loneliness would disrupt the community of faith (Cone, 64). They feared the agony of being alone in a world of hardship and pain.

> I couldn't hear nobody pray,
> Oh, I couldn't hear nobody pray.
> Oh, way down yonder by myself,
> And I couldn't hear nobody pray.

The spirituals lamented a possible loss of community. The suffering would not be too much to bear if you had brothers and sisters to go down in the valley and pray with you, but the burden would be unbearable without their support. The focus of many slave songs on "going home" Cone interprets as an affirmation of this need for community. Home was the place where mother, father, sister, and brother had gone. "To be sure, the slave wanted to make it to heaven so that he could put on his 'golden slippers and walk all over God's heaven'; he wanted to see the 'pearly gates' and the 'golden streets'; and he wanted to 'chatter with the Father, argue with the Son' and 'tell un 'bout the world [he] just come from.' But most of all he wanted to be reunited with his family which had just been broken and scattered in the slave marts" (65).

If the slaves truly believed that God was in control of history, why were they silent about his neglect in ending slavery? The answer is that not all slaves had an unquestioning faith in God. Cone and Levine identify the open rebellion against God exemplified in secular music (the blues). Sterling Brown (1969) records these black songs (215, 216):

> I don't want to ride no golden chariot,
> I don't want no golden crown,
> I want to stay down here and be,
> Just as I am without one plea.

And

> Our father, who is in heaven,
> White man owe me eleven and pay me seven,
> Thy kingdom come, thy will be done,
> And if I hadn't took that, I wouldn't had none.

Cone (1972) notes that the "theological assumption of Black slave religion as expressed in the spirituals was that slavery contradicts God and that He will therefore liberate Black people" (73). But although the slaves were keenly aware of their oppression and lack of freedom, they believed that the same God who delivered the Israelites would deliver them. A central theme in the slave religion and in the development of faith was God's involvement in history and His liberation of the oppressed in bondage. "When the slaves sang, 'Sometimes I'm up, sometimes I'm down, Oh, yes, Lord! Sometimes I'm almost to the ground, Oh, yes, Lord!' they were exemplifying the fact that God was always with them and that 'trouble would not have the last word'" (Cone, 74).

Cone contends that the slaves knew that God was in control and would liberate them (74):

> Do, Lord, remember me.
> Do, Lord, remember me.
> When I'm in trouble,
> Do, Lord, remember me.
>
> When I'm low down,
> Do, Lord, remember me.
> Oh, when I'm low down,
> Do, Lord, remember me.

At the end of slavery, viable institutions controlled by African Americans were created that were geared specifically to the needs of the African American community, and resistance to oppression was expressed in flight and migration (Frankin, 204). But although emancipation changed the legal status of the majority of African Americans, it did not change their core cultural values.

Patsy Mitchner, a former slave interviewed in the 1930s, compared slavery and freedom to two snakes, both of them "full of pisen" (poison); slavery was a "bad thing," but freedom "of de kin we got wid nothin' to live on was bad [too]. . . . Both bit de nigger, an' dey was both bad" (Frankin, 106). "Under slavery, Afro-Americans valued survival with dignity, resistance against oppression, religious self-determination, and freedom. After emancipation, they continued to hold these ideals; and freedom, rather than being an end in itself, became a means for achieving other cultural goals that developed within the slave and free black communities" (ibid., 146).

THE ORAL TRADITION

As a child, Ella Mitchell (1986) marveled over her two grandmothers' eloquent exegeses of the Bible. How could they have gleaned such insights, being barely literate and not having had the benefit of a printed curriculum or trained church schoolteachers? She then understood that the oral tradition in African American culture had been the vehicle for passing on religious insights.

Her observation coincides with one made by Levine, who points out that, even when literate, the slaves favored the songs and prayers from their oral tradition over those in hymn and prayer books. "When Baptist Negroes attended the church of their masters, or when their mistress sang with them, they used hymn books, but in their own meetings they often made up their own words and tunes. They said their songs had 'more religion than those in the books'" (44).

Mitchell points out that the slaves found it necessary to make adaptations in their traditional ways of communicating because of the oppression of slavery; drumming was suppressed, for example. However, the descendants of Africa had a variety of ways to transmit their culture.

Storytelling was one popular form. The story told by Alex Haley in his best-selling book, *Roots,* is an example of the way important historical information was transmitted through the oral tradition (Mitchell, 95). Audience participation was expected, and the stories were enlivened by the mixing in of poetry and music, and even dancing and drumming. These performances might serve any number of very practical functions, "such as a dispute to be settled, a bargain to be driven, a child to be corrected, or a friend to be advised of the error of his/her ways. To say nothing of work made easier by singing, and fields thus converted into classrooms with 'live entertainment'" (ibid., 96).

Proverbs were another form. They peppered conversation and served as pearls of wisdom for the survival of the extended family unit. Mitchell says there was no way for children to escape this ingenious educational system, because they were surrounded by the lessons of their ancestors, dead or living, in such a natural way that they didn't recognize them as lessons.

Traditional African religious gatherings were forbidden, and the authorized worship, supervised by slaveholders, was so unsatisfying that the slaves went underground to worship authentically. Likewise, they developed instructional and socializing techniques for their children that were difficult to police. Parents were required to work from "can to cain't" (sunup to sundown), so the task of transmitting the culture fell on the elderly grandparents, who cared for and taught the children too young to work. "Until they were large enough to work, there was plenty of time to listen to tales and take advantage of the peak learning years" (Mitchell, 99). When the children went into the fields, their education into the culture continued with spirituals, work songs, stories, proverbs, and folktales.

There was no effort on the part of the slaveholders to control the activity in the cabins after sundown. This was a time the slaves could use for reading the Bible or, when that was impossible because of illiteracy, telling stories. Numerous slave narratives "attest to the fact that slave children were exceptionally well trained in devious ways of coping with masters, and in Bible wisdom, prayer and trust" (ibid.).

An important aspect of the slave child-rearing system described by Mitchell was enforced intimacy, analogous to the intimacy of the small African village, so the belief systems of African Americans were more "caught than taught."

> Thus, slave children got their cues for coping by watching their parents and other significant adults at very close range. They were together in cotton and corn fields, in small cabins and in the highly restricted life of the slave quarter. Persons were so close that, blood relations or no, one had to treat all as persons and indeed as kin. Training for coping with tragic mistreatment was thus handed down most effectively with no formal instruction, but lots of casual oral communication (101).

Franklin tells of an effort made by an abolitionist, John Miller McKim, to find out how slave songs originated.

> I asked one of these blacks—one of the most intelligent of them— where they got these songs. "Dey make 'em, sah." "How do they make them?" After a pause, evidently casting about for an explana- tion, he said: "I'll tell you it's dis way. My master call me up, and order me a short peck of corn and a hundred lash. My friends see it, and is sorry for me. When dey come to de praise-meeting that night dey sing about it. Some's very good singers and know how; and dey work it in—work it in, you know, til they get it right, and dat's de way." A very satisfactory explanation; at least so it seemed to me. (45)

Mitchell tells of a little slave girl who, at the age of eight years, saw her mother cruelly beaten and sent away. However, she accepted her mother's admonitions upon her departure and carried them out with calm resolve; because of the mother's faith and unflinching personal dignity, the child accepted the message that this was the way life had to be.

Self-esteem was also taught in the intimacy of the slavery experi- ence. Mitchell says, "The lesson was learned so well that, despite the ravages of dehumanization, very few slaves ever gave up and fully accepted the servile image thrust upon them" (101).

Even though there was precious little time for any adults save the elderly to spend with them, love was lavished on babies and children. According to John Blassingame (1972), "since slave parents were primarily responsible for training their children, they could cushion the shock of bondage for them, help them understand their situation, teach them values different from those their masters tried to instill in them, and give them a referent for self-esteem other than their master" (79). Of course, as Mitchell notes, the message of self-respect and psychic survival could not be communicated openly, so the "caught-not-taught" process was especially useful. "Casual conversation and example could quietly nourish healthy self-awareness in the hearts of even the youngest children" (102).

Children learned early that they were surrounded by danger and potential death. "The gravity of their plight was obvious, and slave parents dared not try to protect their offspring from hard reality. The best evidence of this fact is the sophistication among small children in dealing with situations where survival was at stake" (ibid., 103). The stereotype of slave children as happy-go-lucky is way off the mark. A

African American children who know their culture's worthiness can construct strong self-identities. (Hildegard Adler)

happier aspect of child rearing, which Mitchell describes, was formal religious instruction through teaching the Bible. Such training was regarded not only as spiritual food but also as a means of uplift and an improvement of their condition.

Franklin also identifies education as a key cultural value for African Americans, as illustrated in the following folk song (147).

> When I done been 'deemed en done been tried,
> I'll sit down side de lamb.
> Can't you read? Can't you read?
> When I done been ter heaven den,
> I can read my title clean.
> I's goin' ter git my lesson,
> I's goin' ter read,
> I's goin ter read my title clean.

Among the vehicles of education that Mitchell describes, the unifying thread is the oral tradition brought to the New World from Africa. The Br'er Rabbit stories, for example, taught slave children how to outfox an oppressive system, how to survive life in America.

The oral tradition continued to transmit African American culture even after Emancipation. The enforced intimacy of slavery did not change dramatically under sharecropping or even urban living for the freedmen. There was a new emphasis on formal education. However, reading, writing, and arithmetic "did not take the place of the oral tradition in the deeper matters of how to cope with oppression and in the development of an adequate belief system. In fact, formal education itself was often fused or blended with oral traditional forms of instruction in many creative ways" (Mitchell, 105).

THE PROVERB TRADITION

The proverb is perhaps Africa's richest and most plentiful literary device (Daniel, 1976). Proverbs have served to preserve religious principles and transmit folk wisdom across generations. "There is practically no such thing as a traditional African child who has not been raised on a steady diet of what 'they say.' And throughout Black America, there are many Blacks who use these old sayings to help raise their children by giving oral summations of life's many lessons" (Daniel, 1). Through proverbs, important folk wisdom is transmitted that helps African

American children make sense of the universe and achieve the serenity to cope with events they cannot control.

According to Jack Daniel, Geneva Smitherman-Donaldson, and Jeremiah Milford (1987, 35), proverbs are an index of black cultural continuity and interaction, are significant in the socialization of black children, are central to black children's development of abstract thinking and reasoning, are significant rhetorical devices in arguments, debates, verbal dueling, and other interaction where persuasion and manipulation of the rhetorical situation are paramount, and are indexes of cultural assimilation. Listed below are examples of proverbs (compiled by Daniel, 1976) pertinent to faith, an important African American cultural value. They are listed in the categories assigned by Daniel.

Proverbs about Human Control and Responsibility

- The more you stir mess, the more it stinks.
- If you fall, don't wallow.
- If we send no ships out, no ships will come in.
- If you don't climb the mountain, you can't view the plain.
- If you can't take it, you can't make it.
- If you can't stand the heat, get out of the kitchen.
- Take life as you find it, but don't leave it the same.
- Games can't be won unless they are played.
- When things get tough, remember that it's the rubbing that brings out the shine.
- Where there's a will there's a way.
- Stumbling blocks may be carved into stepping stones.
- Necessity is the mother of invention.

Proverbs about Natural Relationships

- What is done in the dark will come to light.
- The darkest hour is just before the dawn.
- A place for everything, and everything in its place.
- Where there's smoke, there's fire.
- What goes around, comes around.
- What goes up must come down.
- Cream rises to the top.
- A little light in a dark place can serve a large purpose.
- Every dog will have his day.

Proverbs about Taking the Good with the Bad

- You must take the bitter with the sweet.
- Life is not a bed of roses.
- Every good thing has to come to an end.
- You can't be the salt of the earth without smarting some.
- Easy come, easy go.
- You can't eat your cake and have it too.
- You have to crawl before you walk.
- Things that are hard to bear are sweet to remember.
- Into each life some rain must fall.

IMPLICATIONS FOR PARENTS AND EARLY CHILDHOOD TEACHERS

Teachers and parents can use folktales to illustrate the importance of faith and perseverence to African American children. Such stories can teach these children that they can achieve power in the midst of a powerless community. The Br'er Rabbit stories star a rabbit trickster with clear parallels between him versus the fox and the slave versus the slaveholder. There are also numerous folktales that star the slave as trickster.

Teachers and parents should also utilize the body of literature that features black heroes, all the way from the mythical John Henry to Jack Johnson and Joe Louis, who refused to accept the "place" reserved for African Americans. There is also a vast literature about the contributions to society of such African Americans as Jackie Robinson, Marian Anderson, and Booker T. Washington, who emerged from humble beginnings and suffered racial indignities but triumphed in the end. These stories transmit the message to African American children that, although there are quicksand and land mines on the road to becoming an African American achiever in America, they can overcome these obstacles.

These stories help African American children depersonalize oppression when they encounter it and enable them to place their personal difficulties into the context of the overall African American liberation struggle. I am reminded of an occasion when I talked to my minister about the despair of African American students upon encountering racism in a university setting. He asked me to remind them of the racism W.E.B. DuBois must have experienced at Harvard in 1896. I was speechless; he evoked the African American tradition in which I was raised, the faith that has brought us as a people this far along the way.

Proverbs teach African American children the folk wisdom and life skills drawn from the African culture. Teachers and parents should realize that these skills played an important part in the resilience African Americans displayed against overwhelming oppression and should help preserve the foundation of this faith and perseverence.

The African American cultural tradition teaches African American children important lessons about the struggle implicit in human affairs. The tendency of European Americans to distort human history and to paint a picture of never-ending European American victories has robbed white children of legitimate lessons about overcoming adversity. The suicide rate among white males, the highest in the country, is an example of what happens when one has been raised in a culture that expects unending triumphs. When one encounters the defeats and frustrations that are a part of living without having a tradition of overcoming adversity, one personalizes defeat.

In contrast to the suicide rate among white males, the suicide rate among African American females is the lowest in the country. African American females have been given a religious orientation that emphasizes faith, perseverence, and resilience.

Teachers should expose children of other ethnic groups to the literature of the African American culture, so as to give them the benefit of stories that emphasize such resilience. The notion of survival through perseverence is transmitted effectively in a poem by Langston Hughes:

Mother to Son

Well son, I'll tell you:
Life for me ain't been no crystal stair.
It's had tacks in it,
And splinters,
And boards torn up,
And places with no carpet on the floor—
Bare.
But all the time
I'se been a-climbin' on,
And reachin' landin's,
And turnin' corners,
And sometimes goin' in the dark

Teachers can provide books to strengthen African American children's self-image.
(© Janet Brown McCracken)

Where there ain't been no light.
So, boy, don't turn back.
Don't you set down on the steps
'Cause you finds it kinder hard.
Don't you fall now—
For I'se still goin', honey.
I'se still climbin',
And life for me ain't been no crystal stair.

Teachers and parents can find literature from their local library. They can also get in touch with the Schomberg Center for Research in African American Culture, part of the New York City public library system. In addition, the list of readings that follows will be helpful.

READINGS FOR ADULTS

J. H. Cone. 1972. *The spirituals and the blues.* New York: Seabury.

W.E.B. DuBois. 1968 (1906). *The autobiography of W.E.B. DuBois: A soliloquy on viewing my life from the last decade of its first century.* New York: International Publishers.

L. P. Dunn. 1975. *Black Americans.* San Francisco: R & E Research Associates.

V. P. Franklin. 1984. *Black self-determination: A cultural history of the faith of the fathers.* Westport, Conn.: Lawrence Hill.

J. E. Hale-Benson. 1986. *Black children: Their roots culture, and learning styles.* Baltimore: Johns Hopkins University Press.

———. 1990. Visions for Children: African American preschool program. *Early Childhood Research Quarterly* 5:199–213.

L. Levine. 1977. *Black culture and black consciousness.* New York: Oxford University Press.

C. E. Lincoln. 1974. *The black experience in religion.* New York: Anchor/Doubleday.

C. McClester. 1985. *Kwanzaa: Everything you always wanted to know but didn't know where to ask.* New York: Gumbs and Thomas.

E. McNeill, V. Schmidt, and J. Allen. 1981. *Cultural awareness for young children.* Dallas: Learning Tree.

L. E. Nielsen and J. McClain. 1987. *Black history.* Cedar Falls: University of Northern Iowa Press.

H. A. Ploski. 1976. *The Negro almanac.* New York: Bellwether.

J. W. Work. 1915. *Folk songs of the American Negro.* Nashville, Tenn.: First University Bookstore.

READINGS FOR CHILDREN

R. D. Abrahams. 1985. *Afro-American folktales.* New York: Random House.

A. Adoff. 1973. *Black is brown is tan.* New York: Harper.

V. Banks. 1988. *Kwanzaas coloring book.* Los Angeles: Sala Enterprises.

L. Clifton. 1973. *The boy who didn't believe in spring*. New York: Dutton.

A. Dumas. 1982. *Golden legacy*. Seattle: Baylor.

M. Feelings. 1974. *Jambo means hello: Swahili alphabet*. New York: Dial.

D. Freeman. 1968. *Corduroy*. New York: Viking.

————. 1978. *A pocket for corduroy*. New York: Viking.

L. H. Giles. 1982. *Color me brown*. Chicago: Johnson.

N. Giovanni. 1985. *Spin a soft black song*. New York: Hill and Wang.

E. Greenfield. 1974. *She come bringing me that little baby girl*. Philadelphia: Lippincott.

————. 1980. *Daddy is a monster . . . sometimes*. New York: Metheun.

J. Havill. 1986. *Jamaica's find*. Boston: Houghton.

W. Hudson and V. Wilson-Wesley. 1988. *Book of black heroes from A to Z*. Orange, N.J.: Just Us Books.

E. J. Keats. 1971. *Whistle for Willie*. New York: Macmillan.

C. Leslau and W. Leslau. 1985. *African proverbs*. White Plains, N.Y.: Peter Pauper.

L. Lowery. 1987. *Martin Luther King Day*. Minneapolis: Carolrhoda Books.

A. McGovern. 1969. *Black is beautiful*. New York: Scholastic.

P. C. McKissack. 1986. *Flossie and the fox*. New York: Dial.

M. Musgrove. 1976. *Ashanti to Zulu African traditions*. New York: Dial.

M. S. Nolan. 1978. *My daddy don't go to work*. Minneapolis: Carolrhoda Books.

A. V. Sealy. 1980. *Color your way into black history book*. Brooklyn: Association for the Study of Family Living.

J. Steptoe. 1972. *Birthday*. New York: Holt, Rinehart, and Winston.

I. Thomas. 1970. *My street's a morning cool street*. New York: Harper.

————. 1973. *Lordy, Aunt Hattie*. New York: Harper.

J. M. Udry. 1966. *What Mary Jo shared*. Chicago: Albert Whitman.

————. 1970. *Mary Jo's grandmother*. Chicago: Albert Whitman.

M. P. Walter. 1980. *Ty's one man band*. New York: Four Winds.

J. Winter. 1988. *Follow the drinking gourd*. New York: Random House.

CHAPTER NINE

The African American Schoolchild in a Strange Land

A bull does not enjoy
fame in two herds.

African proverb

In this chapter, I consider the literature that examines the interethnic code conflict between African American children and white teachers which results in failure over time for African American children.

THE AFRICAN AMERICAN SCHOOLCHILD AS PARIAH

Ray McDermott (1987, 173) defines African Americans as being a pariah group in American society. F. Barth (1969) says that they are "actively rejected by the host population because of behavior or characteristics positively condemned" by group standards (31). V. P. Franklin has noted that African Americans are considered pariahs because whites no longer need their labor. McDermott's structural inequality thesis holds that the host population works to defeat the efforts of the pariah child to beat the cycle of degradation that is his birthright. Racial markers, low-prestige dialects, school failure, occupational specialties, and lifestyles tag each new generation for low status.

McDermott also sets forth a thesis of achieved

failure, pointing out that simple tagging is a simplistic explanation. Overt ascription is frowned upon legally and in popular ideologies, yet, pariah boundaries remain firm in society and school. Thus even without institutionalized ascription, pariah status survives into each generation. According to McDermott, "the host population does not simply slot a child on the basis of its parentage and then keep a careful eye out for the child so that he never advances a slot. Rather, it seems as if the child must learn how to do it himself; he must learn a way of acting normally which the host population will be able to condemn according to the criteria the hosts have learned for evaluating, albeit arbitrarily, their own normal behavior. Pariah status appears almost as achieved as ascribed" (176).

Each new pariah generation affirms the soundness of this classificatory system, because they learn and exemplify the behavior essential to the system's maintenance. Rather than regarding themselves as blinded by prejudice, the hosts maintain that they use uniform standards of evaluation for all people, regardless of race or ethnic identity. The question McDermott asks is, "How is it that what is there for them to see is in fact there?" (176). He argues that pariah children do not enter school disadvantaged; they leave school disadvantaged.

ASCRIBING STATUS

Ascription of status does not account for all of this disadvantage nor do the inherent characteristics of the pariah population. Clearly, the pariah group regards host behavior as oppressive. Likewise, the host group regards pariah behavior as inadequate. McDermott suggests that the way the two groups find this out about each other is the central problem. Misunderstandings take place very often in the early grades, and the results are disastrous. "Once a host teacher treats a child as inadequate, the child will find the teacher oppressive. Often, once a child finds a teacher oppressive, the child will start behaving inadequately. After such a point, relations between the child and the teacher regress—the objectionable behavior of each will feed back negatively into the objectionable behavior of the other" (178).

McDermott maintains that, in this way, a child achieves pariah status. The miscommunication between the teacher and the child breaks down relations between them until the child begins to form an alternative to the teacher's organization of the classroom in an attempt to become visible. This results in more condemnation, and the teacher then becomes the administrator in charge of failure. "Teachers do not simply ascribe minority children to failure. Nor do minority children simply drag failure along, either genetically or socially, from the previous generation. Rather, it must be worked out in every classroom, every day, by every teacher and every child in their own peculiar ways" (178). In McDermott's view, school failure becomes an achievement, because it is a rational adaptation made by children to human relations in host schools. Children produce pariah-host statuses in their interactions with each other and their teachers.

I have pointed out elsewhere (Hale-Benson, 1986) that African American children are very adept at nonverbal communication and sensitive to affective cues, and McDermott points out that young children upon entering school are more sensitive to relational messages than they are to information transfer:

> School success, an essential ingredient in any child's avoidance of pariah status, is dependent upon high levels of information transfer. In these early stages of school, depending upon how the politics of everyday life are handled, the child defines his relations with his classmates and his teachers. These relations, remember, define the context of whatever information is to be transferred by a communicant. If the wrong messages of relationship are communicated, reading, writing, and arithmetic may take on very different meanings than they do for the child who is more successful in getting good feelings from the politics of the classroom. The wrong messages can result in a learning disability. (McDermott, 181)

Erik Erikson (1968) notes that "it is of great relevance to the young individual's identity formation that he be responded to and be given function and status as a person whose gradual transformation makes sense to those who begin to make sense to him" (156).

The teacher therefore plays an important role in ascribing status and identity to children in the classroom. One example is the division of the class into ability groups. As McDermott says, this division, made to simplify the administration of the classroom, determines the level of work the children engage in, the people they interact with, and the kind of feedback they receive from the teacher. Rarely do children reject their assignment, even if assigned to the lowest status groups. They accept their assignment as if it makes sense. A child who did not accept his assignment might work harder to catch up with the rest of the class.

African American children are very sensitive to messages of relationship and to nonverbal cues. (Richard Bielaczyc, Photography-Media Services, Wayne State University Libraries)

The reason that revolt is rarely attempted, McDermott suggests, is that in schools with *host children the teacher assigns them to groups* using criteria that the children themselves use in dealing with each other and that their parents and the rest of the community use in dealing with children. Essentially, the teacher, the children, and the community are in agreement. Even if a child is placed in a low-status group, it does not have a disastrous effect if it makes sense to the child. "The politics of everyday life in the classroom will be identical to the politics of everyday life outside the classroom and the children's world will be in order" (183). But the ascription of minority children by a host-group teacher does not proceed as smoothly. She will not use the values of the minority community in organizing her classroom.

Through ability grouping, children receive messages of relationship. If bright children are assigned to a lower-ability group, they will reject the messages of relationship from the teacher and demand a reorganization of the classroom and its relationships more in keeping with their self-concepts. If the teacher is insensitive to their demands, which are often subtle, then for the remainder of the year the children will be engaged in small battles with their teacher over their status and identity. The resolution of these battles will determine whether anything gets done in the classroom. Thus we can see that the politics of daily classroom life determine information transfer and the development of abilities and disabilities.

McDermott points out that pariah-host group divisions begin with small political arenas constituted by dyads and slightly larger groups. Abilities and disabilities arise based on a child's tendency to attend to, think about, and manipulate selected aspects of his environment. "Just what parts of an environment are attended [to] and mastered depends upon the social meaning of the environment as recorded in the experiences of the developing child. For example, reading materials can or cannot be attended [to] depending upon whether looking at a book is an acceptable activity in a particular social milieu and whether books contain information helpful in operating in a particular social environment" (184).

A chronic educational problem is the high rate of learning disabil-

The teacher plays an important role in ascribing status and identity.
(Richard Bielaczyc, Photography-Media Services, Wayne State University Libraries)

ities among African American children. Rates of functional African American illiteracy are estimated at 50 percent (Thompson, 1966), compared to 10 percent for white Americans and only 1 percent for the Japanese (Makita, 1968). Explanations for this disproportionality generally suggest some genetic inferiority or cultural deprivation. But McDermott suggests that it is caused by "selective inattention" to instruction developed in the politics of everyday life in the classroom.

The discrepancy between white teachers and African American children regarding the children's status and identity causes the children to psychologically shut down. They ignore reading materials and join their peers in a classroom subculture, which ends up in reading disabilities and school failure. Deprivation theorists generally blame the child or the child's culture. However, achieved-failure theorists suggest that school achievement has been measured using biased standards. McDermott asserts that achievement takes place in a social context; instead of looking at the skills stored in children's bodies, we must look at the social contexts in which the skills are turned into achievements.

Scores on perceptual, intelligence, aptitude, language, and even neurological tests do not reveal much about the mental capabilities of any subject, but they do tell us much about the social processes in which a subject is engaged and about the thinking underlying the social acts to be performed during the test (McDermott, 186). Reading, for example, is an act that may align the African American child with incompatible forces in his social universe, since African American children often do badly on language tests in formal situations and very well in informal situations; the opposite is true for white children (Cazden, 1970).

AN ECOLOGY OF GAMES

Reading is part of the teacher's "ecology of games" (Long, 1958). To read is to buy into the teacher's games and all the statuses and identities that accompany them. Not to read is to buy into peer group games and their statuses and identities. In some sense, reading failure becomes a social accomplishment supported and rewarded by the peer group.

This phenomenon is not measured by tests. What determines whether a child learns to read or not are the statuses and identities available from the teacher and the peer group. McDermott concludes that, "if the teacher and the children can play the same games, then reading and all other school materials will be easily absorbed" (186).

Several researchers (Allitto, 1969; Hostetler and Huntington, 1971; Fishman and Leuders-Salmon, 1972) note the success of teachers who are members of the same ethnic and dialect minorities as their students, and the failure of teachers who are outsiders. When the classroom is divided into two separate worlds, with teachers in one world and children in the other, the teacher's authority and the information she has to transfer are challenged.

A pivotal issue related to reading instruction is the struggle for attention. The politics of everyday life, according to McDermott, get inside a child's body and determine what he perceives; he learns how not to attend to printed information and, as a result, does not learn to read well. The relation between illiteracy and pariah status is clear. A study of gaze direction shows that more than 90 percent of host children fix their eyes on their teacher or on the reading material at a given time (Jackson, 1968). In Harlem elementary schools, however, teachers spend more than half their day calling children to attention (Deutsch, 1963). Attention patterns seem to be the crux of the struggle in pariah education (Roberts, 1970).

In pariah classrooms, to attend to the teacher is to give the teacher a leadership role; to attend to the peer group is to challenge the teacher's authority. Those who attend learn to read; those who do not attend do not learn to read (McDermott, 190).

LANGUAGE CODES

There are subtle but significant changes in language use among African American children as they move through elementary school. Pariah children address pariah people and host people differently. However, it is difficult when the teacher regards you as ignorant for using one language and your peer group rejects you for using the other.

William Labov (1964) distinguishes four stages in the acquisition of nonstandard English: (1) Up to the age of five years, the basic grammatical rules and lexicon are taken from parents. (2) Between age five and age twelve, the reading years, a peer group vernacular is established. (3) During adolescence, the significance of the "dialect characteristics" of the peer group becomes more apparent. (4) At high school age, "the child begins to learn how to modify his speech in the direction of the prestige standard in formal situations or even to some extent in casual speech" (91). The second and third stages are important because, "as children participate in their peer groups, less importance is attached to school games. The more children participate in the ecology of games defined by their peers, the more deviant their linguistic registers; it is these linguistic features which help mark off the peer group from the ecology of the schools" (McDermott, 193).

W. A. Labov and C. Robins (1969) compare language use among three groups in the same community: African American gang members, African American "lames," and white lower-income children. "Lames" are children who, although in contact with gangs, still participate in the teacher's ecology. The three groups' use of language demonstrates a rank ordering that parallels their participation in school, with gang members deviating most from standard English, whites deviating least, and lames falling in between. These linguistic differences do not cause school alienation; rather, they are indexes of the extent to which the children have opted out of school games. Adoption of the peer group's linguistic code and alienation from school develop together.

These writers also show that participation in peer groups and the use of their linguistic codes correlate with reading scores. None of the forty-three gang members read at grade level; most were two years behind the national average.

As McDermott points out, "printed materials appear to send few meaningful cues to those interested in improving their status among their peers" (194). A series of sociometric tests administered to sixth-grade African American children in the lowest achievement track consistently show nonreaders to be at the center of their peer group activities; similar tests of African American fifth graders show nonreaders at the center of most peer group activities (ibid.). "Reading skills do not recommend an actor for leadership. Indeed, the acquisition of such skills can exclude an actor from the peer group ecology of games" (ibid.).

ACHIEVED FAILURE

Pariah children in host classrooms learn in a very subtle way to behave in ways that will acquire them pariah status. They learn to attend to cues from their peers and to disattend to cues from their teachers, such as a demand for attention or to learn a new task, like reading.

McDermott suggests that these attention patterns are deeply programmed in the central nervous system. When the child attempts to attend to cues outside of his normal perceptual patterns, he fails. In this way, when African American children fail to learn to read, it appears the result of neurological impairment. But children are not impaired; they have merely learned over time to attend to different stimuli in a school situation.

COMMUNICATIVE CODE DIFFERENCES

Middle-class teachers attend to middle-class children and label them the most talented and ambitious children in the class (Spindler, 1959). School success follows. Lower-class children over time give up trying and amass "institutional biographies" of failure (Goffman, 1963) as they move through school, because they are unable to give evidence of their intelligence in terms of the limited code that teachers use for evaluating children. African American children are particularly at risk of being overlooked because of a nonrecognition by their teachers of African American culture and its strengths. I have pointed out, in assessing intelligence, elsewhere (Hale-Benson, 1986) that Western social science overly emphasizes linguistic and logicomathematical skills, which must hew to patterns that approximate those used by European Americans to be recognized by the educational system.

Skills that emerge from African American culture are recognized only when they are marketable in the capitalist system, such as the athletic skills of Michael Jordan or the musical skills of Michael Jackson. When these skills are exhibited in early childhood by African American children, they are virtually ignored.

The effect of dividing a kindergarten class *"after the eighth day of school"* (my emphasis), into three "ability" groups—the fast, the slow, and the nonlearners—"became the basis for the differential treatment of the children for the remainder of the school year. From the day that the class was assigned permanent seats, the activities in the classroom were perceivably different from previously. The fundamental division of the class into those expected to learn and those expected not to permeated the teacher's orientation to the class" (Rist, 1970, 423). The teacher's evaluations were rooted in her evaluation of the children's physical appearance and their interactional and verbal behavior. At the table of fast learners were children with lighter skin, neater and cleaner clothes, who were more heavily dressed on cold days. Class leaders and direction givers were also clustered at this table. The children at the other two tables spoke less in class, used heavy dialect, and seldom spoke to the teacher.

By the time all these children were in the third grade, the ones who started out in the lower groups were still in lower groups; once a child is tracked, it is difficult for him to break loose, since the lower his group, the less instructional time he receives. This child is well on his way to amassing his institutional biography, which will follow him through school.

This sorting process continues until only a select few reach college. These "select few make it to college on the basis that they are most like their teachers" (McDermott, 198).

Given Labov's speech data, the children in the lowest group are not neurologically impaired slow learners. In fact, McDermott predicts that by sixth grade, these children will talk the most, be the most popular, and dress more stylishly than the rest of the class. There is nothing wrong with their native ability; they just learn to direct their efforts to achieve away from the school. The reason these children are not selected for school achievement is the result of a communicative code conflict between them and their teachers. If they are not able to work out this code conflict in the early years, the children in the lower groups take flight into their own subculture, which becomes oppositional to the classroom culture.

A key to the construction of an alternative subculture is that children are assigned to the lower group in large numbers and the group thus becomes powerful. There is, anyway, a normal developmental shift away from the teacher and toward the peer group in fourth, fifth, and sixth grades. Therefore, the achievement gap between African American and white children becomes most apparent in these years. Schoolchildren have three choices (McDermott). One, they can take the school as a source of their identity and try to succeed. Two, they can take the peer group as a source of identity; many of these children join gangs by late elementary school. Three, and worst, they can accept the teacher's poor definition of them and their abilities and passively fail through school into pariah status as adults.

Children who dispute the negative messages sent by their teachers and who disrupt the classroom are better off than those who are passive, because they have a better chance of constructing a solid ego and achieving by an alternative route. Children who passively accept subordinate status and do not disrupt the classroom status quo emerge from school with weak egos. "In either response, learning is blocked; in the first case by active selective inattention and misbehavior, in the second case with motivational lag and selective inattention. Neither group learns to read" (McDermott, 199).

McDermott points out that a host-group teacher does not create this code difference. The children and the teacher both participate in ethnic group traditions, which they bring to school. In the early years, teachers make the difference because they are not as adaptable as the children. However, in later years, as the peer group gains strength, the children force a distinction between their code and the teacher's code. In *making their code make a difference,* they learn how to produce pariah status for themselves vis-à-vis the host group.

ETHNIC GROUP IDENTITY AND MOBILITY

McDermott ponders why African Americans do not fare as well as other ethnic groups in working out the politics of the classroom. A possible explanation is found in the work of Robert Havighurst (1976), who suggests a compatibility between the white Anglo-Saxon Protestant American middle-class mainstream and the ethnic cultures of European whites, Jews, Chinese, and Japanese. It seems that African Americans and Hispanics must shed more of the beliefs, values, attitudes, and behavioral styles associated with their ethnicity in order to acquire the culture of the middle-class mainstream. Dual socialization, or a straddling of the two cultures, is required for upward mobility.

At the root of the achievement and disciplinary difficulties of African American children are a lack of understanding on the part of educators of African American culture and child rearing and a lack of recognition of the mismatch between this culture and the European American culture of the school.

According to Bruce Hare (1987), as early as preadolescence, African American children show a trend toward higher self-esteem among peers than white children and higher ratings on the importance of being popular and good at sports. His research corroborates that of Christine Bennett and John Harris (1982), who note that African American children do not differ from white children in general self-esteem or self-esteem in the home but tend toward lower self-esteem in school. This is accompanied by significantly lower reading and mathematics performance. There seems to be a shift from school to peers, which solidifies by late elementary school, as pointed out by McDermott. Given the vulnerability and family turmoil of lower-income African American youth, in particular, this shift toward the positive support of the peer group is a flight from the failure and ego damage of the school.

As early as preadolescence, African American children show a trend toward higher self-esteem among peers than white children. (Richard Bielaczyc, Photography-Media Services, Wayne State University Libraries)

Hare defines African American youth culture as a "long-term failure arena." On a short-term basis, African American youths exhibit competent, adaptive behavior and achieve in the arenas open to them. They are streetwise and excel in playground sports, sexuality, domestic and child-rearing chores, supplementing the family income, and other adult roles at an early age. But even though this youth culture provides alternative outlets for achievement, it offers little hope of long-term legitimate success. Rather, it carries with it the danger of drafting the youths into the self-destructive worlds of drugs, crime, and sexual promiscuity. This is what my father calls "majoring in a minor."

The negative school experiences of African American youth produce this antischool sentiment. The availability of positive peer group experiences and the inability of youths to perceive the long-term consequences of adolescent decisions cause these youths to make what appears to them a logical decision—to shift allegiance from the school to their peers.

> In the long run, of course, they are disproportionately excluded from the legitimate occupational success possibilities. They are also subsequently *blamed as adults* for the consequences of school-system-induced self-protection decisions made during adolescence. In this context, the rising crime, drug, and out-of-wedlock pregnancy rates among Black youth may be seen as a consequence of the interplay of negative schooling experiences as provided by incompetent outsiders, a decline in parental control, and a significant rise in the independence of an attractive peer culture which offers positive strokes and ego enhancement to a vulnerable population. (Hare, 43)

THE CARE OF THE SCHOOLCHILD

The implications of Hare's statement on the consequences of negative schooling experiences are clear for those who are the first teachers and care providers for African American children. The National Black Child Development Institute (1985) raises serious questions about the trend toward placing preschool African American children in urban public schools:

> Are existing public-school-based programs serving the Black family adequately and fostering Black children's growth and development? Can public-school-based early childhood programs still be molded to meet Black children's needs? Can public-school-based child-care

models be developed that will not maintain the discriminatory tradition of our public schools? And can the momentum toward public-
school-based child care be slowed long enough to allow a much
needed and long overdue analysis of the record and implications of
continuing this experiment? (3)

Asa G. Hilliard has observed that the movement toward early
child care in the public schools may serve to misidentify and isolate
nonachieving African American children at an even earlier age. Na-
tionwide, more African American children are categorized as educable
mentally retarded than white children. "EMR is a 'soft' category,
whereas a look at 'hard' categories of assessment, like visually impaired, hearing impaired or mentally retarded, shows almost no dis-
proportion between Black children and white children. EMR is the
category where there is perhaps the greatest imprecision in assessment,
and this usually works to the disadvantage of Black children" (quoted
in ibid., 22).

The solution to the problems facing the African American community will not be found in blaming either the victims or the schools.
The system that keeps African Americans at the bottom of the educational and occupational ladder is extremely complex and has many
interlocking components. It is critical that the schools become more
sensitive to ethnic and cultural groups that do not conform to the
white middle-income model that the schools are prepared to serve.
Only when members of the helping professions demystify African
American culture will solutions be found to the dilemma of achieving
equal educational outcomes for African American children.

CHAPTER TEN

Visions for Children: An Early Childhood Education Program

All of us may not live to see the higher accomplishments of an African empire— so strong and powerful as to compel the respect of mankind— but we in our lifetime can so work and act as to make the dream a possibility within another generation.

MARCUS GARVEY

The base of African American culture is West Africa. The uniqueness of the American slavery experience and the challenge of living thereafter as African Americans created a distinct culture, which has given rise to distinctive expressive and behavioral styles.

THE NEED FOR ETHNIC IDENTITY

George DeVos (1975) says that ethnicity persists in America because of the individual's need for continuity, which, from a psychological perspective, is essential to the development of a sense of self. "Ethnicity . . . is in its narrowest sense a feeling of continuity with the past, a feeling that is maintained as an essential part of one's self-definition. Ethnicity is intimately related to the individual need for collective continuity. The individual senses to some degree a threat to his own survival if his group or lineage is threatened with extinction. Ethnicity . . . includes a sense of personal survival in the historical continuity of the group" (17).

Elsie Moore (1985) points out that ethnicity has its greatest effects in the earliest interac-

Ethnicity is a key
aspect of self.
(© Jeffrey High)

tions between mother and child and continues to have an effect as
parents shape the child's emerging physical and cognitive capacities.
"Therefore, a lifespan perspective on human development requires
analysis of how socialization [acculturation, according to V. P. Frank-
lin] in different ethnic groups affects behavioral development from
childhood throughout later life" (102). Moore notes that the significance of ethnicity has been ignored in conceptual models of human
development. American social scientists have a tendency to describe
children from various ethnic groups in terms of how they deviate from
the European American norm.

Moore compared African American children adopted by white
families with those adopted by African American families and found

that the children adopted by white families scored higher on standardized tests. This is not surprising, given the fact that such tests are highly indexed to the language and culture of middle-class European American families. However, Moore points out that higher test performance alone does not necessarily mean that those African American children will be more effective in their adult roles than traditionally adopted African American children. An agency study of those children at age four, which includes data on social and emotional functioning and cognitive achievement, indicates that African American children adopted by African American families displayed higher levels of social and emotional adjustment than did African American children adopted by white families.

Other scholars have studied the child-rearing attitudes and practices of African American parents and found implications for the construction of a sense of self for African American children. Margaret Spencer (1985) found that many African American parents tend to transcend race in their socialization efforts. The goal, she points out, "seems to be the rearing of 'neutral' children, or 'human beings' irrespective of the continued salience of race on the macrostructural level" (228). The children who made African-American-positive choices on a measure of racial preference and color connotation were older and had knowledge of African American history. The children who made white-positive choices had the following characteristics in their background: parents who do not teach children about civil rights; parents who believe that integration is an enriching experience; a lack of knowledge of black history by both children and parents; parents who believe that the current racial climate is better than in the 1950s and 1960s; and parents who do not discuss racial discrimination.

Spencer found that, for nearly half the children, race dissonance was predicted from specific child-rearing strategies. She suggests that the "race transcendence" position of some African American parents is not compatible with the psychological intervention required to offset the sociocultural factors that place African American children at risk in American society. This humanistic, or race-neutral, posture is at odds with the events the child will encounter over the course of her life.

Leahcim Semaj (1985) points out that a key to helping African American children construct and maintain a positive self-identity is for primary socializing agents (e.g., parents, relatives, teachers) to present evidence confirming the worth of African American culture and people. European American children growing up in a culture that is pro-white and anti–African American do not face this situation; the mass media provide continuous propaganda regarding the superiority of European American culture and people, so the socializing agents of the white child do not need to do anything extra to maintain a positive self-identity. "The dominant position of Euro-American culture enables these agents to draw from other cultures at will without fear of cultural domination. This is because they, on their own terms, filter alien influences through their own cultural mechanisms and discard what they no longer have use for" (183).

Semaj suggests that liberation for African American children is contingent on a socialization that develops a collective, extended self-identity. There is a need for ethnically appropriate parental socialization and Afrocentric early childhood education that can provide African American children with a self-identity that works for them in their existential situation in America.

THE NEED FOR A NEW APPROACH

Early childhood educational and care-giving settings must aim for cultural continuity, not intervention. "The preschool experience must therefore provide a dynamic blend of African-American culture and that culture which is reflected in the Euro-American educational setting. . . . The African-American child who only sees the Euro-American cultural tradition manifested in the preschool environment can only conclude that the absence of visual representation of his culture connotes his essential worthlessness" (Rashid, 1981, 60).

A developmental psychology of the African American child is clearly called for. Likewise, there is a need for an educational model consistent with African American child development. Essential components of such an educational model are (1) the infusion of African American culture into the school curriculum, (2) the development of a culturally appropriate pedagogy, and (3) the replacement of skill-and-drill education with an educational process that imbues African American children with a love of learning and with self-actualization through meaningful work.

Unfortunately, we do not have empirical data to document the long-term effects of Afrocentric programs on children's development and later academic success. However, we do have the data from the research of Jacquelyn Fleming (1985), which reveal that, historically,

Visions for Children.
(Chuck Humel,
Cleveland State
University)

African American colleges do a better job of motivating and preparing African American students than do integrated colleges.

Fleming studied 2,500 African American and white freshmen and seniors over a seven-year period at fifteen colleges, including Spelman College, Ohio State University, and the University of Houston. She found that, even though the African American colleges had very limited resources and many operated under severe financial difficulty, students at those colleges gained more intellectually than did their peers at integrated schools. More African American students are enrolled in white colleges than are enrolled in historically African American colleges, but the largest numbers of African American college *graduates* are produced by historically African American colleges.

Efforts to document the long-term effects of Afrocentric preschool programs have just begun. Visions for Children is a preschool program that emphasizes the special characteristics of African American children, offering a teaching method and curriculum that encourage children to learn the information and skills necessary for upward mobility, career achievement, and financial independence in the American mainstream and, at the same time, to feel pride in their own culture and to identify with and contribute to the development of their own people.

This program is based on the model described in *Black Children: Their Roots, Culture, and Learning Styles* (Hale-Benson, 1986). Visions for Children is a day-care center located in a storefront in Warrensville Heights, Ohio, a suburb of Cleveland, with a 95 percent African American population. The research associated with the program was funded by the Cleveland Foundation. The operation of the program is supported by parental fees. A distinctive feature is the emphasis on teaching young children cognitive skills while strengthening their self-esteem and identity as African Americans.

The teaching method emphasizes African American culture and integrates it in all of its diversity throughout the curriculum. The children learn about Africa and their rich cultural heritage; they learn about African American and African arts and crafts; they listen to folktales and stories written by African American writers; they listen to music and learn about African and African American musicians; they learn about heroes in African American history, like Dr. Martin Luther King, Jr.

Authenticity is maintained by presenting African and African American culture to the children by using original sources, such as authentic African masks at the art museum, and by involving consultants and teachers who have been to Africa. For example, I have visited West Africa and have formally studied African life and culture. For several years, Visions for Children had artists-in-residence teaching dance and drumming who have traveled extensively in Africa and have firsthand knowledge of African culture.

In sum, the children in this program are given the message that they are beautiful African American children who can hold their own in a competitive society.

Visions for Children emphasizes the development of cognitive skills, such as reasoning, memory, problem solving, creativity, and language skills. Progress is assessed using both teacher-made and standardized instruments. Even though standardized instruments can contain inherent biases toward minority children, a goal of this program is to demystify these tests for parents and to help the children perform well on such measures.

There is a strong correlation between language facility and performing well on standardized measures in the professional work world. Therefore, Visions for Children's focus is on language skills. This includes expressive as well as receptive language; too often children receive language through listening but do not have enough opportunity to engage in expressive language. Expressive language includes holding conversations with adults, telling stories from pictures, engaging in sociodramatic play, and responding to questions in complete sentences.

CURRICULUM DEVELOPMENT

Visions for Children is a pioneer effort to pull together a high-quality early childhood education curriculum specifically geared to meet the needs of African American children. This curriculum has an easy-to-follow format that can be easily adjusted in individual programs according to the areas of the curriculum they wish to emphasize. The curriculum can also be adjusted to accommodate more or fewer teachers, larger or smaller groups of children, one room or multiple rooms, short or long days.

Most curriculum schedules in early childhood education texts and activity books designate large blocks of time for undefined activities, such as free play, small-group activity, large-group activity, story time, or activity time. The Visions for Children curriculum is an advancement over these because it combines flexibility and structure. There is an hour-and-a-half period in the morning and an hour-long period in the afternoon for child-directed activities. This gives the children an opportunity to select from a variety of activities the one they will engage in. There is also one thirty-minute period in the morning and one in the afternoon when the children are engaged in free play or teacher-led gross-motor activities. There are other fixed periods, such as breakfast, lunch, snack time, and nap time.

The remaining periods of the day are arranged into activity periods wherein the children rotate among the teachers and engage in small-group activities in each area of the curriculum. Thus, the curriculum offers a balance of child control and teacher direction. Studies show that children gain most from early childhood education programs where teachers have clear objectives in mind for the children (see Berreuta-Clement et al., 1984; Bissell, 1971; and Karnes, Schwedel, and Williams, 1983).

Another feature of the curriculum is that it is planned for use by teachers at the entry level of their careers in early childhood education or child care. Certainly, each teacher must be trained so that each area is taught properly; however, the curriculum provides a panorama of the components of a quality early childhood education. This support may be important for a teacher with minimum training who might have difficulty structuring the day on her own to include all of the things we want young children to know and do.

The teachers in Visions for Children, who live in the Cleveland community, were involved in the development of the curriculum, helping to formulate the monthly themes, to identify the heroes and "sheroes," to plan field trips, and to coordinate and integrate the various streams of the curriculum.

Planning

Several organizational features have been designed to facilitate planning.

Daily Schedule   The daily schedule is designed for flexibility and can be altered when the number of groups of children changes because of increases or decreases in enrollment. It is also altered during the summer, when more outdoor activities are planned and the length of each activity period is shortened.

The daily schedule is designed to be easy for the teachers to follow. It is given for the entire day, and it designates how many activity periods will be devoted to particular curricular areas per week. This can be easily altered to give more or less emphasis to various areas of the curriculum. For example, when preliminary testing revealed low scores on quantitative skills, the daily schedule was altered to allow more activity periods per week to be devoted to mathematics.

Daily Plans   Each Wednesday the teachers are required to submit plans for the coming week for the areas of the curriculum they teach. The teachers specialize in particular areas of the curriculum, and the children rotate among the teachers, as outlined on the daily schedule. I design the daily schedule, but it is revised as needed by the teachers and the director in staff meetings. The children have a "home teacher" they eat meals with, but all of the teachers teach all of the children throughout the course of the day. This creates a family atmosphere in the center.

Monthly Plans Monthly plans were created to require the teachers to add a long-range dimension to their planning. The teachers are required to submit these plans on the second Tuesday of the month for the coming month. The curriculum guide designates each month's objectives, and the teachers identify the ways they will reach these objectives. This long-range planning provides enough time for the teachers to develop the teaching aids and materials needed to teach each unit.

The teachers are also assigned monthly bulletin boards to design on the monthly planning forms. The center displays ten bulletin boards. One, which is labeled VISIONS FOR PARENTS, is designed by the center coordinator. It gives a brief overview of each area of the curriculum, the field trips, and enrichment activities, such as guest speakers or artists-in-residence. Two of the bulletin boards are devoted to displays of children's work. Each of the remaining seven are teachers' bulletin boards, each showing one area of the curriculum.

Monthly Themes An important goal in early childhood education curriculum development is to achieve integration in the curriculum. We have attempted to achieve this in Visions for Children by developing the curriculum component by component and then putting them together, with the goal of achieving integration. The monthly themes provide a mechanism for such integration.

Twelve themes have been identified for each year. The themes have been planned on a three-year cycle, so that a child who enters the program at two years of age will have a variety of themes for each of his or her three years in the program. Eight themes are the same each year and four are new. We believe that some themes bear repeating for the benefit of new children in the program and to allow a deeper treatment for continuing children. In other words, a theme on Africa will have a different yield for a child at the ages of two, three, or four years. The repeat themes are generally indexed to the seasons of the year or aspects of African American culture such as Black History Month or Africa.

The themes integrate the diverse areas of the curriculum. The teachers are encouraged to utilize the curricular objectives for determining the goals of instruction, and to utilize the theme to determine the content of instruction. In other words, the curricular objectives should guide the skills the children are working on, and the themes should guide the information imparted to the children.

The monthly themes should also affect the selection of field trips and enrichment activities. For example, the October monthly theme is Africa, and so during that month a field trip is scheduled to the art museum to see African masks. The enrichment activity is an African party, where the children dress in African costume—coinciding with Halloween. The study of African spirituality replaces the observance of the supernatural usually associated with Halloween. The children also make African drums and masks and participate in African rituals. In this way, the art and music curricula are correlated with the monthly theme.

Weekly Heroes and "Sheroes"   Each week the children study a different person or significant event in African American history. These rotate on a three-year cycle, with certain key figures and events represented each year, such as the birthday of Dr. Martin Luther King, Jr., and the Juneteenth celebration. Juneteenth is a holiday that originated in Texas and is celebrated on June 19. It recalls the day that African Americans held in slavery in Texas received word of the Emancipation. African American Texans celebrate this holiday much like the Fourth of July is celebrated nationally.

The teachers are encouraged to correlate the heroes and "sheroes" with lessons in other curricular areas. For example, when the monthly theme is plants and the hero for the week is George Washington Carver, the science lesson can focus on the peanut and all of the products Dr. Carver created in his research. The intent of this integration is to create an incidental, integrated educational process that flows naturally throughout the curriculum.

Pictures of the heroes and "sheroes" are featured on the bulletin board devoted to the cultural curriculum. Examples of sheroes are Coretta Scott King, Sojourner Truth, Phyllis Wheatley, Lorraine Hansberry, Jane Kennedy, Mahalia Jackson, Mary McLeod Bethune, Nikki Giovanni, and Marian Anderson.

Monthly Field Trips   The monthly field trip is correlated with the monthly theme. Occasionally field trips are planned around important events or exhibits that occur for young children in the community. Field trips we have planned include the Cleveland Zoo, the circus, a dramatic presentation of the life of Harriet Tubman, performances of *Peter Pan* and *The Wizard of Oz,* the Children's Museum, the Holden Arboretum, the Shaker Lakes Nature Center, the Malcolm Brown Art Gallery, and the African-American Museum.

Organization

A central problem in curriculum organization in early childhood education is managing the diversity of the information and skills we try to impart to young children. It takes an extremely skilled teacher to give balanced and integrated attention to all aspects of the curriculum.

As a start toward designing a comprehensive early childhood education curriculum, we have selected five organizing components: (1) physical, (2) communicative, (3) creative, (4) inquiring, and (5) cultural. The first four components were adapted from Stephanie Feeney (1987). The cultural component was added to address the unique thrust of Visions for Children. This list can be expanded or changed to address the focus of other multicultural programs. Thirty-one curricular areas have been identified within the five components:

Physical	Music	Human body
Manipulations	Creative movement	Ecology
Gross-motor	*Inquiring*	Computer science
development	Scientific method	Nutrition
Communicative	Health	*Cultural*
Listening	Safety	African American
Speaking	Social studies	studies
Perception	Mathematics	African studies
Literacy	Physics	African Caribbean
Literature	Chemistry	studies
Writing	Geology	Social skills
Creative	Meteorology	Nonviolent conflict
Art	Astronomy	resolution
	Biology	

At the beginning of each section of the curriculum is a conceptual overview designed to orient teachers to each area they will be teaching and to prepare them to use the latest techniques in early childhood education.

Over a hundred and twenty concepts within the thirty-one curricular areas have been identified, and each has been developed into a specific lesson with a specific instructional objective. This concept is the unit the teacher enters on her daily lesson plan. In the curriculum guide, a brief description of the exemplary activity is given for each objective, so that it is clear to the teacher what the concept is and how it is to be taught. The title of the book the activity is drawn from and the page number where the activity is described is also given. Materials needed to teach the activity are also listed. Other books in the Visions for Children library that teach the same objective are listed.

RESEARCH

The research component of Visions for Children was funded for two years by the Council for Economic Opportunities of Greater Cleveland. It was funded for five years by the Cleveland Foundation.

Comparison of Visions for Children Enrollees with the Control Group

To evaluate the effectiveness of Visions for Children, we selected a day-care center in Cleveland, Ohio, to serve as a control group for the study. This center has provided high-quality child-care services in Cleveland for eighteen years. Its hours of operation are 6:30 A.M. to 5:30 P.M., Monday through Friday, year-round. The center serves children aged eighteen months through eight years, including a full-day kindergarten, after-school and holiday care for school-aged children, and a toddler program for children still in diapers.

Children are enrolled in both Visions for Children and the control group on a family self-selection basis: the parents select the program and pay the fees. The control group has Title 20 funding, which pays for services for lower-income families; Visions for Children provides a sliding-fee scale for lower-income families. Up to 30 percent of its slots are allocated for reduced-fee enrollments; the remaining slots are occupied by children from working-class and middle-class families.

Neither center fits any particular socioeconomic configuration. The primary consideration was that there be no significant difference in the configurations of the two groups. An important consideration in selecting the control group was matching its children with Visions children on the dimension of socioeconomic status, an important variable for African American children. Without such controls, it could be argued that differences in the achievement of the children are due to the socioeconomic characteristics of their families. We used the Hollingshead Four-Factor Index of Social Status, which creates a score based upon parents' education, occupation, sex, and marital status.

An overall *t*-test was conducted on age of subjects in both groups, and the Hollingshead scores determined whether the two groups of children were comparable. The average age of Visions children was 47.13 months; the average age of control group children was 45.00 months. (Only children who fell within the age groups served at Visions were selected for the control group.) There was no significant difference in age. The overall Hollingshead score for the Visions children was 42.05; for the control group children, it was 41.95. The difference was not significant.

The staffs of both programs are racially integrated. At the control group center, the director, who has a master's degree in early childhood education, one teacher's assistant, one teacher who holds a B.A. degree, and one teacher who holds an associate degree are white. The assistant director, three teachers' assistants, and one teacher holding the associate degree are African American. The staff of the control group has more formal credentials than the Visions staff. All of the Visions teachers who are African American have high school diplomas, the minimum standard required by the state licensing agency for a child day-care provider. The center director at Visions, at the time of this writing, had a bachelor's degree in early childhood education.

The structure of the two programs is different. In both programs, the children are divided into small groups, ranging from seven children for the two-to-three-year-olds to fourteen children for the other age levels. The groups at Visions are named after African tribes: Ibo, Fanti, Zulu, Kikuyu, and Kumasi.

The large room used by the Visions program is divided into six areas, where the following activities occur: gross-motor play, housekeeping/dramatic play, block play, sand play, use of computers, circle time, book corner, science, manipulatives, math, music, art, culture, woodworking, writing, easel painting, and chalkboard drawing. There is also a large backyard, with a beautiful lawn and outdoor play equipment: swings, a basketball rim, and a climbing gym. The children and teachers move through the rooms on a schedule. Snack and lunch are served in three areas. The children eat in their groups, family style, with their "home" teacher.

The control group classrooms are self-contained. The children are grouped by age in small groups and have one or two assigned teachers. There is a gross-motor play area used by all the children. The control group schedule is less structured than the Visions schedule, with general time slots indicated on the schedule. The time slots on the Visions schedule are indexed to a specific area of the curriculum with a more clearly designated menu of activities.

Activity time begins in the morning at 9:15 in the control group and at 8:30 at Visions. In the control group, an hour is provided for outdoor play and forty-five minutes for free play in the afternoon. Those who wish to continue free play may do so for another hour and fifteen minutes or they may choose to participate in special activities. Visions provides thirty minutes for free play in the morning and thirty minutes for gross-motor activities in the afternoon, when the children are taught specific skills in the curriculum. Obviously, the control group children spend more time in unstructured activities than Visions children.

In the control group, an hour and ten minutes are devoted to preparation for and eating lunch. The Visions schedule devotes thirty minutes to these activities. Afternoons in the control group are relatively unstructured. Preparation for departure begins as early as 3:30. Visions children continue structured activities until 5:00 o'clock, when they may select activities until their departure at 6:00. There is no "preparation for departure."

Visions has five Apple IIc personal computers and one dot-matrix printer. The control group does not have computers. Visions children use the computers daily for at least thirty minutes. They may also choose to use them during child-selected activities.

The lesson plans used by the control group basically are for a week in advance and indicate each activity with a one-sentence description. Visions lesson plans are more detailed: a one-page planning form states the objective (drawn from the curriculum), the points to be emphasized, materials, the teaching procedure, and extensions. Each teacher completes an average of three lesson plans daily. The children are divided into three groups and rotate among three teachers. Thus each teacher repeats her lesson three times.

The Visions curriculum, contained in a four-inch-thick notebook, is over 500 pages long. The control group curriculum is approximately fourteen pages long and also contains statements of educational philosophy and goals; three pages each describe the objectives for toddlers, three-year-olds, and four-year-olds. Objectives are divided into three categories: relationships, self-esteem, and ego skills.

Attention to African American culture in the control group program varies from classroom to classroom and from time to time. Special attention is paid to Dr. Martin Luther King's birthday and Black History Month. There are a few pictures of African American children on the walls. African American dolls are provided, and stories are read that feature African American children. There is no mention of Africa or African American culture in the curriculum goals or educational philosophy.

African American culture is a central theme in Visions for Children. Many pictures of African American children hang on the walls. The majority of the dolls are African American, although a few are Oriental and Caucasian. The puzzles, books, and puppets are of African Americans pictured in different careers and settings. African American culture is taught three days a week and is included in other curricular areas wherever possible.

Three of the twelve monthly themes are devoted to topics in African and African American culture. The nine remaining themes cover mainstream topics. All of the heroes and "sheroes" are either figures in African American or African culture or took part in important events like the signing of the Fourteenth Amendment to the Constitution.

The Research Design

Standardized tests are used in evaluating the results of Visions for Children. Their use is not intended to convey confidence in their assessment reliability for African American children. Eligio Padilla and Gail Wyatt (1983) provide a fine review of the effects of intelligence and achievement testing on minority group children. I agree with their suggestion that "the major thrust of the testing movement must be the development of criterion-sampling techniques and the elimination of norm-referenced tests. . . . The inclusion of adaptive behavior scales and the consideration of sociocultural factors . . . is the strategy of choice" (435).

However, I also agree with the assertion of Barbara Sizemore, in a personal conversation, that the best way to assure that standardized tests are abolished in America is for all African American children to pass them. Even though we acknowledge the shortcomings and political agendas of standardized tests, we also must recognize that their use is becoming more widespread. I do not recommend that early childhood education programs "teach to the test." However, children who are educated in a culturally appropriate manner should have no difficulty in scoring well on those tests. A key factor in scoring well is exposure to the experiences and vocabulary represented on the test.

To implement the research component of Visions, a literature review was conducted of child development measures that could assess the desired outcome of the program. Instruments were tentatively selected to measure general cognitive ability, behavior, self-concept, ability to delay gratification, and racial attitude. Four consultants reviewed the instruments and the literature associated with them and recommended the final selection. Interestingly, there was no disagreement among the consultants. Not all consultants had a recommendation for a particular category; in several categories, however, more than one consultant strongly recommended the same instruments.

All children enrolled in Visions for Children are tested each year on the child development measures described below. The control group of children is also tested. All children in the study have been tested each year as they matriculated into the primary grades. These data have been analyzed longitudinally to establish the long-term effects of the program and to revise the curriculum.

The data below are for the first two years of testing. Kindergarten scores for the first cohort which are reported in this chapter, provide information on the cognitive abilities of the children at the beginning of the study. These data have been useful for measuring changes in test scores as the children have progressed through the program and elementary school.

Summary of Data Analysis

Listed below are the research questions and the measures used to investigate each question.

Does the Visions for Children Program Result in Measurable Gains in Cognitive Abilities?   This question was investigated using the McCarthy Scales of Children's Abilities (MSCA) (McCarthy, 1972), which provide a measure of children's overall cognitive skills. It is an individually administered test of general cognitive abilities that can be used with children from two-and-a-half to eight years of age; administration time for children under five years of age is approximately forty-five to fifty minutes. The test consists of eighteen individual subtests, which form six scales: verbal, perceptual, quantitative, memory, motor, and an overall general cognitive index (GCI) made up of the verbal, perceptual, and quantitative performance scales. While there is considerable ongoing debate about bias in IQ measures of black children, the MSCA has many assets that counterbalance some of these liabilities. (The majority of my reviewers do not call it an IQ measure.) In general, the psychometric properties of the MSCA are good, and the standardization sample for the test is excellent and fairly recent. In addition, validity and reliability are acceptable. Another strength of the MSCA is that it is appealing to children. Materials are colorful and stimulating, and the individual subtests are relatively short so that the children do not tend to have difficulty attending to task. Also, unlike other measures, the MSCA contains a motor component, with both gross- and fine-motor tasks.

A summary of the measures administered during phase 3 of the Visions research are reported in this chapter. (An analysis of phases 1 and 2 testing is reported in Hale-Benson 1990b.) Visions children scored significantly higher than the control group on five of the six subtests (perceptual, quantitative, memory, motor, and general cognitive). There was a nonsignificant difference between the two groups on the verbal subtest.

Does the Visions for Children Program Cause Children to Become More In-Group Oriented?   There is a tendency for African American children to prefer white physical traits and to attribute more positive characteristics to white people than to African American people. A major question of the study is whether participating in an early childhood education program with an African American cultural component reverses that trend. We used the Preschool Racial Attitudes Measure (PRAM) II (Williams et al., 1975), which is a picture test designed to assess racial bias among preliterate children. It has excellent reliability and validity.

A surprising finding was that, even though both groups of African American children indicated an out-group orientation (more positive characteristics attributed to Caucasians) on the racial attitudes measure, the control group children scored less of a Caucasian orientation than the Visions children. This is surprising, because a major thrust of the Visions program is an Afrocentric perspective.

A conversation with Dr. Harriette McAdoo of Howard University revealed that African American preschool children tend to score similarly to white children until they are about eight years old. Her data reveal that differences caused by educational programs on racial attitudes emerge at that age. We also discussed the possibility that children who score higher on cognitive abilities measures may be more astute at reflecting the attitudes of the general society and that more direct instruction is needed to counteract the messages of the media. We discussed the fact that it is difficult to counteract Eurocentric cultural overtones with a subtle presentation of African American culture like that of Visions.

As a result of these data, steps were taken in the program year following the phase 3 evaluation to engage the children in more direct activities designed to create an in-group orientation, such as mealtime chants and pledges.

Does Visions for Children Result in Distinctive Classroom Behavior? There is evidence in the literature of cultural dissonance between the African American culture and the culture of the schools (Rashid, 1981). The Report of Child Behavior measure (Schaefer, 1987) was administered as a first step in examining relevant dimensions of classroom behavior. This instrument has the virtue of evaluating more normal and less pathological behavior than many other available instruments, many of which seek to identify juvenile delinquency rather than normal classroom adjustment and are biased against African American male children.

Visions children scored significantly higher on this child behavior measure.

Does the Visions for Children Program Enhance Children's Self-Esteem? We sought to answer this question by using the Pictorial Scale of Perceived Competence and Social Acceptance (Harter and Pike, 1984). It has four subscales: cognitive competence, physical competence, peer acceptance, and maternal acceptance. Susan Harter has done some excellent work in the area of self-concept for older children, and this is a recently developed scale for preschool and kindergarten children.

Visions children scored higher on two components of the self-concept measure: assessment of their own cognitive abilities and their teacher's assessment of their physical abilities. The control group scored significantly higher on two components of the self-concept measure: the teacher's assessment of the child's cognitive abilities and the teacher's assessment of peer acceptance. There was a nonsignificant difference between the groups on three components of self-concept: own opinion of peer approval, own opinion of physical abilities, and perception of maternal acceptance.

Does the Visions for Children Program Enhance the Ability of Children to Engage in Sustained Effort for Delayed Rewards? A technique developed by Conrad Schwartz (1981), Delay of Gratification, was used. Teachers rate the children on their ability to defer gratification, an important skill needed for achievement.

The control group scored significantly higher on delay of gratification.

Does the Visions for Children Program Result in Measurable Gains in Reading Readiness? We selected the Metropolitan Reading Readiness Test (1976) as an outcome measure for children entering kindergarten. The test is a group-administered, multiple-skill battery, which takes approximately eighty to ninety minutes for children to complete. There are two levels, with level 1 being appropriate for children beginning kindergarten.

The test is used extensively and has good organization and clarity. In addition, the great deal of psychometric work that has been carried out demonstrates substantial reliability and validity. In general, the test can provide useful screening information on achievement-oriented skills.

The Visions children scored higher on sixteen of the twenty-two subtests, but the difference between the groups was nonsignificant.

Does the Visions for Children Program Result in Measurable Gains in Achievement-Oriented Skills? To answer this question, we used the Stanford Achievement Test (1985). This is an outcome measure for children entering first grade and at the completion of each year of the primary grades. The test is a group-administered, multiple-skill battery.

Children need between ninety minutes and two-and-a-half hours to complete the test. It is recommended that it be given in two to three sittings. The test is used extensively and has good organization and clarity. In addition, the great deal of psychometric work that has been carried out demonstrates substantial reliability and validity. In general, the test can provide useful information on achievement-oriented skills.

Visions children scored significantly higher on visual recognition and vocabulary than the control group. Even though there was not a significant difference on the remaining four tests (sound recognition, comprehension, language expression, and mathematics concepts and applications), Visions children consistently scored higher on all except language expression.

The graduates of both preschool programs have been tested for six years to determine whether they have sustained the gains made through attending either program. An interesting finding has been that, for several cohorts, there was no difference in the scores while they attended preschool but that, as the children reached second and third grades, Visions children tended to outscore the control group. This is a significant trend when you consider that longitudinal studies of Head Start children reveal that their gains are lost by the third grade.

The spirit of Visions for Children is expressed by these words from Mary McLeod Bethune (1938): "When they learn the fairy tales of mythical kings and queens, we must let them hear of the Pharoahs and African kings and the brilliant pageantry of the Valley of the Nile; when they learn of Caesar and his legions, we must teach them of Hannibal and his Africans; when they learn of Shakespeare and Goethe, we must teach them of Pushkin and Dumas" (12).

CHAPTER ELEVEN

Culturally Appropriate Pedagogy

THE CHALLENGE

The future of the nation is on the shoulders of teachers and how they teach kids; the future of the world is in the classroom where the teachers are. If you have any chance to guarantee a positive bridge to the twenty-first century, it is how we educate the children in the classrooms today.

RICHARD GREEN

In this chapter I propose an approach to the education of African American children that springs from an understanding of the exigencies of their development, an approach informed by the dynamic interplay between the historical socioeconomic factors that have shaped their fate in America and the cultural characteristics that are the spiritual essence of African American people.

Bruce Hare (1987) places the blame for the "endangered status" of African American youth on the structural inequality of the American educational and occupational systems. He suggests that theories about the biological and cultural inferiority of African American people serve to justify the race, class, and gender inequalities found in American society. He states further that "the myth of equal opportunity serves as a smoke screen through which the losers will be led to blame themselves, and be seen by others as getting what they deserve. One might simply ask, for example, how can both inheritance of wealth for some and equal opportunity for all exist in the same social system?" (101). Samuel Bowles and Herbert Gintis (1976) point out that unequal distribution of wealth, power, and privilege is, and historically has been, the reality of American capitalism, and that such a system must produce educational and occupational losers.

Hare argues that, in addition to the inherent intergenerational inequality caused by inheritance, the educational system, through its unequal skill giving, grading, routing, and credentialing procedures, plays a critical role in fostering structured inequality in the American social system. The occupational structure simply responds to the schools when it slots people into hierarchical positions on the bases of the credentials and skills given by the schools.

The dire statistics on the problems of African American youths are well known. We consider, in this chapter, strategies that researchers, teachers, parents, ministers, policymakers, and other members of the helping professions can use to address these problems.

African American children are disproportionately located in families characterized by single-parent heads of households, low-paying jobs, or unemployment, any of which causes them to be at high risk for family instability and deprivation. Hare points out that,

> in such circumstances, they are also more likely to fall victim to child abuse, inadequate nutrition, poor health care, drugs, crime, and material deprivation. They are more likely to live in below-par crowded quarters, with relatives other than their biological parents, and in foster care. Given such possibilities as these, it is a wonder that they survive and thrive as well as they do. Fortunately, indicators are that they are loved and feel loved, but there is no denying that many Black youth must also suffer the consequences of the pressures under which they and their parents live. (104)

This structural inequality that Hare speaks of is exacerbated by a nonrecognition of the influence of culture on African American child development. This book has been written to suggest that there is a dynamic blend between historic, socioeconomic, and cultural factors that impinge upon the education of African American children. The cultural factors are indexed to the consequences of participating in life in the African American community, a life that is divergent from the American mainstream.

My goal in writing this book is to stimulate interest in African American child psychology. If foundation executives become interested in this area of inquiry, they might fund projects that create new knowledge in this area. If school superintendents become interested in this area of inquiry, they might form task forces to address the questions. If government officials become interested in this area of inquiry, they might fund think tanks to research the problem. If professional associations become interested in this area of inquiry, they might create conferences on the subject.

AFRICAN AMERICAN BOYS

As we consider creating a comprehensive framework for understanding African American child development, it is critical that we examine how that development is mediated by gender. Agitation by African American intellectual leaders like Jawanza Kunjufu (who was one of the first to draw attention to this issue) has finally focused national attention on the plight of the African American male. Our ability to address specific areas of concern such as the classroom achievement of African American boys will not advance until we understand how their development proceeds. Once we know how to support them through various developmental milestones, we will be able to impact upon the challenges they face.

One explanation for the difficulty African American children have in school is that they are required to master two divergent cultures in order to achieve upward mobility in school and the workplace—the African American culture and the European American culture. African American *male* children, however, may have to master three cultures, because African American males have a culture distinct not only from the white male culture but from the African American female culture as well. This African American male culture is not recognized and may even be condemned by the school because it is not understood.

Most elementary school classes are taught by women, with the result that a female orientation is created in the classroom. As we enter the twenty-first century, inner-city classrooms will increasingly contain a majority of African American children being taught by white female teachers. White female teachers tend to be more comfortable with and knowledgeable about the behavior of white female children and, to a lesser degree, white male children.

Catherine Cornbleth and Williard Korth (1980) provide support for this contention in their study of teacher perceptions and teacher-student interaction in integrated classrooms. Teachers in this study rated white girls as having the most desirable personal characteristics

We need to understand the development of the African American boy. (Mary Jane Murawka, Photography-Media Services, Wayne State University Libraries)

and the highest potential for achievement, rating them highest on descriptors such as *efficient, organized, reserved, industrious,* and *compliant.* African American boys were rated as having the lowest potential for achievement but were rated highest on descriptors such as *outspoken, aggressive,* and *outgoing.*

These data suggest that there is a cultural configuration in classrooms. They also lend support to the notion that, in order to achieve, African American schoolboys must acquire behavioral characteristics incongruent with the culture they bring to school. It is important that we acknowledge this double burden African American boys must bear— to be *white and female* while they are in school. Bartley McSwine has characterized the feeling as going the wrong way down a one-way street.

Robert Bly (1992), a leader of the male movement composed of mostly middle-class white males, says that American males are in a crisis that began during the industrial revolution, when fathers left the home to work. The intimacy and the mentor relationship that was built between fathers and sons as they worked side-by-side on a daily basis was destroyed. Today, fathers spend eight minutes in daily conversation with their children, and so the process by which men help boys become men has disappeared. Women try to raise boys, drill sergeants try to turn boys into men, teenage gang members try to raise each other, but, according to Bly, only an older man who cares about the soul of the boy can show him how to be a man. This older man does not have to be the father, and in fact there are tensions in the father-son relationship. This function is best performed by a community of older men. But today, the community of older men who have traditionally raised the next generation are somewhere in Florida playing golf.

Someone has said that, when white America has a cold, African America has pneumonia. The implication that can be drawn from Bly's conclusions is that the well-being of African American males has been further declining since the 1950s, when the masses became disconnected from the job market during the shift from the industrial to the postindustrial era. This has created the legendary unemployment rate in the African American community that makes it highly unlikely that an African American boy will see an African American man working. Inner-city African American boys have very little contact with successful African American men. It is critical that mentorship programs be developed to create networks to support the development of African American boys.

My brother, Phale Hale, Jr., observes that, in the social services community, there is a lack of coordination of services for target families. Different agencies impact on separate problems of children and families; but the child is an integrated individual, not a fragmented person who needs housing today and food stamps tomorrow. The African American church is in an excellent position to create linkages with other institutions to provide that coordination. Consider the possibilities if the superintendent of a school system were to ask every female head of household with a male child to indicate the church she is a member of. A conference could be called by the school district between the pastors of those churches and the principals of the schools.

A mentorship program could be created modeled after the one

begun in the church I attended in Cleveland, Ohio. Rev. Otis Moss, Jr., pastor of the Olivet Institutional Baptist Church, asked every female head of household with a male child to register her child in a mentorship program. He then invited the men of the church to serve as mentors. More men volunteered to be mentors than there were boys registered. Rev. Moss was able to announce one Sunday morning that there were no fatherless boys in Olivet Institutional Baptist Church. Imagine such a social support network! When a boy is sent to the principal's office for disciplinary reasons, not only would his mother be contacted, but his mentor would also be notified. Conferences could be held in which ministers, principals, and concerned men in the community could think together and plan for supporting the boys in that community.

Activities could be planned such as those of the Simba program, which is like an African American boy scout program, a national organization conducted for African American boys by the men of their communities. These men teach the boys about their African American heritage and culture and give the boys real-life experiences, like visits to a prison or to a Planned Parenthood office. It is important to assist African American boys to build a bridge from their peer culture in order to amass accomplishments in long-term achievement arenas. Both African American boys who are high achievers and those who are low achievers report that their peer groups do not support academic achievement. Thus, as John Ogbu and Ann Woodard (1989) point out, these boys are required to devise elaborate strategies to become achievers and at the same time protect themselves from ostracism by their peers.

Christine Bennett and John Harris (1982) studied the high number of suspensions and expulsions of African American boys from school. They found that African American boys have a high sense of personal efficacy but a low sense of school efficacy. Conflict ensues when their inefficiency in negotiating the culture of the school clashes with their out-of-school feelings of competence. The result is Hare's conclusion— that African American boys then express their competence only in out-of-school arenas.

It is critical for school districts to establish for African American boys the goal of attaining the baccalaureate degree. Robert Staples (1985) identifies the college-educated African American man as a success model: 90 percent of them are married and living with their spouses. Even though we know that on the average college-educated

African Americans earn less than white high school graduates, they still live longer and have a higher quality of life than their less well educated counterparts in the African American community. So another important issue for teachers and school psychologists to address is how to increase the numbers of African American men who enroll in and graduate from college. An important means to that end is for high school counselors to become familiar with the success rates of African American colleges (Fleming, 1985) and the variety of colleges to choose from.

A promising approach to fostering achievement among African American boys is to complement cultural values and attitudes already present in the African American culture. For example, there is an emphasis on sports in the African American culture; attention could be given to strenthening the role of the coach in enhancing African American male achievement. Rather than bemoaning the interest African American boys have in sports, as some leaders do, more study should be directed to effectively channeling that interest. Successful coaches like John Thompson of Georgetown University, who have produced winning teams and African American male college graduates, should be studied and emulated.

Strengthening the bond between achievement in sports and academic achievement is logical, given the fact that in some universities virtually every African American man enrolled is on an athletic scholarship. While some focus on the exploitation of the African American male athlete and his disastrous academic failure rate (which is a worthwhile concern), it might be equally worthwhile to consider that sports is the primary vehicle for delivering African American males to college at all. Such a perspective would allow us to bring more energy to bear on how to productively utilize athletics. Studies show that a person who attends college for one semester is better off than one who never attends.

AFRICAN AMERICAN GIRLS

I have discussed issues in the development of African American girls in detail elsewhere (Hale-Benson, 1986). The educational challenges these girls face are encompassed in the general discussion of the burden of acting white. In general, African American girls fare better academically than African American boys. The pecking order in integrated

African American girls
have greater access
to role models
than African
American boys.
(Mary Jane Murawka,
Photography-Media
Services, Wayne State
University Libraries)

classrooms is white girls first, white boys second, African American girls third, and African American boys last. Twice as many African American women as men enter and graduate from college. In general, African American girls have greater access to role models and mentoring than African American boys. However, the greatest barrier I see to adult success among African American girls is a high fertility rate at a young age.

The majority of babies born in the African American community are to mothers between twelve and twenty years of age. African American middle-class women have a lower fertility rate than white middle-class women, and African American professional couples are not even reproducing themselves. African American women have the lowest educational level and are among the lowest income earners in our society. Girls give birth at a time when they are unable to be financially independent and at a time when their bodies are not well prepared for childbirth. These young mothers do not receive adequate prenatal care, and their children do not receive adequate postnatal care.

It is a very difficult struggle for an adolescent girl to complete her education and raise a child or children. William Julius Wilson (1987) points to the growth in the number of never-married African American women that has resulted from the joblessness of African American men. In the present situation, where African American women cannot be assured of marriage as a means of financial support, it is critical that African American girls delay childbirth until they have enough education to be economically self-supporting.

Why adolescents continue to conceive and give birth to children is a complex issue. More study should be devoted to this problem and more programs designed to address it. Some African American sororities have created laudatory programs in which a big sister relationship is created between a professional African American woman and a single teenaged girl in the community who has had a baby. But more work should be done to intervene at earlier ages to prevent teenage childbearing.

SCIENCE AND MATHEMATICS

A part of connecting African American children to the future is to monitor whether the curricula of schools that serve African American children are preparing them to acquire technological skills that will prepare them for employment in the 1990s and beyond.

The National Urban Coalition (Beane, 1985) has developed an initiative designed to enable African American children to take courses in the higher math and science sequences, beginning with first-year calculus and first-year physics. Without these sequences, African American children are tracked away from high-paying technological careers. Statistics show that, in the 1990s, 60 to 80 percent of career fields will be eliminated for those with poor mathematics preparation. In 1982, 62.8 percent of the jobs offered to college graduates were in the engineering sciences. This figure is expected to increase to 80 percent in the 1990s. This field requires preparation in advanced mathematics.

A study done in 1980 and 1982 of high school seniors who had taken math and science courses in grades ten through twelve reveals that 60 percent of Asian Americans and 30 percent of whites had taken trigonometry, calculus, and other advanced math courses; only 11 percent of African Americans had taken these courses. Furthermore, 27 percent of the Asian American and 13 percent of the white seniors had taken first-year physics. Only 5.5 percent of African American seniors had taken first-year physics.

These figures stand in contrast to a National Assessment of Educational Progress report (1983), which includes items designed to assess the attitudes of thirteen-year-old students toward science: 47 percent of white students and 50 percent of African American students indicated positive attitudes toward science. Further, the National Urban Coalition says that 15 percent of third-grade African American students expressed an interest in technical occupations.

A study should be done on why these positive attitudes and interests are not translating into achievement in these arenas. The National Urban Coalition's explanation is that, in textbooks, African American children do not see people who look like them doing math and science. There also may be an overemphasis on civil rights heroes in the African American community. Role models in technological careers need to be made more visible to African American schoolchildren.

FAMILY LIFE AND SCHOOL ACHIEVEMENT

Reginald Clark (1983) dispels myths about the limitations of family structure or income on children's school achievement. Working mothers, broken homes, poverty, racial or ethnic background, and poorly educated parents are the usual reasons given for the academic problems of poor urban children. But Clark emphasizes total family life, stating that the most important indicators of academic potential are embedded in family culture.

To support his contention, Clark conducted ten intimate case studies of African American families in Chicago. All of the families had income at the poverty level and were equally divided between one-parent and two-parent families. All were likewise equally divided in terms of having produced either a high-achieving or a low-achieving child. Clark made detailed observations on the quality of home life, noting how family habits and interactions affect school success and what characteristics of family life provide children with "school survival skills"—a complex of behaviors, attitudes, and knowledge essential to academic success. The success-producing patterns in the families of high achievers are (200):

• Frequent school contact initiated by the parent,
• Stimulating and supportive schoolteachers,
• Parents who are psychologically and emotionally calm with the child,
• Parents who play a major role in the child's schooling,
• Parents who expect the child to get postsecondary training,
• Parents who have explicit, achievement-centered rules and norms,
• Parents who establish clear, specific role boundaries and status structures, with parents as the dominant authority,
• Siblings who interact as an organized subgroup,
• Infrequent conflict between family members,
• Parents who frequently engage in deliberate achievement-training activities.

It is critical to do further case studies, like the ones of my parents, to understand why people with comparable backgrounds become either high achievers or low achievers. School psychologists, teachers, counselors, ministers, and other members of the helping professions can use such information to help parents inculcate school survival skills in their children.

The solution to the problems facing African American schoolchildren will not be found in blaming either the child or the school. The system that keeps African Americans at the bottom of the educational and occupational ladders is extremely complex and has many interlocking components. Schools need to become more sensitive to ethnic and cultural groups that do not conform to the white middle-class model. Only when members of the helping professions are able to understand the ways the African American culture intersects with the mainstream culture will solutions be found to the problem of achieving equal educational outcomes for African American children.

CURRICULUM PLANNING FOR YOUNG CHILDREN

There is relative agreement that one can evaluate a preschool child at the end of the school year and designate him as being "not ready for kindergarten" or "not functioning at age level." However, we are not in agreement about what he should be taught at three or four years of age during the school year to escape those designations.

It is my contention that children who come to school from European American middle-class families participate in a culture that prepares them to receive the educational experiences that schools are prepared to deliver. The more a child is different from that culture, whether it is because of ethnicity or socioeconomic factors, the more points of mismatch the child encounters upon school entry.

Many of the early childhood curricular models that emphasize "socialization," "discovery," "child-initiated learning," or "child-centered instruction" work quite well for children who have a family background that complements such programs. However, for children whom this society has placed at risk for school success, it is critical that we plan preschool experiences that will truly provide the background for success in kindergarten.

I had the occasion to observe a classroom of four-year-olds in a public school designed for children at risk for success in kindergarten. What I saw in terms of curricular planning was a make-it-up-as-you-go-along day. The children did finger plays. They played with puzzles. They had snacks. They went outside. The teacher read a story. They turned on a record and sang along. They did finger painting. While these were all worthwhile activities, there was little consideration given to which activities would be chosen in which combination over the course of the school year. Each classroom varied from the other, providing only random experiences to the children. If one teacher liked to do art, then the children did a lot of art. If the teacher next door liked music, then those children did a lot of music. If another teacher swore by play, then the children went outside a great deal. If one teacher swore by language arts, then she read to them a lot. The principal could not say with a great deal of certainty what was being delivered to the children.

It seems that educators need to engage preschoolers in activities that are planned, that are developmentally appropriate, and that we know result in success in kindergarten and beyond. We know a whole compendium of things that are appropriate to do with young children. However, I am not as sure that we know how to organize those things into a curriculum that works.

There has been some misunderstanding of the implications of developmentally appropriate activities for curricular planning. Some educators interpret that to mean that a good program is one in which the child aimlessly follows his interests. Certainly, active hands-on involvement is a cornerstone of a developmentally appropriate curriculum. However, the teacher should play an active role in planning these experiences for the children. I pointed out earlier that studies (Berreuta-Clement et al., 1984; Bissell, 1971; and Karnes, Schwedel, and Williams, 1983) show that children gain most from early childhood education programs where teachers have clear objectives in mind for the children.

Teacher-initiated instruction has been incorrectly interpreted as having two-year-olds sit and work on dittoed sheets. It has also been interpreted to mean giving four-year-olds first-grade experiences. I am suggesting that we can engage two-, three-, or four-year-old children in developmentally appropriate activities that are planned and initiated by the teacher. The literature on African American children shows that the most important activities in the classroom are those between the child and the teacher and the child and his peers (Hale-Benson, 1986). School systems, educational coordinators, preschool directors, and others need to help develop overall curricular planning that will allow teachers to select developmentally appropriate activities for children.

A CULTURALLY APPROPRIATE PEDAGOGY

My future work will be devoted to designing an educational practice embedded in African American culture. The effective-schools model, designed by the late Ronald Edmonds, addresses the administration of schools to produce results for children. The Comer model, designed by James Comer, emphasizes the restructuring of relationships within schools and between parents and schools. It seems appropriate that we now give attention to instructional practices within the classroom. The first step in creating a culturally appropriate pedagogy is the recognition that there is a distinctive African American culture.

Everyone who is interested in obtaining money or votes from the African American community knows that there is a distinctive African American culture. Specialists in advertising, marketing, public relations, politics, journalism, television, theater, and motion pictures have long targeted messages to the African American community. No longer do we see an African American doing a toothpaste commercial like a white person previously did it. And in recognition of the amount of money African Americans spend on fast food, McDonald's TV advertising shows a rapping french fry and hip-hop cheerleaders. Politicians know that the best place to appeal for the African American vote is in African American churches, using the rhythm, inflection, intonation, and emotional overtones that characterize the African American rhetorical style. Politicians also evoke the symbolism that African Americans resonate to, inevitably singing the praises of Dr. Martin Luther King, Jr. Educators seem to be the last ones to consider that they can use a culturally salient vehicle to get their message across.

African Americans transform every cultural mode—language, music, religion, art, dance, problem solving, sports, writing—with a kind of "soulfulness." African American children are exposed to a great deal of stimulation from the creative arts: such visual arts as posters, paintings, and graffiti; such audio arts as phonographs, radios, and tape players; such video arts as television and films; and such fashion arts as hairstyles, hats, scarves, jewelry, clothes, makeup, and a general orientation toward adornment of the body that grows out of the African heritage.

Performance also permeates African American expressive style. African American children learn at an early age how to perfect performer roles. They see this expressiveness in African American preachers, athletes, singers, and dancers and also among ordinary African Americans.

Scholars of African American culture show that its roots lie in traditional West African culture (Akbar, 1976; Banks, 1976; Dixon, 1976; Franklin, 1984; Gutman, 1976; Jones, 1979; Levine, 1977; Smitherman, 1977; Wilson, 1972; Young, 1970). An analysis of their descriptions suggests at least nine interrelated dimensions of African American culture. These are outlined by Wade Boykin (1983) as follows:

1. *Spirituality:* an essentially vitalistic, rather than mechanistic, approach to life which carries the conviction that nonmaterial forces influence people's everyday lives

2. *Harmony:* the notion that one's fate is interrelated with other elements in the scheme of things, so that humankind and nature are harmonically conjoined

3. *Movement:* an emphasis on the interweaving of movement, rhythm, percussion, music, and dance, which are believed to be central to psychological health

4. *Verve:* a propensity for relatively high levels of stimulation and for action that is energetic and lively

5. *Affect:* an emphasis on emotions and feelings, together with a special sensitivity to emotional cues and a tendency to be emotionally expressive

6. *Communalism:* a commitment to social connectedness, which includes an awareness that social bonds and responsibilities transcend individual privileges

7. *Expressive individualism:* the cultivation of a distinctive personality and a proclivity for spontaneous, genuine, personal expression

8. *Oral tradition:* a preference for oral/aural modes of communication, in which both speaking and listening are treated as performances and in which oral virtuosity—the ability to use alliterative, metaphorical, and graphic forms of spoken language—is emphasized and cultivated

9. *Social time perspective:* an orientation in which time is treated as passing through a social space rather than a material one, in which time can be recurring, personal, and phenomenological

Boykin also suggests that the African American home environment provides an abundance of stimulation, intensity, and variation. A relatively high noise level exists, with the television playing a significant portion of the time and with constant stereophonic music playing. Usually large numbers of people occupy a living space, and a variety of activities are taking place at once. This condition has been called "overstimulation" and has been thought to create "conceptual deafness" by some social scientists (Marans and Lourie, 1967; Goldman and Sanders, 1969; Wachs, Uzgiris, and Hunt, 1971). However, Boykin believes this stimulating home environment produces the greater psychological and behavioral "verve" that is found among African American children compared to white middle-class children. Exposure to constant stimulation, he argues, leads to chronic activity. Therefore, African American children have increased behavioral vibrancy and an increased psychological affinity for stimulus change and intensity.

It has been pointed out by a number of scholars that schools are rather unstimulating and monotonous places (Silberman, 1970; Holt, 1964). Boykin suggests that factors like investigatory exploration, behavioral change, novelty, and variability have not been incorporated into the classroom. Further, the reason white children are more successful than African American children at academic tasks is that they have a greater tolerance for monotony. White children might not perform as well if they were faced with format variation and stimulation or if they were asked to utilize movement more. Likewise, perhaps African American children are not as successful in school because they are more intolerant of monotonous, boring tasks and the sterile, unstimulating school environment.

Boykin concludes that affective stimulation and vervistic stimulation are necessary for the African American child to be motivated to achieve in an academic setting. Without this stimulation, African American children are turned off and seek other arenas for achievement and expression. "Perhaps we can facilitate the academic/task performance of the African American child if we increase the 'soulfulness' of the academic task setting."

There is no counterpart in European American culture for gospel music, jazz music, rap music, and hip-hop dancing. There is no counterpart in European American culture for the preaching style of the African American minister, which is highly dynamic compared to the lecturelike presentation of the white minister. The preaching style of the African American minister has emotional overtones that build to a climax, called the "whoop" in religious lexicon. This whoop is the orgasmic climax of the sermon, which often is accompanied by the minister going into an ecstatic state. The congregation often responds with verbal chants, shouting, and physical movements (now called "holy dance"). There is an undeniable African American preaching style; it "connects" with an African American congregation. If I showed videotapes of several African American preachers preaching, an African American audience could judge which ones "have it" and which ones do not. Even though the audience may vary in the sophistication with which they could identify the features of a good sermon (content, voice, rhetorical style, whoop), they could all judge whether the entire presentation "set the church on fire."

If it is plausible that there is an African American preaching style, then it is equally plausible that there could be an African American teaching style, which would connect with the culture of African American children, inspire them, motivate them, and capture their imagination. This statement in no way implies that only an African American could utilize such a style. Just as southern white evangelists have approximated the African American preaching style and used it in their ministries, and as white rhythm-and-blues musicians and white artists like the New Kids on the Block have utilized African American musical styles, so European American teachers can utilize African American culture when it is in the interest of their students to do so.

INCARCERATION EDUCATION

The point that I want to emphasize is that, if African American children were in the best schools where white middle-class children are routinely educated, there would be a disconnection. If that is true, then how much more tragic is the situation in the schools in which most African American children are found?

I have had an opportunity to observe in schools in several large American cities what I call *incarceration education*. In such schools, the teachers should receive certification for "lining up and walking down the halls," because a great deal of time is being spent on perfecting those activities. There are elaborate rituals and record-keeping around who lines up first and last and the facial expressions and body language that are appropriate. It seems to me that as much energy is used for that ritual as is used for instruction.

An important index of the quality of a school environment is the extent to which the children appear happy and relaxed, with body language that conveys the same. In incarceration education, the children seem to be receiving training to become inmates. They cannot greet others as they walk down the halls; they must keep their eyes facing forward. And they must adopt an unnatural posture for walking in line. Some children have been reprimanded and notes were sent home for "talking at lunch"! Apparently, the children are to be task-oriented even at lunch and are to refrain from talking so they can finish their meal quickly.

Further, the predominant instruction in these classrooms is called "skill and drill," or "drill and practice." The children do dittoed sheets, workbook sheets, and chalkboard work. Then the teacher goes over the dittoed sheets, the workbook sheets, and the chalkboard work. In the morning, the teacher writes on the chalkboard the pages in the textbook the children should read and the questions at the end of the chapter that they should complete. In essence, the children teach themselves. If a child conveys in any way how boring this is, he is assigned to write, "I will not do (whatever it is I just did)" again and again. As I was observing one such class, the class departed for another activity. An African American boy emerged from the closet and asked the student teacher if he could get a drink of water. In disbelief, I asked what he was doing in the closet. She said that, as punishment, this child had to do his writing in the closet all day.

Opening exercises should include poems, songs, instrumental music, dance, and physical activities to focus children's minds and bodies spiritually and physically. (Richard Bielaczyc, Photography-Media Services, Wayne State University Libraries)

One could cut the tension in this classroom with a knife. I thought about my precious son and how I would never allow him to be enrolled in a classroom with this much tension. I wondered where the parents were and whether they had seen this. I remembered that the children were bused and that it was possible the parents had never been there. Then, a more chilling thought was, What if they did come here? This is school as I experienced it in the 1950s. This is school as my mother experienced it in the 1930s. They would probably conclude that this is school as it is supposed to be.

The reality is that children destined to be the leaders of tomorrow are not being educated in skill and drill, as inner-city African American children are. I thought about Doris Kearns Goodwin's book, *The Fitzgeralds and the Kennedys* (1987), which describes how Joseph P. Kennedy carefully crafted the education of his sons. As I looked at the children seated before me in that classroom, I wondered where those children were going to work when they became adults. They seemed to me to be throw-away children. The girls are destined to be on public assistance, the boys to be unemployed or in prison.

The factories, for all practical purposes, are closed. We no longer have a need for a large population of unskilled workers. Poorly educated people cannot obtain employment as they once did. We know now what characteristics will be required for people to be economically viable in the twenty-first century: we need people who can think, who have imagination, who can solve problems; people who are creative, innovative, and have vision; people who are self-starters, who can work independently.

For many African American schoolchildren, there is a disconnection between the abilities being developed in school and those they will need to be economically viable, to function independently as adults, and to make a creative contribution to the society.

There have been some well-intentioned efforts to improve educational outcomes for African American children by church organizations and groups such as the Nation of Islam. There have been some successes, because the teachers sincerely cared for the children and taught them conscientiously. However, often they required young children to dress in uniform, to sit in assigned seats and do seatwork, with instruction oriented to tests and a rigid, militaristic atmosphere. Because there were positive outcomes in terms of the children's achievement and few competing models for African American children, over time this highly structured and rigid form of education was considered to be "the way" to produce outcomes for African American children.

ARTISTIC TEACHING

I gave a lecture at a Sunday school in Kentucky recently. When one of the Sunday school teachers asked how they could motivate African American children to work toward a goal when they were not being paid or graded, I responded, "hobbies." Because we don't receive grades or money for our hobbies, they stimulate us to develop our intrinsic drive for excellence. We might work to perfect our photographic skills because we have an internal criterion for beauty. Or we might work to acquire a comprehensive stamp collection because of our inner vision of a completed collection.

Imagine a school that incorporated into instruction the features of hobbies. Imagine a school whose children are busily at work on independent projects. Imagine a school that has no basal readers, textbooks, or dittoed sheets but plenty of literature, math manipulatives, science experiments, art supplies, enriching speakers, field trips, projects, thematic units, and internships. Artistic teaching as it is employed in the Waldorf method of education is highly compatible with the Afrocentric instructional strategies described here. First of all, the arts are incorporated into instruction by the classroom teachers and not taught solely by special art teachers. Colored chalk is used on the chalkboards. There are no textbooks. The children record their work in large blank books, which serve as workbooks. Their work is recorded using crayons and colored pencils and embellished with their own art. The children use various art media such as paint, clay, and beeswax to interpret their experiences in all areas of the curriculum.

Children at all grade levels in Waldorf schools participate in opening exercises, which include poems, songs, instrumental music, dance, and physical activities that focus their minds and bodies spiritually, ideologically, and physically for the work of the day. These schools project a spirituality that is soothing to the soul. Each classroom has a nature table, which provides a spiritual focus. The walls are pastel, and the floors are often carpeted. Instead of window shades and venetian blinds, there are curtains at the windows. Instead of bulletin boards, there is framed art and displays of the children's art.

Roeper City and Country School in Bloomfield Hills, Michigan, is a school for gifted children. Its preschool through fifth-grade classrooms contain no desks lined up facing the chalkboard. Instead, the classrooms resemble living rooms. There is comfortable furniture: a sofa, a loveseat, and an easy chair, with rocking chairs in the primary grades. There are lamps on the teachers' desks and small tables where groups of children work. This is what I call a child-friendly and teacher-friendly educational environment.

We need an educational process for African American children that imbues them with a raison d'être—a reason for being. We need an educational process that is the first step toward the identification of interests and meaningful work. Abraham Maslow (1968) identifies the steps toward becoming a self-actualized person, one of them being the identification of and involvement with meaningful work. People who engage in work in which they can use their natural talents are the most happy.

Children should not grow up only to awaken each day and think that they have to go to their slaves' jobs. Or to awaken on Friday and think, Thank God it's Friday, so I can get drunk this evening. Someone has said that you should love the work you do so much that you would do it for free, but because you do it so well, people pay you to do it. One's work should be paid fun!

Further, I believe that substance abuse and premature sexual activity among young people arises because they are incarcerated in school all day and then go home to unstructured street time. These children do not have their minds engaged constructively. When one does not have one's mind on anything, the only thrill is titillating the body. Unstimulating instruction causes a disconnection from school for African American children and begins their search for physical thrill seeking.

Henry Levin (1988) has developed a concept of accelerated learning. He points out that when a student is behind his peers in school, the usual school response is to slow the student down further through remedial education. Then everything that is meaningful in terms of educational content is removed, and he is subjected to drilling on a set of isolated, unrelated concepts. Levin maintains that, when a student is behind, the only hope he has to catch up is to accelerate or concentrate his education; so the first thing that educators should do is to set a deadline for the student to get caught up. Second, the educational content should be made relevant to the student's experiences, and the instruction should be made extremely interesting. The student who is behind needs more, not less, interesting instruction than the person who is ahead. The predominant mode of instruction should be projects, hands-on activities, lessons that stress the interrelationship of concepts, and real-life experiences, not the repetitious drill and practice of dittoed sheets.

In our educational system, the only children who receive instruction that makes sense are those enrolled in schools and programs for the gifted and talented. They not only receive an accelerated education, they receive a qualitatively different type of education than the

Classrooms should be furnished comfortably, like living rooms, to reduce the institutional atmosphere. (Mary Jane Murawka, Photography-Media Services, Wayne State University Libraries)

average child. I believe with John Dewey that the education that is best for the best of us, is best for the rest of us.

My father would quote Benjamin Mays, who said, "When a man is ahead of you in a race, the only way that you can catch up is either for him to slow down; for someone to give you a lift; or for you to run faster than he. You cannot depend upon him to slow down. You cannot depend upon a lift. So, you had better get out there running." A step toward that end is the design of a culturally appropriate pedagogy for African American children in which teaching strategies are an outgrowth of their culture and which will connect them to the future. This pedagogy will stimulate intrinsic motivation and start African American children on the road to a lifelong love of learning.

DEVELOPMENTALLY APPROPRIATE PRACTICES

A starting point for this pedagogy is for elementary school teachers to acquaint themselves with *Developmentally Appropriate Practices in Early*

Childhood Programs Serving Children from Birth through Age 8, which is available through the National Association for the Education of Young Children (NAEYC) in Washington, D.C. Even though this document addresses classroom management and instructional issues through third grade, the practices it discusses can inform education throughout the lifespan; education for children of all ages will be enhanced when paper-and-pencil tasks are reduced and a playful, exploratory, hands-on, investigative learning process is introduced.

My earlier book, *Black Children,* explores in depth two issues particularly salient to African American children. First, empirical research has documented that African American children are more kinesthetic than white children. Second, African American children are reared with an affective orientation.

The following story exemplifies the first issue. My five-year-old son's teacher observed that he was very territorial about his space and often got into conflicts with white children who invaded his space. He also was often punished at school for infractions during whole-class meeting time in the morning.

I decided to observe him in Sunday school to see how he behaved

A teacher-friendly, child-friendly educational classroom. (Mary Jane Murawka, Photography-Media Services, Wayne State University Libraries)

Classroom for gifted children: an educational environment that is best for the best of us is best for the rest of us. (Mary Jane Murawka, Photography-Media Services, Wayne State University Libraries)

in an out-of-school setting. I took him to his class, returned fifty minutes later, and was amazed to see him sitting in the same seat, attending to the lesson. He was rocking a little in his chair and squirming, but he was not distracting the other children, and he was generally sitting quietly. I could not believe that he was capable of sitting for that length of time.

On the way home from church, I questioned him about why he was able to sit still for so long. He said, "It was easy Mommy, I had my own chair. All I had to do was sit up straight and keep my feet on the floor." Why did he have difficulty in his classroom at school? "Because it is hard work, Mommy." "What do you mean? Is the work too difficult for you?" "No, I mean that it is hard work to sit on the floor; I have to cross my legs; I can't touch anybody; and the teacher says that I have trouble finding my space." A light came on: I thought, Whoop, there it is! Perhaps his adjustment in the classroom could be partly solved if he were allowed to sit on a chair during meeting time instead of crossing his legs on the floor. He might be saved from developing a self-concept of not fitting into the classroom, of standing in the hall for punishment.

I have also noticed a black male greeting-fighting ritual between my son and his friends. When he and two of his friends engaged in what seemed to their mothers to be fighting, they exclaimed that they were really playing! But the white boys my son plays with at school react totally differently toward aggression: if my son hits them, they invariably do not hit back, whereas, the black boys give tit for tat. Consequently, my son moves between two worlds, one black and one white. My dilemma as a parent is that, on the one hand, I do not want him to be physically aggressive toward anyone and I do not want him to be considered hard to manage at school. On the other hand, I do not want to turn him into a "white boy" who cannot function with African American boys, because the African American culture is his true emotional world. This is a real dilemma African American parents face in raising their children in integrated settings.

Another aspect of this kinesthetic orientation is the practice of sitting African American children in assigned seats and requiring them to sit all day with little opportunity to move. I am amazed as I visit school districts and speak with teachers to note that they do not recognize how critical it is that children have free play (recess), physical education, and creative movement (dance). I have spoken with teachers who have voted to eliminate recess because they want more instructional time. In one excellent science and mathematics magnet school, the director noted with pride that they have no recess. But educators who believe that they enhance children's education by eliminating physical activity are misguided. This is developmentally inappropriate for all children and fatal for African American children, particularly boys.

At the Roeper School, the children have a rotation of six special classes—library, science, music, art, dance, and physical education—with one class each day. Notice that dance and physical education have equal standing with science, music, and art. In addition to dance and physical education, the children have outdoor recess twice daily. This is developmentally appropriate.

I visited a school as a part of student teacher supervision in which the children were assigned to a portable unit outside of the school building. There were thirty-two second-grade children in the classroom; twenty-four of them were African American boys. These boys were required to sit in their seats all day and were "bouncing off the walls." They could get out of their seats only to go to the bathroom, and the bathroom was only two feet away from them, right there in the portable unit.

Before the teacher and the student teacher left the classroom to go to a conference room with me, the teacher briefed the relief teacher. She identified what seemed to be all of the boys in the classroom as having "lunch detention," meaning that they were required to go home for lunch. They were being punished for earlier stampeding out of the portable en route to the lunchroom: the first boy ran over a little girl, and there was a twenty-four-boy pileup. "When you operate like a *gang*," she said, "you must be punished like a gang."

I asked the teacher whether lunch detention was a developmentally appropriate punishment considering the stress it would place on the working-class families in that community, who would have to arrange to be at home to provide lunch for their children. Developmentally appropriate practices extend to parents as well as to children. She was hostile: "These parents need to know what these children they send over here to us are doing."

In the conference, the teacher told me that the student teacher was not adept at disciplining the children. I commented that General Colin Powell, assisted by the army, the navy, and the marines, would be needed to discipline those boys given the way the classroom was organized. I asked whether she felt that she as a teacher had a responsibility to organize her classroom in a developmentally appropriate manner so the boys could experience success. I then inquired about how recess and physical education were scheduled. She responded that they have recess every other semester when it is *their year for recess*. And it was not her class's year for recess. The playground was a big mud hole, anyway, so it offered no opportunity to even throw a ball around. There was no playground equipment.

I suggested that she have the children push their seats back and do ten minutes of aerobics in the morning and ten minutes in the afternoon to expend energy. Waldorf teachers, for example, use excellent opening exercises, which are physically and mentally stimulating, to help the children concentrate and focus in preparation for the day's activities. This teacher, however, thought that her children would make too much noise pushing their seats back. Could they do aerobics standing next to their seats? I recalled that on a nine-hour flight to Alaska I and the other passengers had done aerobic exercises sitting in our seats—and it felt wonderful. If it is possible to do aerobics in an airline's seat, it is possible to do aerobics standing next to one's seat in a classroom.

The teacher responded that the children are territorial and would get into fights. I then suggested she take the children on a five-minute walk in the morning and again in the afternoon, but she countered that the children were poor and didn't have proper hats and gloves. When I offered to have my church purchase hats and gloves for each child in her classroom, she refused, stating that the children's parents were proud and would be offended. I suggested that she did not have to send the clothing home; she could just keep them in a box in the classroom for the walks. But obviously, we had reached an impasse.

Next I went to the principal, who promptly informed me that he was to retire in two years, which seemed to be an announcement that he was already in retirement. He explained that the school was over-crowded, which was true; they were serving about a thousand children in a building built for six hundred. I brought up things he and the teacher could do to improve the success chances for the boys in that classroom.

First of all, I recommended that he more equally distribute boys and girls in the second-grade classrooms so that one classroom was not predominantly girls and one predominantly boys, as was the case. There is nothing wrong with a mostly boys classroom, but the teacher should have the personality and sensitivity to deal with them. This teacher clearly did not. I also suggested that a classroom full of boys should not be housed in a portable unit because opportunities for the boys to stretch their legs and walk around were so restricted. At least in the main building, they could stretch their legs walking to the bathroom. Additionally, the special teachers came to the portables, instead of the children going to them, which further restricted the children's opportunity to move about.

It was interesting that the teacher said that at lunchtime she had to get out of the portable unit because she couldn't stand to be in it any longer. This doesn't sound like a teacher-friendly learning environment. And the principal mentioned that when the cleaning crew tried to clean the portables in the evenings someone in the community *shot* at them. Also, vandals had torn pieces of the roof off of the building. Did he consider that perhaps some of the people shooting at the portables were boys who had to sit in them all year? No one was shooting at the main building!

Black Children also develops in detail the affective orientation found in African American child rearing: the most important learning for African American children in the classroom is that mediated by people—their teachers and their peers. So the biggest crimes against African American children are the large class sizes and imbalanced teacher-child ratios that are found in most school districts. NAEYC recommends the following ratios: for four- and five-year-olds, two adults to no more than twenty children; for six- to eight-year-olds, no more than twenty-five children with two adults, one of whom may be a paraprofessional and no more than eighteen children to one teacher. Groups can include three chronological ages, with individualized movement in separate subject matter areas. At the Roeper School, class ratios are two adults for up to nineteen children. Groups include two chronological ages, in stages. The children stay with the same teachers for two years. Of course, Roeper is a private school; most public schools have a class ratio of between twenty-five and thirty-four children to one teacher. However, it is important to go on the record—to the public, to school boards, to state legislatures, and to parents—that these class sizes are developmentally inappropriate.

The children in the Roeper School are taught math and language arts in groups of one teacher to four children. I have observed reading groups in predominantly African American schools with twenty-four children to one teacher and thirty minutes for each reading group. Most of the schools I have visited have only had two reading groups for a classroom of thirty-four children.

In the classroom in the portable unit mentioned earlier, I suggested that the teacher divide the children into at least three reading groups. She responded that she could not come up with ninety minutes of seat work to give to the children who were not in the reading group in session. I pointed out to her that six of the twenty-four boys could not read at all. She stated (and it was confirmed by the language arts supervisor) that she was required to assign every second-grade child a second-grade book, even if the child could not read the book.

The furniture is outdated in many classrooms where African American children are found, and chairs are connected to the desks. Without single chairs, the flexible groupings and seating arrangements in a developmentally appropriate school like Roeper are not possible. To my horror, I found that when these twenty-four children in one group had reading, they had to sit on the dirty floor because there were not enough chairs for them to sit close to the teacher. They knew they were not supposed to sit on a dirty floor because none of them sat flat with their legs crossed; they sat on their knees, trying to juggle their books. And yet, we have national conferences and summits pondering the question of why African American children cannot read: all we have to do is to go into some classrooms and the answer is there for us to see.

In another classroom the children were divided into two reading groups: seventeen children in the lower-ability group and thirteen in the higher-ability group. One would think that the lower-ability group would be the smallest so that the children could receive more individual attention. The children were seated in rows instead of the intimate semicircle around the teacher that we are accustomed to for reading groups. The children in the fourth and fifth rows away from the teacher were in a world of their own; they could not hear what was going on and were not involved in the lesson.

I shall never forget an incident when I was observing the student teacher. She was having difficulty with two African American boys who were having trouble sitting still and waiting for their turn in a reading group of thirteen children. The student teacher abruptly took the book of one boy, closed it, and reprimanded him. The charge: reading ahead in the story! He was not hitting anyone with the book; he was not distracting anyone; he was not interrupting the discussion; he was simply trying to cope with being in a group too large and with having to wait too long for his turn.

The challenge we face when we are assigned to classrooms with large numbers of children is how to reduce whole-class teaching and large reading groups and how to provide time for learning to occur in small groups. One suggestion is to involve the instructional aides in *instruction*. In the skill-and-drill classrooms I have observed, instructional aides grade dittoed and workbook sheets, cut out pumpkins, set up the filmstrip projector, and do other tasks that do not involve them directly with the children.

Upon entering a classroom at Roeper, a school where instruction is developmentally appropriate, one cannot tell who the lead teacher is or who the assistant teacher is based upon what they are doing with the children. The instructional aides should not be described as being the "teacher's helper" or "teacher's aide." They are not there to help the teacher; *they are there to teach the children.*

The teacher in a classroom with too many children should organize the volunteer parents to work with children in small groups so the teacher can spend time with other small groups. Volunteers from churches and civic groups should be brought into the classroom; older children can tutor younger children. Whatever temporary strategies we devise, we must remember that large class sizes are inappropriate for African American children and that, within those large classes, huge reading groups (of more than seven or eight children) are inappropriate.

CURRICULUM GUIDES AND
THE PHILOSOPHY OF EDUCATION

It is essential that every school district, and perhaps every school, have a curriculum guide that states the consensus of those educators about how they believe children learn and how they intend to teach them. The process of clarifying their vision can provide a spiritual frame of reference for their work. In too many cases, a school system teaches whatever the textbook series in each subject matter area is teaching. In such systems, the textbook is not a tool that the teacher is using to teach what she and her colleagues have clarified as being important: the textbook is the curriculum guide.

The time has come for educators to think about the kinds of people we are trying to produce through the educational process. In my visits to school districts, I have seen the slogan, "Every child can learn," at first glance a beautiful, inspirational sentiment. However, consider the Roeper School's goals for its children, as stated by Chuck Webster, its head: "Our goals for the children are for them to: (1) understand themselves; (2) find meaning in their world; (3) construct their futures; (4) have an impact on their world." When you then consider "Every child can learn," it seems condescending and one-dimensional. Is anyone thinking about the kind of African American children we are trying to produce? Does anyone care? Are we interested in creating an educational process for African American children where they can have a creative impact on our society, or do we intend for them to iron other people's clothes and serve as a buffer for the economy?

When we engage children in skill-and-drill activities throughout their educational career, they become skill-and-drill people!

On an ABC news documentary entitled "Common Miracles: The New American Revolution in Learning," Peter Jennings said that "education is how a society hands out its life chances. How it gives people options. Philosophers sometimes say the best definition of freedom is a good range of options. A new revolution in learning would give many more Americans real freedom."

VALUES

The time has come to clarify the values that must permeate the educational process. I think that we can agree that we want to produce children who are responsible and honorable. Roeper School has a goal of empowering children, enabling them to take responsibility for decisionmaking in their lives.

It seems appropriate to close with words of W.E.B. DuBois (1968); they were written in 1906, but they ring true today:

> And when we call for education, we mean real education. We believe in work. We ourselves are workers, but work is not necessarily education. Education is the development of power and ideal. We want our children trained as intelligent human beings should be and we will fight for all time against any proposal to educate black boys and girls simply as servants and underlings, or simply for the use of other people. They have a right to know, to think, to aspire. (251)

Bibliography

Akbar, N. 1976. Rhythmic patterns in African personality. In *African philosophy: Assumptions and paradigms for research on black persons,* edited by L. King, V. Dixon, and W. Nobles. Los Angeles: Fanon Center Publications.

Allitto, S. 1969. The language issue in communist Chinese education. In *Aspects of Chinese education,* edited by C. Hu. New York: Teachers College Press.

Banks, J. 1976. Crucial issues in the education of Afro-American children. *Journal of Afro-American Issues* 4:392–407.

Barrett, L. 1974. African religions in the Americas. In *The Black experience in religion,* edited by C. Eric Lincoln. New York: Anchor Press/Doubleday.

Barth, F. 1969. Introduction to *Ethnic groups and boundaries,* edited by F. Barth. Boston: Little, Brown.

Beane, D. 1985. *Mathematics and science: Critical filter for the future.* Washington, D.C.: American University, Midatlantic Center for Race Equity.

Bennett, C., and J. Harris III. 1982. Suspensions and expulsions of male and black students: A study of the causes of disproportionality. *Urban Education* 16:339–423.

Berreuta-Clement, J. R., L. J. Schweinhart, W. S. Barnett, A. S. Epstein, and D. P. Weikert. 1984. *Changed lives: Effects of the Perry Preschool Program on youth through age 19.* Ypsilanti, Mich.: High Scope Press.

Bethune, M. M. 1938. Clarifying our vision with the facts. *Journal of Negro History* 23:12.

Bissell, J. 1971. *Implementation of planned variation in Head Start.* Washington, D.C.: U.S. Department of Health, Education, and Welfare, Office of Child Development.

Blassingame, J. W. 1972. *The slave community.* New York: Oxford University Press.

Bly, Robert. 1992. *Iron John.* New York: Vintage.

Bowles, S., and H. Gintis. 1976. *Schooling in capitalist America.* New York: Basic Books.

Boykin, A. W. 1977. Experimental psychology from a black perspective: Issues and examples. In *Final report from the third conference on empirical research in black psychology,* edited by William Cross. Washington, D.C.: National Institute of Education.

———. 1978. Psychological behavioral verve in academic/task performance: Pretheoretical considerations. *Journal of Negro Education* 47:343–54.

————. 1979. Black psychology and the research process: Keeping the baby but throwing out the bathwater. In *Research directions of black psychologists,* edited by A. W. Boykin, A. J. Franklin, and J. F. Yates. New York: Russell Sage.

————. 1983. The academic performance of Afro-American children. In *Achievement and achievement motives,* edited by J. Spence. San Francisco: Freeman.

————. 1986. The triple quandary and the schooling of Afro-American children. In *The school achievement of minority children: New perspectives,* edited by U. Neisser. Hillsdale, N.J.: Erlbaum.

Branch, T. 1988. *Parting the waters: America in the King years, 1954–1963.* New York: Simon and Schuster.

Brazelton, T., B. Koslowski, and E. Tronick. 1971. Neonatal behavior among urban Zambians and Americans. *Journal of Child Psychiatry* 15:97–107.

Brown, S. 1969. Negro folk expression: Spirituals, seculars, ballads, and work songs. In *The making of black America: Essays in Negro life and history,* edited by A. Meier and C. Rudwich. New York: Atheneum.

Cazden, C. 1970. The situation: A neglected source of social class differences in language use. *Journal of Social Issues* 26:35–60.

Clark, R. M. 1983. *Family life and school achievement: Why poor black children succeed or fail.* Chicago: University of Chicago Press.

Comer, J. 1988. *Maggie's American dream: The life and times of a black family.* New York: New American Library.

Cone, J. H. 1969. *Black theology and black power.* New York: Seabury.

————. 1972. *The spirituals and the blues.* New York: Seabury.

Coons, J. 1970. *Private wealth and public education.* Cambridge: Harvard University Press.

Cornbleth, C., and W. Korth. 1980. Teacher perceptions and teacher-student interaction in integrated classrooms. *Journal of Experimental Education* 48:259–63.

Daniel, J. 1976. *The wisdom of Sixth Mount Zion from the members of Sixth Mount Zion and those who begot them.* Pittsburgh: Limited Edition Publications.

Daniel, J. L., and G. Smitherman. 1976. How I got over: Communication dynamics in the black community. *Quarterly Journal of Speech* 62:26–39.

Daniel, J. L., G. Smitherman-Donaldson, and J. Milford. 1987. Makin' a way outa no way: The proverb tradition in the black experience. *Journal of Black Studies* 17: 482–508.

De Anda, D. 1984. Bicultural socialization: Factors affecting the minority experience. *Social Work* (March–April): 101–7.

Deutsch, M. 1963. The disadvantaged child and the learning process. In *Education in depressed areas,* edited by A. Passow. New York: Teachers College Press.

DeVos, G. 1975. Ethnic pluralism: Conflict and accommodation. In *Ethnic identity: Cultural continuities and change,* edited by G. DeVos and L. Romanuci-Ross. Palo Alto: Manfield.

Dixon, V. 1976. Worldviews and research methodology. In *African philosophy: Assumptions and paradigms for research on black persons,* edited by L. King, V. Dixon, and W. Nobles. Los Angeles: Fanon Center Publications.

Dixon, V., and B. G. Foster. 1971. *Beyond black or white.* Boston: Little, Brown.

DuBois, W.E.B. 1961 (1903). *The souls of black folk.* Greenwich, Conn.: Fawcett.

————. 1968 (1906). *The autobiography of W.E.B. DuBois: A soliloquy on viewing my life from the last decade of its first century.* New York: International Publishers.

Ebony magazine. November 1987, 68–74. Interview with August Wilson.

Erikson, E. 1968. *Identity: Youth and crisis.* New York: Norton.

Feeney, S. 1987. *Who am I in the lives of children?* Columbus, Ohio: Charles E. Merrill.

Fishman, J., and E. Leuders-Salmon. 1972. What has sociology to say to the teacher? In *Functions of speech in the classroom,* edited by C. Cazden et al. New York: Teachers College Press.

Fleming, J. 1985. *Blacks in college.* San Francisco: Jossey-Bass.

Fowler, J. 1981. *The stages of faith.* New York: Harper and Row.

Franklin, V. P. 1984. *Black self-determination: A cultural history of the faith of the fathers.* Westport, Conn.: Lawrence Hill.

Gitter, A., G. H. Black, and D. I. Mostofsky. 1972. Race and sex in perception of emotion. *Journal of Social Issues* 28:63–78.

Goffman, E. 1963. *Stigma.* Englewood Cliffs, N.J.: Prentice-Hall.

Goldman, R., and J. Sanders. 1969. Cultural factors and hearing. *Exceptional Children* 35:489–90.

Goodwin, D. K. 1987. *The Fitzgeralds and the Kennedys.* New York: Simon and Schuster.

Gutman, H. 1976. *The black family in slavery and freedom, 1750–1925.* New York: Pantheon.

Guttentag, M. 1972. Negro-white differences in children's movement. *Perceptual and Motor Skills* 35:435–36.

Guttentag, M., and S. Ross. 1972. Movement responses in simple concept learning. *American Journal of Orthopsychiatry* 42:657–65.

Hale, J. E. 1991. The transmission of cultural values to young African American children. *Young Children* 46:7–15.

Hale-Benson, J. E. 1986. *Black children: Their roots, culture, and learning styles.* Baltimore: Johns Hopkins University Press.

————. 1990a. Visions for Children: African American preschool program. *Early Childhood Research Quarterly* 5:199–213.

————. 1990b. Visions for Children: Educating black children in the context of their culture. In *Going to school: The African American experience,* edited by K. Lomotey. Albany: State University of New York Press.

Hare, B. 1987. Structural inequality and the endangered status of black youth. *Journal of Negro Education* 56:100–110.

Harter, S., and R. Pike. 1984. Pictorial scale of perceived competence and social acceptance for young children. *Child Development* 55:1969–82.

Haskins, J., and H. F. Butts. 1973. *The psychology of black language.* New York: Barnes and Noble.

Havighurst, R. J. 1976. The relative importance of social class and ethnicity in human development. *Human Development* 19:56–64.

Henderson, D. H., and A. G. Washington. 1975. Cultural differences and the education of black children: An alternative model for program development. *Journal of Negro Education* 44:353–60.

Hilliard, A. 1976. *Alternatives to IQ testing: An approach to the identification of gifted minority children.* Final Report. Sacramento: California State Department of Education.

Holt, J. 1964. *How children fail.* New York: Dell.

Hostetler, J., and G. Huntington. 1971. *Children in Amish society: Socialization and community education.* New York: Holt, Rinehart, and Winston.

Hughes, Langston. 1926. Mother to son. In *Selected poems of Langston Hughes.* New York: Knopf.

Jackson, P. 1968. *Life in the classroom.* New York: Holt, Rinehart, and Winston.

Jones, J. M. 1979. Conceptual and strategic issues in the relationship of black psychology to American social science. In *Research directions of black psychologists,* edited by A. W. Boykin, A. J. Franklin, and J. F. Yates. New York: Russell Sage.

Karnes, M. B., A. M. Schwedel, and M. B. Williams. 1983. In *Consortium for longitudinal studies* "As the twig is bent" . . . *lasting effects of preschool programs.* Hillsdale, N.J.: Erlbaum.

Kozol, Jonathan. 1991. *Savage inequalities.* New York: Crown.

Kuhn, C. M., H. E. Joye, and E. B. West. 1991. *Living Atlanta: An oral history of the city, 1914–1948.* Athens: University of Georgia Press.

Labov, W. A. 1964. Stages in the acquisition of standard English. In *Social dialects and language learning,* edited by R. Shuy. Champaign, Ill.: National Council of Teachers of English.

————. 1969. The logic of nonstandard English. *Florida FL Reporter* 7: 60–75.

Labov, W. A., and C. Robins. 1969. A note on the relation of reading failure to peer-group status in urban ghettos. *Florida FL Reporter* 7:54–57.

Lemann, N. 1991. *The promised land.* New York: Knopf.

Lester, J. 1969. *Look out whitey! Black power's gon' get your mama!* New York: Grove.

Levin, H. 1988. *Accelerated schools for at-risk students.* Berkeley, Calif.: Center for Policy Research in Education.

Levine, L. 1977. *Black culture and black consciousness.* New York.: Oxford University Press.

Lieberson, S. 1980. *A piece of the pie: Black and white immigrants since 1880.* Berkeley: University of California Press.

Lightfoot, S. L. 1988. *Balm in Gilead: Journey of a healer.* Reading, Mass.: Addison-Wesley.

Lincoln, C. E. 1974. *The black experience in religion.* New York.: Anchor/Doubleday.

Long, N. 1958. The local community as an ecology of games. In *Politics of social life, 1963,* edited by N. Polsby et al. Boston: Houghton-Mifflin.

McCarthy, D. A. 1972. *Manual for the McCarthy Scales of Children's Abilities.* New York: Psychological Corporation.

McDermott, R. 1987. Achieving school failure: An anthropological approach to literacy and social stratification. In *Education and cultural process: Anthropological approaches,* 2d ed., edited by G. Spindler. Prospect Heights, Ill.: Waveland.

Makita, K. 1968. The rarity of reading disability in Japanese children. *American Journal of Orthopsychiatry* 38:599–614.

Malinowski, B. 1954. *Magic, science, and religion, and other essays.* Garden City, N.Y.: Doubleday.

Marans, A., and R. Lourie. 1967. Hypotheses regarding the effects of child-rearing patterns on the disadvantaged child. In *The disadvantaged child,* edited by J. Hellmuth. Seattle: Special Child Publications.

Maslow, A. 1968. *Toward a psychology of being.* Princeton, N.J.: Van Nostrand.

Massari, D., L. Hayweiser, and J. Meyer. 1969. Activity level and intellectual functioning in deprived preschool children. *Developmental Psychology* 1:286–90.

Metropolitan Reading Readiness Tests. 1976. New York: Harcourt Brace Jovanovich.

Mitchell, E. R. 1986. Oral tradition: Legacy of faith for the black church. *Religious Education* 81:93–112.

Moore, E. 1985. Ethnicity as a variable in child development. In *Beginnings: The social and affective development of black children,* edited by M. Spencer, G. Brookins, and W. Allen. Hillsdale, N.J.: Erlbaum.

Morgan, H. 1976. Neonatal precocity and the black experience. *Negro Educational Review* 27:129–34.

National Assessment of Educational Progress. 1983. *The third national mathematics assessment: Results, trends and issues.* Denver, Colo.: Education Commission of the State.

National Black Child Development Institute. 1985. *Child care in the public schools: Incubator for inequality?* Washington, D.C.: NBCDI.

National Science Foundation. 1984. *Women and minorities in science and engineering.* Washington, D.C.: NSF.

National Urban Coalition. See Beane, D. 1985.

Newmeyer, J. A. 1970. Creativity and nonverbal communication in preadolescent white and black children. Ph.D. diss., Harvard University.

Ogbu, J., and A. Woodard. 1989. Minority status and literacy. Paper prepared for the Conference on literacy among black youth: Issues in teaching and schooling, University of Pennsylvania.

Padilla, E. R., and G. E. Wyatt. 1983. The effects of intelligence and achievement testing on minority group children. In *The psychosocial development of minority group children,* edited by G. J. Powell. New York: Brunner/Mazel.

Piestrup, A. 1974. *Black dialect interference and accommodation of reading instruction in first grade.* Monograph 4. Berkeley: University of California, Language Behavior Research Laboratory.

Rashid, H. 1981. Early childhood education as a cultural transition for African American children. *Educational Research Quarterly* 6:55–63.

Roberts, J. 1970. *Scene of the battle: Group behavior in urban classrooms.* New York: Doubleday.

Rohwer, W., and W. Harris. 1975. Media effects on prose learning in two populations of children. *Journal of Educational Psychology* 67:651–57.

Rist, R. 1970. Student social class and teacher expectations. *Harvard Educational Review* 40:411–51.

Sarason, S. B. 1973. Jewishness, blackishness, and the nature-nurture controversy. *American Psychologist* 28:962–71.

Schaefer, E. S. 1987. Maternal prenatal, infancy, and concurrent predictions of maternal reports of child psychopathology. *Psychiatry* 50:320–31.

Schwartz, J. C. 1981. *Measuring individual differences in self-control and self-regulation in childhood.* ERIC Document 204008.

Semaj, L. 1985. Afrikanity, cognition, and extended self-identity. In *Beginnings: The social and affective development of black children,* edited by M. Spencer, G. Brookins, and W. Allen. Hillsdale, N. J.: Erlbaum.

Silberman, C. 1970. *Crisis in the classroom.* New York: Vintage.

Smitherman, G. 1977. *Talking and testifying. The language of black America.* Boston: Houghton-Mifflin.

Spencer, M. B. 1985. Cultural cognition and social cognition as identity correlates of black children's personal-social development. In *Beginnings: The social and affective development of black children,* edited by M. Spencer, G. Brookins, and W. Allen. Hillsdale, N.J.: Erlbaum.

Spindler, G. 1959. The transmission of American culture. In *Education and culture,* edited by G. Spindler. New York: Holt, Rinehart, and Winston.

Stanford Achievement Test. 1985. Monterey, Calif.: McGraw-Hill.

Staples, R. 1985. Black male/female relationships. In *Proceedings of the conference on the black family,* edited by J. Hale-Benson. Cleveland, Ohio: Olivet Institutional Baptist Church, 31–35.

Thompson, L. 1966. *Reading disability.* Springfield, Ill.: Charles C Thomas.

Wachs, T., L. Uzgiris, and J. M. Hunt. 1971. Cognitive development in infants of different age levels and from different environmental backgrounds: An explanatory investigation. *Merrill Palmer Quarterly* 17:283–316.

Warren, E. H. 1983. *Brownridge M. B. Church, 1863–1983.* Privately published.

Williams, J. E., et al. 1975. Preschool Racial Attitudes Measure II. *Educational and Psychological Measurement* 35:3–18.

Wilson, A. 1988. *Joe Turner's come and gone: A play in two acts.* New York: New American Library.

Wilson, T. 1972. Notes toward a process of Afro-American education. *Harvard Educational Review* 42:374–89.

Wilson, W. J. 1987. *The truly disadvantaged.* Chicago: University of Chicago Press.

Work, J. W. 1915. *Folk songs of the American Negro.* Nashville, Tenn.: First University Bookstore.

Young, V. H. 1970. Family and childhood in a southern Georgia community. *American Anthropologist* 72:269–88.

Zigler, E., W. Abelson, and V. Seitz. 1973. Motivational factors in the performance of economically disadvantaged children on the Peabody Picture Vocabulary Test. *Child Development* 44:294–303.

Zigler, E., and E. Butterfield. 1968. Motivational aspects of changes in IQ test performance of culturally deprived nursery school children. *Child Development* 39:1–14.

Index

Library of Congress Cataloging-in-Publication Data

Hale, Janice E., date
    Unbank the fire : visions for the education of African American
children / Janice E. Hale.   .
        p.   cm.
    Includes bibliographical references and index.
    ISBN 0-8018-4821-0 (hard : alk. paper). — ISBN 0-8018-4822-9
(pbk. : alk. paper)
        1. Afro-American children—Social conditions. 2. Afro-American
children—Education.   I. Title.
E185.86.H23   1994
370'.089'96073—dc20   94-2864

1943